JOURNEY TO THEATRE & DRAMATIC ARTS

College Admissions & Profiles

Rachel A. Winston, Ph.D.

ISBN 978-1946432643 (hardback); 978-1946432636 (paperback); 978-1946432650 (e-book)

LCCN: 2022905602

Lizard Publishing, 7700 Irvine Center Drive, Suite 800, Irvine, CA 92618 *www.lizard-publishing.com*

Lizard Publishing creates, designs, produces, and distributes books and resources to provide academic, admissions, and career information. Our mental process is fueled by three tenets:

- Ignite the hunger to learn and the passion to make a difference
- Illuminate the expanse of knowledge by sharing cutting edge thinking
- Innovate to create a world that makes the transition from dreams to reality

We work with academic leaders who transform the educational landscape to publish relevant content and advise students of their educational and professional options, with the aim of developing 21st-century learners and leaders. We also work with students to publish their books and present widely diverse ideas to the college/graduate school-bound community. With headquarters in Irvine, California, Lizard Publishing works virtually with authors to edit, publish, and distribute both hard copy and paperback books.

This book was published in the U.S.A. Lizard Publishing is a premium quality provider of educational reference, career guidance, and motivational publications/merchandise for global learners, educators, and stakeholders in education.

Book design by Michelle Tahan *www.michelletahan.com*

Book formatting by Obinna Chinemerem Ozuo

Book website: *www.collegefashionprograms.com*

LIZARD PUBLISHING

This book is dedicated to Dennis Boutsikaris who served as my husband's lifelong role model. My husband got the opportunity to play the lead in his high school play since Dennis was performing professionally. Afterward, my husband served in the Marine Corps during the Vietnam War. Dennis went on to have an amazing acting career. Though my husband appeared in three movies afterward, he always looked to Dennis as his star.

I also want to dedicate this book to the hundreds of talented directors, actors, musicians, choreographers, and backstage personnel with whom I performed in musicals at Montgomery Blair High School (Silver Spring, MD) and Syracuse University. Their creativity, genius, and dedication left an indelible impression.

Best wishes to everyone who chooses theatre and delights new audiences in each and every performance.

ACKNOWLEDGMENTS

There is never enough room to acknowledge every person. Numerous people contributed to my perspective about theatre. Students, performers, faculty, directors, counselors, admission directors, and researchers assisted in enhancing my knowledge base or taught me indelible lessons. Over a lifetime of experiences working with students and actors, I am wiser and more worldly.

I gratefully acknowledge Michelle Tahan, Jasmine Jhunjhnuwala, E. Liz Kim, and Jacqueline Xu, as well as my family, friends, colleagues, and professors. It is with profound gratitude that I also acknowledge those performers I have known in the theatre world.

As a faculty member in the UCLA College Counseling Certificate Program, I met many dedicated counselors who spend their life serving and supporting students. Meaningful contributions to the book have been made indirectly by admissions representatives, college counselors, and faculty members who took a special interest in this book's success.

I would also like to thank the thousands of students I have taught, counseled, or supported in my nearly four decades of service.

> *"If I see so far, it is because I stand on the shoulders of giants."*
> *— Isaac Newton*

Isaac Newton once said, "If I see so far, it is because I stand on the shoulders of giants."

A few of those giants whose broad shoulders lifted me higher and helped teach invaluable lessons include: Mark Wolf, Danny Casey, Zayd Kuba, Davis Ferrero, Marissa Kotch, Rachel Richardson, Davis Ferrero, Grant Smith, Morgan Higgins, Corina Lee, and Jackson Ellison.

Finally, there would be no book on theatre schools and no career college admissions counseling without the support of Robert Helmer, whose tireless efforts support me every single day.

ABOUT THE AUTHOR

D r. Rachel A. Winston is a tireless student advocate. She has served the educational community as a university professor, college advisor, statistician, researcher, author, cryptanalyst, motivational speaker, publishing executive, and lifelong student. As one of the leading experts in college counseling and an award-winning faculty member, Dr. Winston has spent her lifetime learning, teaching, mentoring, and coaching students. Her counseling practice centers around college admissions, college essays, portfolios, and intellectual conversations about life and career pursuits.

She started college at thirteen and graduated from college programs in such widely ranging disciplines as chemistry, mathematics, computers, liberal arts, international relations, negotiation, conflict resolution, peacebuilding, business administration, higher education leadership, interpreting, college counseling, and publishing. Throughout her education, she attended and graduated from Harvard, University of Chicago, GWU, UCLA, Syracuse, CSUF, CSUDH, Pepperdine, Claremont Graduate University, and Gallaudet University.

Her position working in Washington, D.C. on Capitol Hill and with the White House in the 1980s took her to approximately a hundred universities training campaign managers at colleges from Colorado to California, thoroughly dotting the western states. Later, she led college tours with students and their families on road trips throughout the United States. She has taught or counseled thousands of students over her career and speaks at conferences and academic programs throughout the world.

As a professor and avid writer for numerous publications, she won the 2012 McFarland Literary Achievement Award, Bletchley Park Cryptanalyst Award, and numerous other awards, including Faculty Member of the Year, Leadership Tomorrow Leader of the Year, and college service and leadership awards. While studying Human Capital at Claremont Graduate University, she was a scholarship recipient at the Drucker School of Management. She was also elected to the statewide Board of Governors for the Faculty Association for California Community Colleges, where she served on the executive committee.

She also served as a faculty member for the UCLA College Counselor Certificate Program, the Director of Mathematics at Brandman University, and Embry Riddle Aeronautical University, Chapman University, Cal State Fullerton, and a handful of California Community Colleges, including Cerro Coso College where she represented the entire faculty as the Academic Senate President and retired in 2016. Over her career, she taught mathematics online, on television, live interactive satellite, telecourses, and in large and small lecture halls.

AUTHORS' NOTE

You are reading this book because you are considering admission to colleges where you open the doors to the world of theatre. Whatever route you took to get to this point, you are in the right place. Right now, you need to gather information to make informed decisions.

While many people offer advice, suggestions differ. Friends will tell you the 'right' way or the way their neighbor was accepted. Graciously accept this anecdotal information, pursuing theatre with your heart and mind as you commit to learning more.

Dig deeper to consider current, expert information from counselors who have worked with hundreds of students. Changes in programs, curricula, requirements, and links happen each year.

Doublecheck each program's specifics yourself. Each school's profile information is current as of March 2022. However, since researching this book, changes may have taken place. There are other college guidebooks written by talented and experienced counselors, though none like this book on theatre. Nevertheless, I admire and cheer on their efforts.

> *"We are what we think. All that we are arises with our thoughts. With our thoughts, we make the world."*
> *— Buddha*

This resource about colleges, admissions, profiles, and lists is different in that it also provides unique tidbits. I hope you find the information valuable. Your job is to begin early by assembling lists of possible schools to consider. Create a road map and set yourself on a clear path.

If you see an error in this book or even a suggestion for a future edition, please write to Dr. Rachel A. Winston at collegeguide@yahoo.com. We will fix the entry with the next printed version. All of that said, this book was written with you in mind.

There is a wealth of information on the Internet with free downloads, FAQs, testimonials, and offers to help you with your applications. Some of these advisors are knowledgeable and can help you. Unfortunately, students and parents hunt around the web, searching for a tremendous number of hours to seek the information they need. This book aims to resolve this problem with college admissions data and profiles to make your search easier.

For now, though, I assume you want to attend college to study theatre and are exploring this book to find a program that will get you on your way toward your goal. You are undoubtedly a talented candidate who is willing to work very hard. Whether your goals include regional shows, Broadway, or international stages, keep believing that anything is possible. There is a perfect character fit for you.

As you investigate colleges, you might find that some programs are listed in the School of Theatre, School of Drama, School of Acting, or School of Music. Either way, this book will help you reach your goal. Investigating these programs, applying, prescreening, auditioning, and writing personal statements for each college will require research to determine which is right for you and the specific reasons you are a good fit.

While you might believe that theatre programs are relatively similar, each college's nuances make them very different. These small differences may seem confusing. My goal with this book is to demystify the information and process.

CONTENTS

CHAPTER 1

THE WORLD IS YOUR STAGE: ENTER AND PERFORM

"All the world's a stage, And all the men and women merely players; They have their exits and their entrances, And one man in his time plays many parts."

– **William Shakespeare**, *As You Like It*

The allure of the theatre beckons both the actor and the audience. Actors, hearing their calling, train themselves to embody all facets of their characters. Meanwhile, audiences come to witness that mesmerizing transformation as they watch the story unfold. Even when patrons have read the play or previously watched the performance, every retelling tugs on heartstrings, arousing feelings that lay deep inside. From the onset, there is a mystical moment when the theatre is silent, the suspense builds, and the curtain opens.

Plays are told with structure and form, building to a crescendo of tension. In Sophocles' *Antigone*, retold through the centuries in the form of a play, opera, and ballet, the audience senses the spellbinding tragedy of family, honor, and the tug-of-war between divine and societal laws. This 5th century B.C. story holds timeless lessons, causing the audience to consider their duty to honor higher moral commandments. The king, Creon, must decide between moral goodness, empathetic humanity, and governance of the state and its political forces – both Antigone and Creon end up as tragic victims. The director's production devices suspensefully highlight the dramatic conflict along with Sophocles' cynicism.

Performances of stories like *Antigone* can be gripping. We also know the story of Oedipus, ruler of Thebes, who murders his father, marries his mother, and realizes that he is the "unclean thing…The dirt that breeds disease." After his mother commits suicide in shame, he gouges out his eyes, blinding himself. Then, Creon, his half brother-in-law, banishes him from the city. No matter how much we know about the play or how many times we have seen the reenactment, when actors retell the story, audiences remain glued to the edge of their seat.

Thus, powerful stories, connect to our emotions, transforming what we know to our hopes, dreams, emotions, and fears. Cultural, civic, and interpersonal ruminations come alive in scripts and dramatic re-enactments. The stories told on stage present the good and bad in life. Thus, the stage is a metaphor for life as everyone lives on a stage, performing in their own play. It's humbling.

Shakespeare provided his own commentary.

> "All the world's a stage,
> and all the men and women merely players:
> they have their exits and their entrances;
> and one man in his time plays many parts ..."

—*As You Like It,* Act II, Scene 7, 139–142

Behind the curtain, a different kind of magic happens. Costumes and sets create mood and ambiance, sensationalising grand moments like the balcony scene in *Romeo and Juliet* depicting societal barriers that can thwart love. Using mood and tempo to build an arc, three witches lead readers to wonder if Macbeth is simply a pawn, controlled by demonic chess players, forced to live out their prophecy, or the Chessmaster of his own life who takes out the bishops and rooks in his path to be the King of Scotland. When the show begins and the curtain rises, excitement builds as the actors begin their onstage performance in the glow of scintillating lights, donning dramatic costumes, amidst a captivating set.

Iconic sets like the chandelier in *Phantom of the Opera*, dramatic moments like the helicopter scene in *Miss Saigon*, and a carnivorous, human-eating plant in *Little Shop of Horrors* bring theatre to spectacular glory. Audience members experience the dynamic sight and sound display.

Plays inspired audiences. With the play's script as the inspirational source, *Network* set and lighting designer Jan Versweyveld explained that the studio serves as the central element in the set design. However, the story needed other spaces for the characters' professional lives and a separate area for their social lives of bars, restaurants, and home. Rob Howell who won Tony Awards for both Best Scenic Design of a Play and Best Costume Design of a Play two years in a row for *The Ferryman* in 2019 and *A Christmas Carol* in 2020 used stone walls, a wrought-iron stove, and an intimate, but simple runway design to bring these shows to his audiences.

Meanwhile, costume designers enchant audiences, Superwoman dons an indelible red, white, and blue outfit, accessorized with a gold belt, and Dorothy dazzles the Munchkins with her spectacular ruby red slippers. Identifiable masks like the iconic masterpiece designed by Maria Björnson and worn by the Phantom in *Phantom of the Opera* or the outfits designed by Paul Tazewell and showcased by the *Hamilton* cast stand out in our memories.

As you pursue your goal in theatre, you will explore all aspects of the stage, learning fine details of how sets are constructed, costumes are assembled, accessories added, and props are envisioned to add flair that realistically portrays your character. While you intensely study acting, diction, and stagecraft, have fun using your creative talents, and live each moment fully, developing invaluable skills that are transferable to other jobs you might choose. As you transition, remember that life is a journey, not a destination. Theatre is a thrill ride of grand proportions.

Learning basic sewing skills could come in handy if you need to fix a costume quickly. Knowing a bit about carpentry could help you repair a loose board on a set if you are practicing after hours or build creative spaces in a home or office. With the transferrable skills you learn studying technical theatre, even Halloween sets and costumes can be remarkably fun to produce.

Many actors working in theatre, musical theatre, and film have a Bachelor of Fine Arts (BFA) or Master of Fine Arts (MFA), though this degree is not necessary to earn a role, and half of the performers on Broadway do not have a college degree. Nevertheless, somewhere down the line, a college education is valuable and some of the best actors on stage continue to train, study with coaches, and develop new skills throughout their life.

You can earn your degree in theatre arts, musical theatre, or music, though some attend liberal arts colleges studying dramatic writing, literature, or history. Either way, a bachelor's degree gets you started with general skills to fine-tune your craft while diversifying your talents. Before, during, and after your educational foundation, you just need experience.

The journey you are taking will have its ups and downs, but you will have stories to tell for the rest of your life. American drama critic Alexander Woollcott once said, "There's no such thing in anyone's life as an unimportant day." Attending Hamilton College and serving in World War I, he treasured each remarkable day. You can too. Enjoy this magical experience.

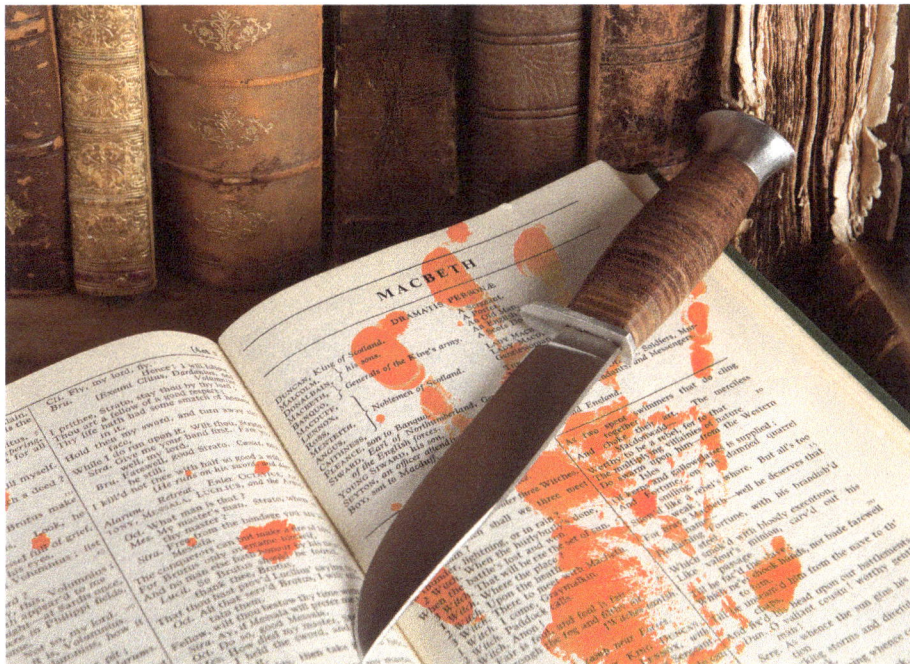

IMAGINE THE "SARAH SIDDONS" AWARD IN ALL ABOUT EVE OR THE BLOODY KNIFE IN SHAKESPEARE'S MACBETH

Acting is not simply pretending to be someone else. In fact, the heart of any role is in the impassioned expression of human nature. Actors must embody a character and bring its essence to life in words, diction, and song. There is a certain *je ne sais quoi*, a mysteriousness that captures the lives of people during a certain moment in history.

To understand Thornton Wilder's Pulitzer Prize-winning *Our Town*, actors must internalize the period of time at the turn of the last century. Through the wisdom of dramaturgs, actors and crew members can be more in tune with the play, its interpretation, and the essence of what the playwright meant when he said, "Our claim, our hope, our despair are in the mind—not in things, not in 'scenery.'"

This partly explains why Wilder's play had little in the way of scenery and the main character, the stage manager, interacted with the audience. Wilder writes,

> We all know that something is eternal. And it ain't houses and it ain't names, and it ain't earth, and it ain't even the stars . . . everybody knows

in their bones that something is eternal, and that something has to do with human beings. All the greatest people ever lived have been telling us that for five thousand years and yet you'd be surprised how people are always losing hold of it. There's something way down deep that's eternal about every human being.

Emily, who dies early in the play says, "Does anyone ever realize life while they live it...every, every minute?" The line says much about each person and each day. Everyone should live every minute. So too, actors must live in and enjoy the present. Sometimes that means feeling the ghosts, spirits, and supernatural in *Macbeth* and sometimes it means returning to the Earthly world to say one last thing to your mother, as Emily docs in *Our Town*. "Mama, just for a moment we're happy. Let's really look at one another!...I can't. I can't go on. It goes so fast. We don't have time to look at one another. I didn't realize. So all that was going on and we never noticed."

Meanwhile, the audience comes along for the ride from highs to lows and back as actors and crew members creatively perform as a team. Stage design helps tell the story through lighting, sound, effects, costume, scenery, and props. All the while, actors must embrace the following seven Cs of theatrical shows.

1. Creative
2. Clear
3. Concise
4. Compact
5. Communication
6. Collaboration
7. Complete

Creativity is fundamental. Afterward, the story's visual imagery needs to be told clearly so that people can see the story and internalize the mood, meaning, purpose, time period, socioeconomic climate, and emotion. The elements of a story are folded into one or more sets of visual pieces – moving parts in a jigsaw puzzle that, alone, says little, but together illuminates the entire picture.

At the same time, the show is not long. The limited timeframe necessitates brevity and conciseness. While plays, musicals, films, and commercials can range in duration, each has a beginning, middle, and end. Films, plays, and musical theatre must complete the entire thought with all components fitting together.

The stage or scene is compact in space. All of the action needs to happen within the frame of the stage or a lens. Yet, these components are confined to spatial limitations within the given area. While theatrical stages range in size, film locations can be much larger. Nevertheless, there are still bounds on action scenes that can take place on set. Every image, costume, or set piece that is needed to tell the story must be within the borders.

Shows do not take place in a vacuum. They are visualized and constructed as a team. Not only must the actors, choreographers, costume designers, and those in technical theatre know the story and understand the context, but they must also communicate effectively with the director at the start. From the very beginning, there should be a clear line of communication.

Collaboration is essential. Actors must listen attentively and propose ideas, though the performance must be conceptualized with the director's leadership. Consultation with other cast and crew members is also necessary. By discussing opportunities for improvement, pitfalls in design elements, and financial and spatial limitations, the team can efficiently and effectively produce the synergy to craft the best representation of the story.

In the end, the story must be complete. Whatever needed to be communicated must have its rise and fall. The costumes and sets must reflect the perspective, conflict, climax, resolution, and overall theme.

Theatres are alive, buzzing with activity. Although the pandemic presented challenges to in-person plays and musicals, films continued to be created and theaters returned to enthusiastic audiences. Omicron's December 2021 last-minute heartbreaking shutdown disappointed thousands, though the song "No Day But Today", in the musical *Rent* reminds us,

There's only us,
There's only this,
forget regret,
or life is yours to miss.
No other road,
no other way,
No day but today.

Historically, theatres have always bounced back, even in the most catastrophic times. Shows and styles may change; budgets may tighten; designs may reflect the momentary mood.

While few alive today will ever forget the impact the pandemic had on life, liberty, and disparity, people will remember that "somewhere over the rainbow, bluebirds fly." We, too, will fly again, as will theatre. Unfortunately, the saddest moments will not completely disappear.

Theatres took a huge hit, stopping production teams. However, theatre, with its inspiring performances will come back stronger as will those who brought energy and life to the stage. People will again hunger to be inspired with messages that transcend the heartwrenching anguish of disease and war. Shows will return.

Actors will rehearse. Costumes will be created and stitchers will resume their roles. Feverish tech crews will construct sets, create props, paint miniature villages, and move tons of material. We will all move on and audiences will again be moved and thrilled.

In Arthur Miller's *Death of a Salesman*, Willy Loman says, "I'm gonna show you and everybody else that Willy Loman did not die in vain. He had a good dream. It's the only dream you can have - to come out number-one man. He fought it out here, and this is where I'm gonna win it for him."

Though Willy was a tragic hero in the play, there is something about Willy that captivates our imagination. Willy cannot admit to his mistakes and never achieves the success he desires. Furthermore, he never appreciated what he had. If everyone can take Emily's advice, we can appreciate the one life we get to live, stop, look around, and be grateful for what we have rather than what we do not. Ultimately, theatrical showcases will return worldwide, and life will continue despite adversity, challenges, and global strife as we keep striving for our dreams.

The song "Seize the Day" from the musical *Newsies* tells us,

Now is the time to seize the day

They're gonna see there's hell to pay

Nothing can break us

No one can make us quit before we're done

One for all and all for one!

Ultimately, theatre will return worldwide, and life will continue despite adversity, challenges, and global strife as we keep striving for our dreams.

CHAPTER 2

EXPECTATIONS AND TRAINING: ACTING CLASSES AND DRAMATIC ROLES

"If you were born with the ability to change someone's perspective or emotions, never waste that gift. It is one of the most powerful gifts God can give—the ability to influence."

– Shannon L. Alder

BORN TO INSPIRE

With your gift to impact audiences profoundly and emotionally, you have the power to inspire. You offer a unique stage presence and a multitalented skillset. Meanwhile, within your audience, there are kernels of greatness just waiting to germinate into a garden of flowers.

Each performance could be the instant in which those seeds begin to grow, providing the water and fertilizer for those flowers to blossom. You may not know who is in that night's audience, but there is a person you do not see and will never meet who is moved in ways that are unknowable. In a split-second moment, an audience member, far away in the darkness of row X, latches on to your words and feelings, transforming their life and their future into new and exciting possibilities.

With as much practice as you have had thus far, you still need in-depth training - personal, professional, experiential - where you can deeply feel what you have not yet felt and sense what you do not yet know is inside of you. In college workshops, acting classes, and dramatic roles, you will summon thoughts from the depths of your humanity in ways you do not realize and are not yet comprehendible.

Can you feel the desperate and immediate loss of your home, school, and possessions in Ukraine, huddled endlessly without food in a country where you do not speak the language? Can you endure the pain of a slave picking cotton or sweating on a summer's day as an ironworker? Getting into character as a victim of a strangler, a struggling artist, comedienne, coal miner, war medic, or sex slave takes practice. Most of you do not have each of those experiences, but over time you will dive into the depths of your humanity to conjure those feelings within you.

The road to theatrical performance is neither straight nor predictable. Think of it like Dorothy's yellow brick road. You are off to see the Wizard, skipping merrily to some upbeat music, when you stumble upon a field where a scarecrow hangs from a pole. You knew that somewhere over the rainbow, big city lights and a grand theatre were just ahead. Theatres beckon you to enter, but you are now in a cornfield in Munchkin Country helping a lonely straw-stuffed gentleman off of the pole. You continue along your path as you find a tin man and a lion. Your road takes twists and turns as you fall asleep in a field of poppies, missing a grand opportunity, or are carried away in the beaks of birds to some never, neverland.

Given that acting contracts are short-term, a performer's value only lasts while they are healthy and free of injury. Life's successes rest perilously on ability and showmanship. During college, freelance work typically begins in a small company where actors gain professional experiences and could be discovered. Later, actors may write their own plays, create their own shows, or audition among many other talented actors. One day, a part fits you like a glove, and you are simply a perfect match for the character.

Personal character is essential in the acting world since actors spend so much time together, interacting personally and professionally while sharing emotional experiences on and off the stage. Relationship building and collaboration are essential as actors strive for value-centered living while seeking the essence of their moral fabric and developing lifelong relationships. Toxic personalities, prima donnas, and drama queens often blend like oil and water.

Thus, actors must be able to:

1. Take direction from the director and stage manager
2. Work well with the choreographer, blending seamlessly with other dancers
3. Be punctual and reliable, attending scheduled rehearsals
4. Work as a team on and off the stage
5. Show up at all costume fittings and props rehearsals
6. Understand how their character fits into the play's story
7. Memorize lines, songs, dances, and timings
8. Learn their role independently and collectively
9. Improvise, perform, ad-lib
10. Project their character's persona confidently and convincingly
11. Assist where necessary, supporting cast and crew members
12. Laugh

THEATRE'S MULTI-DISCIPLINARY TRAINING

You are embarking on a thrilling, demanding, and disciplined pursuit. You will work with extremely skilled performers who started when they entered elementary school. Some have performed professionally on stages worldwide and will blow you away with their abilities. However, rarely are drama students equally skilled in singing, dancing, and acting.

Don't be surprised. Some thespians are amazingly talented. Do not let their abilities bring you down or make you feel as if you are not good enough. You may significantly improve during college with the right training. Besides, your enthusiasm and talent will show through in your auditions. Furthermore, many directors and college talent scouts are more interested in your potential, commitment, and attitude.

Coursework may include theatre and camera presentation along with an in-depth study of Shakepeare and scenes in contemporary plays. Required courses might also include voice, movement, diction, dialects, dramaturgy, and theatre history. In addition, you will need to have a basic understanding of technical theatre, lighting, props, and costumes. Choices of electives like voice-overs, commercials, clowning, new media, and stage combat may open new doors for you. On the other hand, you might consider courses in directing, stage artistry, and theatre management

READING AND UNDERSTANDING PLAYS

Goodreads offered a list of the "Top 100 Stage Plays of All Time.[1]

1. *Hamlet*
2. *Macbeth*
3. *The Importance of Being Earnest*
4. *Waiting for Godot*
5. *Romeo and Juliet*
6. *A Midsummer Night's Dream*
7. *Othello*
8. *King Lear*
9. *Antigone*
10. *Death of a Salesman*
11. *A Doll's House*
12. *A Streetcar Named Desire*
13. *The Crucible*
14. *Rosencrantz and Guildenstern Are Dead*
15. *Oedipus Rex*
16. *Our Town*
17. *Pygmalion*
18. *Who's Afraid of Virginia Woolf?*
19. *The Tempest*
20. *Cat on a Hot Tin Roof*
21. *The Cherry Orchard*
22. *The Glass Menagerie*
23. *A Raisin in the Sun*
24. *Twelfth Night*
25. *Cyrano de Bergerac*
26. *The Merchant of Venice*
27. *Much Ado About Nothing*
28. *Angels in America*
29. *The Misanthrope*
30. *Arcadia*
31. *Long Day's Journey into Night*
32. *Amadeus*
33. *Lady Windermere's Fan*
34. *No Exit*
35. *Richard III*
36. *Dr. Faustus*
37. *Lysistrata*

---

1   https://www.goodreads.com/list/show/13581.Goodreads_Top_100_Stage_Plays_of_All_Time

38. *Tartuffe*
39. *Arsenic and Old Lace*
40. *An Ideal Husband*
41. *A Man for All Seasons*
42. *The Threepenny Opera*
43. *Glengarry Glen Ross*
44. *The Seagull*
45. *Fences*
46. *Faust*
47. *West Side Story*
48. *The Taming of the Shrew*
49. *Medea*
50. *Mother Courage and Her Children*
51. *The Miracle Worker*
52. *The Winter's Tale*
53. *Uncle Vanya*
54. *Endgame*
55. *Medea*
56. *The Oresteia: Agamemnon, The Libation Bearers, The Eumenides*
57. *Caligula*
58. *A View from the Bridge*
59. *Hedda Gabler*
60. *Arms and the Man*
61. *The Bald Soprano*
62. *Equus*
63. *Noises Off*
64. *Henry V*
65. *Twelve Angry Men*
66. *Blithe Spirit*
67. *Saint Joan*
68. *Sweeney Todd: The Demon Barber of Fleet Street*
69. *The Zoo Story*
70. *The Frogs*
71. *King Henry IV*
72. *Julius Caesar*
73. *Phèdre*
74. *An Enemy of the People*
75. *The Playboy of the Western World*
76. *An Inspector Calls*
77. *Hedda Gabler*
78. *The Caucasian Chalk Circle*
79. *Richard II*
80. *The Children's Hour*
81. *Pirates of Penzance*
82. *The Lion in Winter*
83. *The Iceman Cometh*
84. *Dancing at Lughnasa*
85. *The Elephant Man*
86. *Major Barbara*
87. *Betrayal*
88. *Blood Wedding and Yerma*
89. *The Homecoming*
90. *Six Characters in Search of an Author*
91. *Dead Shambles*
92. *Edward II*
93. *The Inspector General*
94. *American Buffalo*
95. *Mourning Becomes Electra*
96. *M. Butterfly*
97. *Deathtrap*
98. *The Birthday Party*
99. *The Three Sisters*
100. *Master Harold…and the Boys*

PREPARE AHEAD OF TIME

Drama students must have the ability to perform. Intensive college training will enhance these skills. Since colleges must choose between talented thespians, most applicants must demonstrate their skills in pre-screening videos. Video your performances to showcase your acting abilities.

Many students do not consider taping their acting lessons, vocal coaching, dance instruction, or rehearsal choreography. However, even especially strong practice sessions posted on YouTube or Vimeo can give admissions officers an idea of your talents, skills, and training. Photographs, like a headshot or a screen capture of you on stage, may come in handy when you are applying to college, creating a resume, or producing a one-sheet. There are times when you feel bright, light, and effortless in your body and mind. Those unpredictable times may offer you the best photo-ops.

For your prescreen video, find a time when your studio room is quiet and empty, possibly before anyone arrives or after everyone has left. You can get a friend or family member to capture the recording or bring a camera and a tripod. A recording studio is best for monologues. Regardless, if this is not possible, locate an acoustically sound room, or some other quiet place where you can create the environment you desire.

PRE-SCREENING AND AUDITION PREPARATION

Whether you are preparing your monologues, work with your theatre teacher or a private coach. Someone who is a trained listener can hear whatever you miss. Remember, your goal is to put your best foot forward. Iron out the kinks in your performance before you press submit.

PROFESSIONAL THEATRE OR COLLEGE OR BOTH

Note: Some colleges do not allow their students to perform professionally while they are enrolled in their college program.

Nevertheless, uber-talented theatre students often hunger for the big stage and gain professional experiences while studying at school. Particularly in theatre hubs, like New York, Los Angeles, Atlanta, Chicago, Cleveland, Dallas, Philadelphia, Washington, D.C., students do not want to wait for their big break. However, colleges often want students to focus on academics. This situation presents a tricky space between college and professional theatre, resulting in students mulling over their future while living in the present.

Students believe that it could not hurt to try when casting sheets open. Besides, in their mind, they can rehearse and practice between classes and perform in weekend and evening shows that are outside of class time. Yet, being in a professional cast often necessitates missing a class or turning down a role at the university. Additionally, with dual commitments, something often has to give. Homework is frequently the loser, and academic performance may drop. Resolution of the conflict often leans to the professional stage rather than the college.

A college could decide professional theatre concurrently with college is not acceptable. Universities could pull a scholarship that was predicated on performing in college shows. However, the rules that guide a student's ability to perform outside of school are frequently listed in the college catalog. Students must do their due diligence and decide.

Many theatre directors or division deans believe that students should choose. Do you want to perform professionally now or focus on your college education - one or the other? They might tell students that if they miss a class, rehearsal, or show due to an outside professional commitment, they may not remain in the program. While theatre directors or division deans are reticent about professional theatre during the school year, they often encourage students to perform each summer and during winter break.

Every college is different. Some actually encourage students to audition while in school. Review each college's catalog to see their specific requirements or contact someone at the school. No matter what, there is a program for you out there. This book only reviews a fraction of the theatre programs due to space limitations, but the profile section provides enough information to get you started on your search.

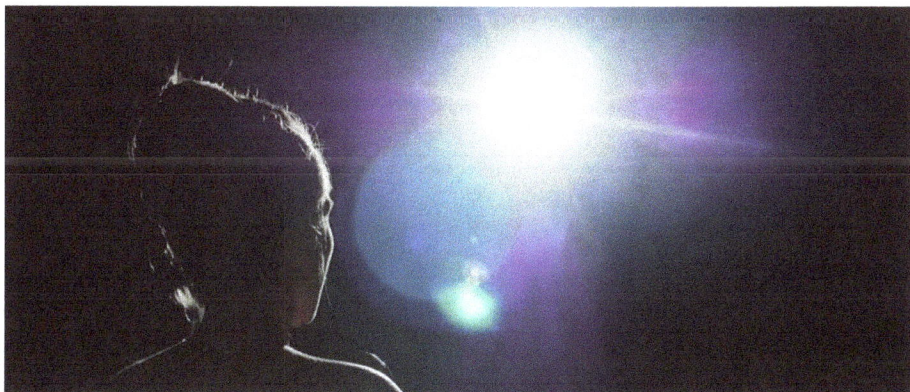

CHAPTER 3

ACADEMIC SKILLS: FOUNDATIONAL KNOWLEDGE FOR TELEVISION, FILMS, AND PLAYS

"I wish I had read more and majored in literature rather than theatre. I think I would have been a better artist for it. I am trying to play catch-up now."

– Idina Menzel

S tudents applying to college programs in theatre are expected to be dynamic, multidisciplinary, and extraordinarily talented. However, since majoring in theatre is more than just studies in acting, students must possess intellectual curiosity for literature, dramatic writing, history, sociology, psychology, economics, communication, and foreign language.

The liberal arts offer a valuable core of knowledge, preparing students for life. This importance is no different for theatre students. Liberal arts classes offer students a range of academic studies from which they can view the world. This interdisciplinary foundation is the core essence of knowledge to build a future and a life that extends beyond auditioning, casting, and acting.

Connecting the past to the present delivers a sense of captivating tension, underlying frustrations, and societal conflict to audiences. Pulitzer Prize winner, Lin-Manuel Miranda, who wrote the book, music, and lyrics for the musical *Hamilton*, studied at Wesleyan University in Connecticut. Wesleyan University's President, Michael Roth, explained that *Hamilton* makes "the past come alive in ways that expand possibilities in the present." This is a key skill for everyone involved in theatre.

Simply learning how to conduct research, write clearly, and use technology is valuable. However, the academic skills in developing scholarly papers not only aids in personal self-expression but in delving into big picture concepts and fine-tuned grammar. When an individual writes an e-mail, letter, or paper, others know whether the person has strong English skills. Knowing proper English is not a necessity in theatrical performance if you know your lines, but a person's written communication speaks loudly.

Students learn to collect, organize, and synthesize information in imaginative ways that inspire new points of creativity and opportunity. While diving into problem-solving and critical thinking students can test their ideas, tossing them around with classmates and professors, improving skills in collaboration, interpretation, and originality. Thinking outside of the box in small group discussions can refine character portrayals, remove philosophical biases, and clarify what lies under the surface of the story.

Academic skills also allow students to have a more global and historical worldview. Students who study world history can delve into the past to understand prejudices and challenge today's intellectual thinking. Taking liberal arts classes can teach skills that can help eliminate bias and bigotry. Thespians profoundly shape our world, bringing people together and offering new ways of thinking.

Although students applying to BA or BS programs will take approximately one-third to one-half of their credits in the liberal arts, even BFA students will typically take one-quarter of their classes in required humanities and social science courses to better understand time periods, social conditions, and environmental contexts that set the stage for each show.

Thus, pursuing theatre is not just the ability to perform, although auditions will focus on performance quality and skill development. Some schools may require tangential skills like the ability to play the piano or understand dramatic literature. Imagination is also essential. Students must be able to dream and envision bold and provocative new worlds. Without hesitation, they must step into new complex settings fresh and renewed.

Initiative is also essential. Listening, attentiveness, and taking direction are all important. However, going one step further demonstrates the commitment to practice, rehearse, and get things right. You can wait until a fitter checks sizes and seams or you can check that costumes fit, ensuring there are no tears or missing accessories. Remember, you are the one going on-stage and a hole or trailing tulle fabric could mean you might trip or have some other kind of accident.

While some students believe that their one moment in time will evaporate if they do not perform professionally as a teenager, training the mind is equally important as training the body. Disciplined preparation in artistic talent is often not sufficient. The ability to read, write, analyze, and interpret characters, sociocultural lifestyles, and political atmospheres is immensely helpful.

Ambition is sometimes seen as derogatory, particularly when egos get involved and students are not kind to others in the competitive environment. However, ambition is essential. You must be willing to go the extra mile since other standouts will. Only the best, brightest, and most focused students will get past the first call. Directors look for those who collaborate as team players and support the artistry of fellow students while also looking for those people who are "in it to win it."

"NOTHING CAN DIM THE LIGHT WHICH SHINES FROM WITHIN." - MAYA ANGELOU

Lucille Ball, whose entertainment career on television and Broadway spanned nearly sixty years, explained that becoming a successful performer requires confidence. She said, "Love yourself and everything else falls into line." Winning the Cecil B. DeMille Award and two stars on the Hollywood Walk of Fame, she said in her training, "All I learned in drama school was how to be frightened."

Nevertheless, academic skills will take you far. While many theatre success stories include award-winning actors who never went to college, there is a certain sense of respect in the industry for the smart, disciplined, prepared, and flexible. Scholarship can help you succeed if you decide not to continue with theatre, or you are unable to because of some unforeseen reason. Albert Einstein once said, "The value of an education in a liberal arts college is the training of the mind to think something that cannot be learned from textbooks."

Studying and performing in theatre demands resilience and flexibility. Even with all good intentions, unexpected events happen with sets, costumes, or lights. Regardless, actors go on stage to perform. Not all shows are flawless; sometimes there are imperfections. Grace and mercy must be extended if unfortunate events unfold, or important details are left out. When the milk spills, it cannot be returned to its carton.

Interpersonal communication, thus, is an equally important academic and social skill. Everyone in theatre must be patient and deliver written and verbal messages thoughtfully. Broken relationships due to irrational or inappropriate outbursts are hard to repair. Individuals must communicate effectively and ensure that the intended receiver gets the delivery of information. George Bernard Shaw once said, "The single biggest problem in communication is the illusion that it has taken place."

Likewise, actors must emote lines with the feeling, sensitivity, and comprehension of the conceptions to be conveyed and the underlying meaning of the words. Actors must deliver lines with appropriate feeling, sensitivity, and comprehension of the ideas to be conveyed. College students build upon any deficient skills or learn new talents.

However, the most important aspects of academic and artistic training are conceived with passion. When a student is driven to work hard and learn new skills, they can overcome most areas in which they are not quite as skilled. Directors in theatre, television, and film worldwide look for the most expressive, committed, talented, and passionate artists. If you have interests beyond the arts that make you interesting, knowledgeable, and wise, you can make a tremendous impact on audiences as well as with fellow cast members.

Review websites and research programs. Look through official publications, but also review the internet, YouTube, and past shows. Contact someone in the theatre department to learn more about specific details in programs you want to pursue. This is your future. Jump in and learn about the environment to find the best fit for your undergraduate college or conservatory education.

CHAPTER 4

THEATRE EXPERIENCES: INTERNSHIPS FOR HIGH SCHOOL, COLLEGE, AND BEYOND

"I'd be more frightened by not using whatever abilities I'd been given. I'd be more frightened by procrastination and laziness."

– Denzel Washington

ACKNOWLEDGMENT OF THE PANDEMIC'S IMPACT ON THEATRE

To begin, the pandemic's impact on theatre cannot go unnoticed. Theatres around the world were impacted by COVID-19 and its numerous repercussions. Theatres were shuttered. Though many that could survive the financial impact reopened, casts, crew, and directors needed to find alternative opportunities, retrain, or use their skills in creative ways. Internships were difficult to find for students who counted on gaining experience. Many school plays and musicals were canceled. However, new opportunities opened. Schools resumed. Theatre programs from high school to graduate school began once again.

INTERNSHIP LOCATIONS

Some geographical locations lend themselves better to theatre opportunities. Larger cities where there are big stages or where the region's donors support theatre offer more chances to obtain internship experiences. However, colleges with theatre programs also provide their students with internal opportunities to gain experience.

For example, New York City offers the greatest diversity of theatre internship options. In addition, nearby areas in New Jersey, Connecticut, Long Island, and Westchester County also offer significant opportunities for internship experience and professional positions. Some colleges in the New York and New England areas have a close affiliation with major theatres. For example, the University of Connecticut is connected to the Hartford Stage where the Metropolitan Opera offers study abroad opportunities with University of the Arts London's Wimbledon College of the Arts in the United Kingdom.

London is a mecca for theatre. An internship or semester abroad at a school, particularly in London to train as an actor in West End theatres, would be a phenominal oppotunity. Though the theatre community suffered during the pandemic, London theatre will rebound with the robust support of patrons of the arts.

Other locations where there are significant opportunities for theatre include:

Atlanta	Miami/Ft. Lauderdale
Austin	Minneapolis/St. Paul
Boston	Philadelphia
Chicago	Phoenix
Cleveland	Portland
Dallas/Ft. Worth	San Diego
Hartford	San Francisco/Oakland/Berkeley
Los Angeles/Orange County	Washington, D.C./Maryland/Virginia

ArtsAmerica also explains, "But even some cities and towns that don't have an especially large or active year-round theatre scene are noteworthy for festivals and other events; one famous example is Louisville, Kentucky, where the Actors Theatre of Louisville hosts the annual Humana Festival of New American Plays."[1]

Look through TheatreWorksUSA for some of the many opportunities available: *https://twusa.org/about/work-with-us/*

AMERICANS FOR THE ARTS INTERNSHIP

If you are committed to arts education in the United States there are numerous opportunities to support students. One of those is with Americans for the Arts where you can make a difference. Undergraduates, recent graduates, and graduate students are invited to apply and become a part of the team. This internship can be for college credit or as an hourly-paid position. Apply online through their portal.

Americans for the Arts also has a program called Diversity in Arts Leadership Internship, which seeks applicants from underrepresented groups who are passionate about community arts and education leadership. Locations for these internships are in New York City, New Jersey, Nashville, Boston, Sarasota, and Raleigh-Wake County.

---

1   Arts America, "Theater," *Arts America,* n.d., http://artsamerica.org/genres/genres-theater/

Additional Opportunities for Underrepresented Groups Include:

CALIFORNIA

- **The Getty Center** offers summer internships to undergraduates of culturally diverse backgrounds who reside or attend college in Los Angeles County.

- **Stanford Institute for Diversity in the Arts** - *Community Arts Fellowships* engage artists, students, and the local community collaboratively to create performance and visual art that examine the complex intersections between race, diversity, and social action.

- **Film Independent - *Project Involve*** offers up-and-coming film professionals from under-represented communities the opportunity to hone skills, form creative partnerships, utilize free or low-cost production resources.

COLORADO

- **The Diversity in the Arts Internship Program (DITA)** is a cohort of diverse arts and culture interns that learn from and support art and culture nonprofits in the diverse Denver metro community.

ILLINOIS

- **Steppenwolf Theatre -** *Multicultural Fellowship is* for early-career persons of color interested in working in arts administration.

- **Greater Baltimore Cultural Alliance - *Urban Arts Leadership Program*** supports historically underrepresented, particularly those of color, in the management of cultural and artistic organizations.
- **The Walters Art Museum** offers a research and fellowship program for training and diversifying the fields of art history and museum practice.

NEW YORK

- **The New York Foundation for the Arts** has a classified section with various opportunities and is especially good for finding internships with galleries in New York.
- **Studio in a School - *ARTS Intern Program*** provides opportunities for college undergrads to learn about museum professions through internships in museums and cultural institutions.
- **4A - *Multicultural Advertising Intern Program*** allows students to work at prestigious advertising agencies, interact w/ advertising professionals, and gain credentials in arts management, production, and planning.
- **Center for Communication - VICE Cencom Fellowship** ensures greater access to careers in journalism for the next generation of innovative storytellers.
- **Pentacle - *Cultivating Leadership in Dance*** provides a structured internship program working closely with dance artists/choreographers and non-profit organizations.
- **International Radio & Television Society (IRTS) - *Summer Fellowship Program*** brings together to train & educate the next generation of media & communication professionals.
- **ArtTable - *Diversity Internship Initiative*** provides opportunities and mentorship for GRADUATE students from underrepresented backgrounds to aid their transition from academic to professional careers.
- **The CUNY Cultural Corps** creates opportunities for CUNY students and CUNY recent graduates to work in NYC's cultural sector.
- **The PENCIL Internship Program** provides NYC area students with access to career readiness training, connections to professional mentors, and the opportunity to secure a paid summer internship.
- **American Ballet Theatre Internship Program** expands ethnic and cultural diversity in classical ballet. ABT is committed to facilitating inclusive programs through its Project Plié initiative.

- **Creative Catalyst Fellowship** allows participants to gain experience and develop visionary leadership in paid fellowships in residence at our partner organizations.

PENNSYLVANIA

- **Philadelphia Museum of Art** *Honickman Diversity Internship* provides students from diverse backgrounds with exposure to the inner-workings of a major metropolitan museum.

VIRGINIA

- **Wolf Trap -** *Diversity Initiative Internship Program* provides opportunities for promising young professionals, especially those from cultural or ethnic backgrounds underrepresented in arts management.

WASHINGTON, DC

- **Smithsonian –** *Minority Awards Program* aims to increase participation of groups who are underrepresented in the museum field.
- **Archives of American Art -** *Horowitz-Fraad Minority Internships* provides professional experiences in archival science, information management, museum studies, art administration, art history, and cultural studies.
- **Arena Stage -** *Allen Lee Hughes Internship Program* provides the highest standard of training through immersion in the art and business of producing theatre.
- **The National Museum of African American History and Culture** offers internships and fellowships for college, recent graduates, and graduate students opportunities to work closely with professionals and scholars in the museum field.

MULTIPLE CITIES

- **T. Howard Foundation -** *Diversity in Media & Entertainment Internships* provides minority students who are interested in media & entertainment with internships, networking opportunities, professional development training, scholarships, mentors, and more.

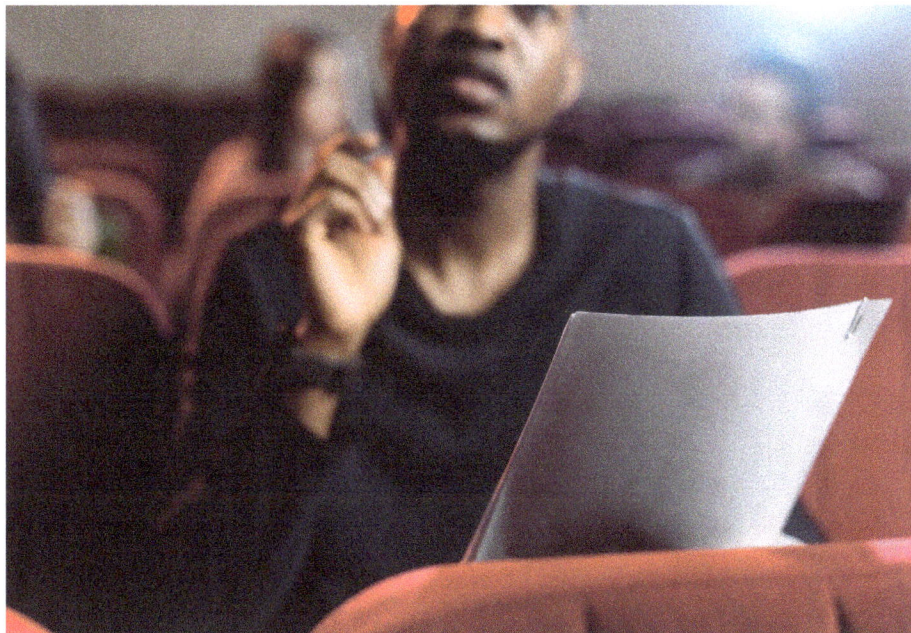

CASTING OPPORTUNITIES WITH THEATER WORKS USA

Theater Works USA (TWUSA) constantly looks for performers, holding auditions year-round. TWUSA is eager to find actors prepared to tour North America for two to six months. Contracts under American Actors' Equity Association's TheaterWorksUSA are available for actors signed as Assistant Stage Managers. Submit basic information, resume, and headshot to: twusa.org/about/work-with-us/.

You must be 18 years old to audition, though there are both Equity and Non-Equity calls. Auditions and rehearsals are held in New York City. You will have the opportunity to become a member of Actor's Equity Association, although this is not a requirement. Duties include load-in, load-out, props, and costumes.

SUMMER INTERNSHIPS IN ARTISTIC SERVICES, AUDIENCE SERVICES, CASTING LITERARY, STAGE MANAGEMENT, AND THEATRE OPERATIONS

One hundred internships are highlighted at https://www.playbill.com/article/over-100-theatrical-internships-you-can-apply-for

A few include:

Lincoln Center – New York, NY - Performance Marketing

Manhattan Theatre Club – New York, NY - Artistic and Literary, Individual Giving, Company Management, Marketing Analytics, Marketing, Business, Casting, Production Management, and Stargate Theatre

Signature Theatre – New York, NY – Artistic, Literary, Development, Special Events, Company Management, Business Management, Company Management/ General Management, and Marketing

MCC Theatre – New York, NY – Audience Services, Development, Education and Public Engagement, Operations, Marketing, and Executive Office

Atlantic Theatre – New York, NY - School Education, School Artistic, and School Administration

Roundabout Theatre Company – New York, NY – Artistic, Literary, Audience Services, Development, Education Intern, Facilities/House Management, Finance, Human Resources, Management, IT, and Marketing

Telsey & Company - New York, NY - Casting

Stewart/Whitley - New York, NY – Casting

Tara Rubin Casting - New York, NY – Casting

5th Avenue Theatre – Seattle, WA – Artistic, New Works, Development, Education/Engagement, Company Management, Marketing/Communications, Casting, and Production Intern

La Jolla Playhouse – La Jolla, CA – Artistic, Philanthropy, Special Events, Administrative Education, YP@LJP Summer Program, Company Management, Marketing, Public Relations, Production Intern, and Stage Management

Steppenwolf Theatre Company – La Jolla, CA - Education

Steppenwolf Theatre Company – Chicago, IL – Literary, Fundraising/ Development, Theatre Management, Marketing, Public Relations, Artistic/Casting, Production Intern, Electrics, Properties, Scenic Art, and Sound

American Repertory Theater – Cambridge, MA – Access and Equity, Fundraising/Development, Education, Community Engagement, and Public Relations

SUMMER TRAINING & INTERNSHIPS –
MIDDLE SCHOOL & HIGH SCHOOL

In theatre, students learn by doing. Thus, initial and necessary experiences are often in school and community-based theater programs. Some of the following internships are for acting, musical theatre, technical theatre, and backstage opportunities. However, there are numerous summer options for students to pursue their dream and hone their craft. The following are a few of the summer options.

- ArtsBridge Summer Drama Programs
- AMDA (American Musical and Dramatic Academy) High School Summer Conservatory (Los Angeles and New York)
- Boston Conservatory
- Broadway Artists Alliance Summer Intensives
- BroadwayEvolved NYC Summer Intensive
- Carnegie Mellon University, Pre-College Drama
- Emerson College
- Florida State University
- French Woods Festival of the Performing Arts
- Idyllwild Arts Teens & Kids Summer Program
- Interlochen Arts Camp
- Ithaca College Summer Theatre Intensive

- La Jolla Playhouse Conservatory
- Marymount Manhattan
- Muny/Webster Intensive – St. Louis, Missouri
- Neighborhood Playhouse, Six Week Summer Acting Intensive
- Northwestern University, National High School Institute (Cherubs)
- NYU, Tisch, Summer High School
- Oklahoma City University
- Paper Mill Playhouse, Summer Musical Theater Conservatory
- Penn State University
- The Performing Arts Project (TPAP) – Wake Forest University
- Perry-Mansfield Intensives
- Rutgers Summer Conservatory
- Southeastern Summer Theater Institute (SSTI)
- Stagedoor Manor
- Stella Adler Teen Summer Conservatory
- Syracuse University, Summer College
- Texas State University, NEXUS Musical Theatre Pre-College Intensive
- UCLA, Acting and Performance Summer Institute
- University of Cincinnati, College Conservatory of Music
- University of Michigan, MPulse Summer Performing Arts Institutes
- University of North Carolina School of the Arts
- University of Southern California High School Summer Conservatory
- Walnut Hill School for the Arts

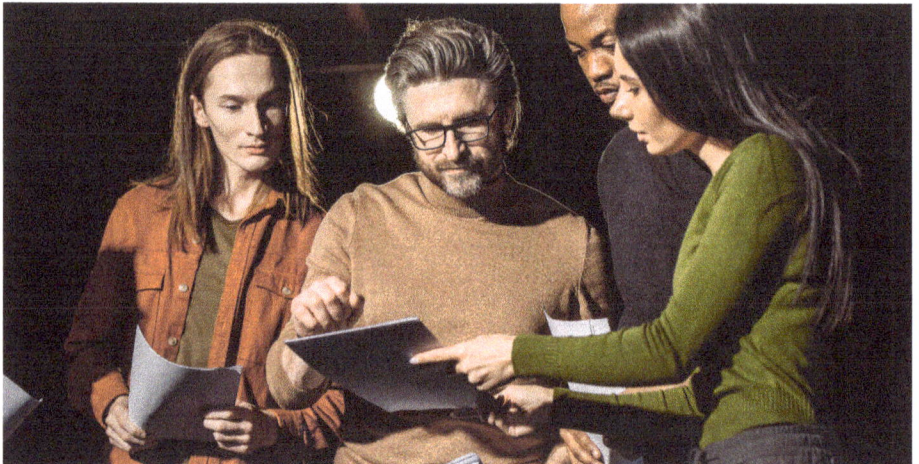

FESTIVAL JOBS AND INTERNSHIPS

ALABAMA

Alabama Shakespeare Festival
Location: Montgomery, AL
Career Opportunities: Positions open as available across the spectrum of theatre positions.[2]

CALIFORNIA

Marin Shakespeare Festival
Location: San Rafael, CA (Dominican University)
Paid Positions:[3] Stage Manager, Assistant Stage Manager, Carpenters, Costume Designers, Costume Assistants, House Manager/Assistant House Manager, Lighting Designer, Master Carpenter, Master Electrician, Prop Designer, Scenic Painters, Set Designer, and Wardrobe Supervisor
Volunteer Positions:[4] Carpenters / Scenic Painters, Costume Helpers, Dressers, Technicians, Sound and Light Operators, and Ushers.

Location: Santa Cruz, CA (University of California, Santa Cruz)
Internships: The summer season opens for intern applications in late fall and closes in February. Applications will be reviewed in February.[5] For more information, contact intern@santacruzshakespeare.org

Will Geer Theatricum Botanicum
Location: Topanga, CA
Internships:[6] Acting, administration, technical design, education and production – we have an internship for every aspect of Theatricum's operation.

COLORADO

Colorado Shakespeare Festival
Location: Boulder, CO (University of Colorado, Boulder)
Positions/Internships: For positions as they open, see https://cupresents.org/about-cu-presents/job-opportunities/

Casting for the following summer season is announced in October. Colorado Shakespeare Festival hires AEA actors on two to three show contracts and non-AEA

---

2   Alabama Shakespeare Festival, "Career Opportunities," *Alabama Shakespeare Festival*, n.d., https://asf.net/careers/

3   Marin Shakespeare Company, "Job Openings," *Marin Shakespeare Company*, n.d., https://www.marinshakespeare.org/jobs/

4   Idaho Shakespeare Festival, "Volunteer," *Idaho Shakespeare Festival*, n.d., https://idahoshakespeare.org/volunteer/

5   Santa Cruz Shakespeare, "Internship," *Santa Cruz Shakespeare*, n.d., https://santacruzshakespeare.org/internship/

6   Will Geer's Theatricum Botanicum, "Internships," *Will Geer's Theatricum Botanicum*, n.d., https://theatricum.com/internships/

actors on one, two, or three show contracts. Live auditions or video submissions are held in October. Two contrasting monologues, no more than two minutes (each should be less than one minute).

Creede Repertory Theatre
Location: Creede, CO
Professional Positions:[7] Numerous positions are open for each summer form May – July, including stage management, technical, carpentry, costume, first hand, sound, lighting, electrician, artisan, paint, props, and stitcher.

CONNECTICUT

Goodspeed Musicals
Location: East Haddam, CT
Paid Production Apprenticeships: Positions are available in Stage Carpentry, Technical/Construction, Prop Run Crew, Costume Shop, Stitchers, Wardrobe, and Electrics. Most 2022 apprenticeship positions are paid minimum wage. To apply, submit cover letter, resume, availability and list of three references to jobs@goodspeed.org.[8]

Actors – Equity video submissions for three musicals. All principal roles will be understudied ($1,008 weekly minimum). Video audition, headshot, resume.

IDAHO

Idaho Shakespeare Festival
Location: Boise, ID
Volunteer/Paid/Apprenticeship Positions: Production & Technical Positions, Volunteers, Apprenticeship Program, Workshops, Residences, Casting, Directors & Designers, and Acting Company.

Actors may submit headshots, resumes, and video auditions (include Shakespeare and contemporary monologues and a song if you sing) at any time of the year. EQUITY and non-EQUITY actors are considered.

ILLINOIS

Illinois Shakespeare Festival
Location: Bloomington, IL (Illinois State University)
Internships: Acting, Company Management, Lighting/Electrics, Prop Shop, Scenic Artist/Paint Shop, Scene Shop/Carpentry, Sound Shop, and Stage Management. "Interns will participate in an internship class once a week for professional development and education. Interns will be registered for THE 398 - Professional Practice in Theatre at Illinois State University…The Illinois Shakespeare Festival will pay for the tuition and fees for up to six credit hours of THE 398 and assist students

7   Creede Repetory Theatre, "Work With Us," *Creede Repetory Theatre*, n.d., https://creederep.org/work-with-us/

8   Goodspeed Musicals, "Job Opportunities," *Goodspeed Musicals,* n.d., https://www.goodspeed.org/about/career-opportunities

in transferring this credit to their home academic institution.

"Our summer 2022 course will be facilitated by Dr. Ann Haugo and Dr. Derek R. Munson. Interns will meet with their mentor and the production manager every three weeks. Mentorship meeting goals are to provide structured feedback for each individual, discuss any programmatic challenges they are having, and to set goals for the internship experience.

"Current enrollment in a college program with an anticipated graduation date of August 2022 or later. Ability to commit to the full summer season. All internships are full-time commitments."

MAINE

Theater at Monmouth
Location: Monmouth, ME
Internships: "Each year, early career theatre artists, technicians, and administrators start their professional journey at Theater at Monmouth. Members of the intern and apprentice company work alongside artists and professionals to produce the summer season at one of the nation's only classical repertory theatres."[10]

MASSACHUSETTS

Barrington Stage Company
Location: Pittsfield, MA
Internships/Jobs:[11] The listing in early 2022 included these positions: Lighting and Sound Technician, Scene Shop Operations Manager, Scenic Carpenter/Welder, Scenic Carpenter, Charge Scenic Artist, Scenic Artist, Stitcher, Associate Wardrobe Supervisor, Wardrobe Technician, Light Board Operator, Electrician, Audio Supervisor, Sound Board Operator (A1), Sound Technician (A2), Properties Supervisor, Assistant Properties Supervisor, Properties Artisan, Stage Crew Chief, Stage Crew.

Berkshire Theater Festival
Location: Pittsfield/Stockbridge, MA
Internships and Jobs: https://www.berkshiretheatregroup.org/Join%20Our%20Team/#Year-Round_Job_Opps

Shakespeare & Company
Location: Lenox, MA
Internships: In addition to exclusive lectures, career guidance, and the possibility

---

9   Illinois Shakespeare Festival, "Internship Program," *Illinois Shakespeare Festival*, n.d., https://illinoisshakes. com/employment/internships/

10   Theater at Monmouth, "Work With Us," *Theater at Monmouth,* n.d., http://theateratmonmouth.org/about-us/ work-with-us/

11   Barrington Stage Company, "Job Opportunities," *Barrington Stage Company*, n.d., https://barringtonstageco. org/about-the-company/jobs/

of a capstone project, "Interns receive one-on-one mentoring from within their department and experience with professional artists and staff...Internships are available year-round, typically 15- or 16-week duration, but if one of the tracks below is not perfect for an applicant, programs of custom duration or areas of interest can be developed as well."[12]

Actors are sought for the season. All roles will be understudied. Virtual auditions (may change). Auditions are for Equity actors, no non-union acting roles are available. Auditions include a Vimeo submission with contrasting monologues, a headshot, and a resume.

Williamstown Theatre Festival
Location: Williamstown, MA (Williams College)
Internships: "Tony Award-winning Williamstown Theatre Festival's summer season offers a variety of career opportunities for theatre professionals at all levels of experience.... In the summer of 2021, salaried positions will be compensated at a range of $684 to $750 per week. Hourly positions will be compensated at a rate of $13.50 to $15.00 per hour."[13]

NEW YORK

Adirondack Theatre Festival
Location: Glen Falls, NY
Internships: "ATF's professional internship program offers rigorous, hands-on educational opportunities for current students and early career professionals seeking an introduction to careers in the professional theatre. Our goal is to provide interns with practical experience in the shop, rehearsal room, backstage and in the front office as well as valuable networking opportunities with working theatre professionals."[14] Internships available in administration, artistic, production, carpentry, electrics, sound, props, paint, and wardrobe.

Apply by February 1st. Chorus roles are possible for interns as well. "While interns are assigned specific departments and mentors, they are also expected to learn and work outside their chosen area of expertise. We hope to provide the intern with a well-rounded experience designed to inform them of all the various jobs required to mount a professional production." Interns may receive either course credit or a weekly stipend.

Hudson Valley Shakespeare Festival
Location: Garrison, NY
Internships/Training: "While most theater training programs are unpaid (or charge

---

12 Shakespeare & Company, "Jobs and Volunteering," *Shakespeare & Company,* n.d., https://www.shakespeare.org/jobs-and-volunteering/interns

13 Williamstown Theatre Festival, "Work & Learn," *Williamstown Theatre Festival,* n.d., https://wtfestival.org/work-learn/

14 Adirondack Theatre Festival, "Professional Theatre Internships at Adirondack Theatre Festival," *Adirondack Theatre Festival,* 2021, https://www.atfestival.org/opportunities/internships/

tuition), we're proud to pay educational stipends to participants and, in most cases, offer local housing, reducing barriers to employment in the arts. Our Conservatory Company training program, Production and Administrative Internships and Directing Fellowships offer exceptional practical experience through collaboration, hands-on learning, and mentorship."[15]

Powerhouse Theater
Location: Poughkeepsie, NY (Vassar College)
Training Program: The summer 2022 training program is five weeks encompassing the theatre process while observing and participating in shows.[16]

Shakespeare in the Park
Location: New York, NY
Freelance Positions: Stitchers/Costume Department – stitching and finishes to costumes - $25/hour
Scenery Department – Hard-working carpenters, scenic artists, and props run crew. Construction/painting experience required - $25-$27/hour.[17]

OREGON

Oregon Shakespeare Festival
Location: Ashland, OR
Internships: "Internships are designed to provide participants with a learning opportunity within our artistic, production, and administration areas…Prior theatre experience is not required. This is a 2- to 4–month experience that is designed to provide a professional development opportunity for emerging artists and aspiring arts administrators. Recipients are paired with an OSF company member and receive mentorship in their respective discipline.

"Internships are unpaid learning opportunities. Housing and travel are not provided for Internships…Candidates for Internships must be a high school graduate or have at least one year of work experience. Applicants interested in an Internship in Stage Management and any of the production areas must have at least one year of experience in their specific area of interest, a year of experience in an academic environment will be considered."[18]

Actors – AEA required for auditions – Contact Oregon Shakespeare Festival in July for open call auditions for the following summer repertory season.

15 Hudson Valley Shakespeare Festival, "Professional Training," *Hudson Valley Shakespeare Festival*, n.d., https://hvshakespeare.org/education/training/

16 Vassar College, "Powerhouse Theater Training Program," *Vassar College*, n.d., https://www.vassar.edu/powerhouse/apprentices/

17 The Public, "Employment & Internships," *The Public*, n.d., https://publictheater.org/footer/employment--internships/

18 Oregon Shakespeare Festival, "Internships," *Oregon Shakespeare Festival*, n.d., https://www.osfashland.org/en/work-with-us/FAIR/Internships.aspx

40

Pennsylvania Shakespeare Festival
Location: Center Valley, PA
The 2022 Season includes productions of A Chorus Line, Fences, Little Red, Every Brilliant Thing, The River Bride (reading) and Much Ado About Nothing.
Internships: There are numerous Stage Management (SM) tracks. Interns work alongside Equity SMs. Responsibilities include prop tracking, feeding lines, backstage deck, run crew, lifting, props, repairing, construction, carpentry, and foreman shadowing. Specialty skills will be learned on the job. SM and Carp interns must be go-getters in a fast-paced environment. Salary $300/week.
Costume Design – **First Hand Assistant** to the Cutter/Draper – Experienced in pattern layout/cutting/sewing. Salary $475/week. **Costume Shop Craftsperson** – assists with crafts, including millinery, footwear, jewelry, masks – must be self-motivated, manage multiple simultaneous projects. and able to read/interpret sketches. Salary $425/week. **Stitcher** – Intermediate/Advanced sewing by hand/maching, including alterations, construction, and finishing. Salary $340/week. **Costume Shop Intern** and **Costume Shop Management Intern** – Assists the costumer design staff while working following instructions and working independently. Salary $300/week. **Wardrobe Crafts** and **Wardrobe Stitcher**– Salary $340/week. **Wardrobe Intern** and **Wig and Makeup Dresser** – Salary $300/week

Texas Shakespeare Festival
Location: Kilgore, TX (Kilgore College)
Internships:[19]
Costume Intern / Wardrobe: May 20 - August 3   Salary: $1,500 / double occupancy dorm housing / 14 meals a week. Minimum Requirements: undergraduate costume technology training required and/or one year of professional experience. **Costume and Wig Stylist Intern:** May 20 - August 3 Salary: $1,500 / double occupancy dormitory housing / 14 meals a week. Minimum Requirements: undergraduate training in wigs and hairstyling preferred and/or one year of professional experience working on wigs and hairstyling. **Properties Intern:** May 20 - August 3 Salary: $1,500 stipend / double occupancy dorm housing / 14 meals a week Note: Properties Interns are assigned primarily to the properties department, but may also be reassigned, as needed, to other technical areas. **Scenic Carpenters:** May 16 - August 3   Salary: $4,400 stipend / up to $300 / double occupancy dorm housing / 14 meals a week Minimum Requirements: Experience with various scenic construction techniques and materials; strong woodworking skills. **Scene Painting Intern:** May 20 - August 3 Salary: $1,500 stipend / double occupancy dorm housing / 14 meals a week. Minimum Requirements: Fundamental experience in scenic treatments including, but not limited to, faux finish, carving, texturing, aging, and distressing. The candidate should also be comfortable working at heights above

---

19 Texas Shakespeare Festival, "Costume Department," *Texas Shakespeare Festival,* n.d., https://www. texasshakespeare.com/costumes

16'. **Lighting Intern:** May 20 - August 3   Salary: $1,500 stipend / double occupancy dorm housing / 14 meals a week. Minimum Requirements: Assist with the hang, focus, and strike of electrics and special effects for all productions; program and run the lighting console for shows as assigned; assist with the maintenance and upkeep for all lighting inventory and systems. **Stage Management Intern**: May 20 - August 3 Salary: $1,500 stipend / double occupancy dorm housing / 14 meals a week. Minimum requirement: one year undergraduate stage management training. **Stage Management Intern:** May 20 - August 3 Salary: $1,500 stipend / double occupancy dorm housing / 14 meals a week. Minimum Requirement: minimum one year undergraduate stage management training.

Review the website for audition opportunities in the fall. Even though they have more than a thousand submissions, some of those who audition get a spot. Casting is completed in late February. The Texas Shakespeare Festival also has a fall Roadshow Educational Tour.

UTAH

Utah Shakespearean Festival
Location: Cedar City, UT
Inernships: May/June – July/September Draper:[20] May – July - Oversees all construction of costumes for assigned show. Works in direct relationship with costume designer. **First Hand:** Works with the draper to construct and supervise construction of costumes. Supervises costume technicians. **Technician:** Constructs all costume pieces assigned by first hand. Contracts are May 2–July 2 or June 1–July 13. **Wardrobe:** Works on the run of assigned productions assisting in preparation and maintenance (laundry and repair) of costumes. **Assistant Costume Crafts Supervisor:** Assists with the operation of costume crafts including scheduling of fittings and attending fittings; helps interpret costume designer's sketches and ideas and assists with problem-solving and engineering of costume crafts items. **Crafts Technician:** Assists senior crafts technician in the construction of all accessories or special costume projects. **Junior Artisan/Stage Crew:** Responsible for the building and fabrication of stage and rehearsal properties for assigned productions. Works with the prop team to complete shop improvement and organizational projects as assigned. **Scenic Carpenter**: Constructs and loads in all scenic set elements for assigned productions. Completes shop improvement and organization projects as assigned. **Junior Carpenter/Stage Crew:** Constructs and loads-in all scenic set elements for assigned productions. Responsible for running, storage, and maintenance of scenery for assigned productions. **Scenic Artist:** Responsible for painting and finishing of all scenic elements for assigned productions. **Junior Painter/Stage Crew:** Responsible for painting and finishing of all scenic elements for assigned productions. Responsible for running, storage, and maintenance of paints for assigned productions. **Deck Carpenter:** Responsible for load in, running, organization of storage, and maintenance of scenery and props for

---

20   Utah Shakespeare Festival, "Employment," *Utah Shakespeare Festival*, n.d., https://www.bard.org/employment

a theatre (Engelstad, Randall, or Anes). Works with scenery director on stage crew schedule and necessary adjustments. **Junior Carpenters/Painters/Prop Interns:** Responsible for load in, running, storage, changeovers, and maintenance of scenery and props for assigned productions. **Stage Crew:** Responsible for load in, running, storage, and changeovers of scenery and props for assigned productions.

VIRGINIA

American Shakespeare Center
Location: Staunton, VA
Drama Club: "With Shakespeare's text as our touchstone and his technology as our laboratory, the Drama Club meets once a week in 12-week terms to explore Shakespeare's wordcraft and stagecraft through play, building confidence and expanding creativity by working together to craft and rehearse a final performance of Shakespearean scenes at the Blackfriars Playhouse."[21]
American Shakespeare Center holds Equity auditions each year. Submit your headshot and resume to be considered for upcoming seasons.

Appalachian Festival of Plays and Playwrights
Location: Abingdon, VA (Emory & Henry College -10 min away)
Internships: The Association of the Barter Theatre with Emory & Henry College "offers theatre majors opportunities for professional internships, mentoring, workshops, and master classes throughout their college career. Barter staff members and artists often serve as adjunct faculty and guest artists in the Theatre Department. In addition, E&H theatre majors have the opportunity to attend professional rehearsals, participate in "talk backs" with the actors and crew after Barter performances, and serve as understudies in Barter Theatre productions. With this partnership, Emory & Henry Theatre Department offers students the combined strengths of a small liberal arts college and the type of pre-professional experiences often found only in large conservatories."[22]

WEST VIRGINIA

Contemporary American Theater Festival
Location: Shepherdstown, WV (Shepherd University)
Internships: "Apply for a specific department based on your strengths and passions as a theater artist. You may apply for no more than two departments [carpentry, costumes, electrics, props, scenic arts, sound] but if hired, you will only be assigned to one. Internships usually begin in late May and end in early August, running 8-10 weeks."[23]

---

21 American Shakespeare Center, "Drama Club," *American Shakespeare Center*, n.d., https://americanshakespearecenter.com/education/drama-club/

22 Barter Theatre, "Emory & Henry College," *Barter Theatre*, n.d., https://bartertheatre.com/emory-henry/

23 Contemporary American Theater Festival, "Internships," *Contemporary American Theater Festival*, n.d., https://catf.org/internships/

American Players Theatre
Location: Spring Green, WI
Positions: Stitchers, Wigs, Stage Management, Carpentry, First Hand, Lighting, Production[24]

INTERNATIONAL

ONTARIO, CANADA

Shaw Festival
Location: Niagara-On-The-Lake, Ontario, Canada
Camps and Training Programs: While there are no internships, per se, there is training, including a summer stage combat class.
Stratford Shakespeare Festival
Location: Stratford, Ontario, Canada
Camps and Training Programs: While there are no internships, per se, there are summer camps and training programs for students of all ages.

---

24 American Players Theatre, "Employment," *American Players Theatre,* n.d., https://americanplayers.org/about/employment

CHAPTER 5

UNIVERSITY OPTIONS: WHAT COLLEGE PROGRAMS ARE BEST FOR THEATRE, DRAMATIC WRITING, AND DIRECTING?

"Movies will make you famous; television will make you rich; but theatre will make you good."

– **Terrence Mann**

In the United States, more than 600 colleges offer degrees in theatre, about 475 offering a 4-year degree. More than 11,000 students each year earn a degree in some area of the dramatic arts. Although this book only profiles about one-sixth of these schools and only those U.S. colleges with bachelor's degree programs, there are undoubtedly many with excellent faculty and facilities in your local area. Thus, Yale, for example, which has an amazing MFA program, is not included. Nevertheless, many undergraduate schools provide thorough training from which you can choose.

Everyone has heard about the top colleges for theatre - NYU, Juilliard, Carnegie Mellon, Northwestern, Ithaca, Penn State, Elon, Florida State, Texas State, and the University of Michigan. Yet, there are many more excellent programs. The colleges that offer the most bachelor's degrees in theatre each year are:

1. New York University
2. Texas State University
3. Northwestern University
4. University of California, Los Angeles
5. University of Central Florida
6. Cal State Fullerton
7. University of California, Irvine
8. Muhlenberg College
9. Florida State University
10. Virginia Commonwealth University

Also, when you get to the master's level, Yale, Columbia, Brown, American Conservatory Theatre, and USC are top-notch. These MFA programs offer students opportunities for personalized training, smaller classes, wise faculty, performance roles in on-campus shows, and unique programs.

You might even want to study theatre abroad. Though international programs are not profiled in this book, some of the best include the London Academy of Music & Dramatic Art, Guildhall (London), Royal Academy of Dramatic Art (London), and the National Institute of Dramatic Arts (Sydney). The following are the top 10 colleges on the 2021 QS World University Rankings for the Performing Arts.

1. The Juilliard School (U.S.)
2. Royal College of Music (U.K.)
3. Royal Conservatoire of Scotland (U.K.)
4. Royal Academy of Music (U.K.)
5. Conservatoire National Superieur de Musique et de Dance de Paris (France)
6. New York University (U.S.)
7. Universitat fur Musik und Darstellende Kunst Wien (Austria)
8. Norwegian Academy of Music (Norway)
9. Sibelius Academy, University of the Arts Helsinki (Finland)
10. Hong Kong Academy for Performing Arts (Hong Kong SAR)

Some small colleges produce acclaimed successes. Lisa Kron, playwright and lyricist of the Tony Award-winning musical *Fun Home,* graduated from Kalamazoo College, while Anaïs Mitchell, who wrote and composed *Hadestown,* won 8 Tony Awards, graduated from Middlebury College.

Since there are many excellent opportunities, here are twelve schools you might consider outside of New York City.

SPOTLIGHT ON 12 NON-NEW YORK CITY PROGRAMS

MICHIGAN AND ILLINOIS

Northwestern University (private, Evanston, IL)

Northwestern offers holistic training in the dramatic arts combining theatre literature, critique, and theory with practice in acting, voice, movement, dance directing, design, stage production, playwriting, and dramaturgy. Students gain valuable skills with forty productions per year in Northwestern's multi-stage Wirtz Center for the Performing Arts. Theatre majors choose from music theater, playwriting, acting, design, and stage management. Additionally, many students study abroad at the British American Drama Academy in London.

University of Michigan (public, Ann Arbor, MI)

With one of the top theatre programs in the United States and the world, U-M students have access to premier trainers, professors, and performers in an intense conservatory-style environment. Students must be book smart, people smart, and performance smart. With the possibility of a dual degree, students are encouraged to explore their interests and collaborate with others. The University of Michigan's extensive network of alumni offers unparalleled connections.

NORTH CAROLINA, PENNSYLVANIA, AND VIRGINIA

Carnegie Mellon University (private, Pittsburgh, PA)

The 3% acceptance rate for CMU's conservatory-style program is daunting. However, the program is fantastic. Options for additional study include directing, stage/production management, video/media/scenic design, production technology, dramaturgy, and sound/lighting. Students can take wide-ranging courses like "Art of Cabaret" and study at Sydney's National Institute of Dramatic Art, The Moscow Art Theatre, London's Drama Centre, and famed programs worldwide.

Elon University (private, Elon, NC)

Elon's professionalization in theatre begins from the start of the student's education with onstage opportunities from day one. With conservatory-style training, sixteen students are accepted each year to prepare for film, stage, and television. Student auditions are held starting in the first semester with musicals, one-act plays, dance performances, vocal ensembles, and impromptu groups. BFA students can participate in classical studies in Greece and residencies in London while seeing shows and weekend travel to Spain, France, and Portugal. Seniors take a two-semester seminar on the "Business of Show" followed by opportunities to meet with agents and casting directors.

Penn State University (public, State College, PA)

Penn State emphasizes academics, performance, and study abroad. From contemporary plays, film, and new media to classical plays, musicals, and Shakespeare numerous performance opportunities exist. With a student-faculty ratio of less than 1 to 4, students get individualized attention in a high-performing, dynamic environment. Penn State's theatre program commissions writers through the unique New Musicals Initiative. Other opportunities include the Master Class Series, and MusicPoal Theatre Wellness Center. Additionally, students are encouraged to spend a semester at the Theatre Academy London.

Shenandoah University (private, Winchester, VA)

Though a smaller conservatory school, its reputation for turning out some of the top theatre students is astounding. Shenandoah's program is the second-oldest in the country. Known as a "pop/rock school" whose performers earn roles in contemporary Broadway shows. While mastering storytelling, students also learn branding, marketing, web design for artists, the "Business of the Business", and "Prep for the Profession". The faculty are Broadway veterans and industry professionals

CONNECTICUT, MASSACHUSETTS, AND NEW YORK (NOT NYC AREA)

Emerson College (private, Boston, MA)

Emerson College has its theatre right on Boston Common where thousands of people come for fresh air, peace of mind, and artistic performances. Emerson College's approach is to hone student's skills in musical theatre. Senior showcases in Boston and New York City allow students to perform for current industry leaders. Many students take summer theatre positions in New York, New England, and destinations across the country. Preparation includes self-reliance, audition training, teamwork, stamina, fitness, entrepreneurship, technique, and the nomenclature of the theatrical arts. Students are encouraged to attend combined auditions like SETC, NETC, StrawHats, IOC/Outdoor Drama, NHPTA, and UPTAs.

Ithaca College (private, Ithaca, NY)

Ithaca College is one of the top programs in the country for musical theatre with rigorous training and a focus on performance. Students participate in 20 hours of studio training per week along with classes, auditions, rehearsals, and performances. Students take private voice lessons and vocal repertoire classes while gaining skills in piano, scene study, movement, ballet, jazz, and modern dance. Students can study British drama and culture at Ithaca College's London Center and take workshops and masterclasses. During a one-week field studies trip to New York City, students connect with alumni working in the industry.

Syracuse University (private, Syracuse, NY)

Syracuse University partners with Syracuse Stage, a professional theatrical company. Syracuse University offers students training in all areas of musical theatre with shows produced by the university as well as opportunities to train professionally and earn points toward Equity membership through Syracuse Stage. In a thorough performance-oriented program, students gain opportunities to train and practice individually and in group settings in acting, dance, and voice. Students train to be artists, while also learning to read, analyze, and interpret a script and a score. Students master the entire theatrical and musical canon, learning how to vividly bring to life their individual piece of the puzzle while collaboratively working to perfect each show.

Wesleyan University (private, Middletown, CT)

Merging theory, scholarship, and practice, Wesleyan graduates theatre-makers who are proficient n classical works as well as contemporary plays. Students cross specialties by learning directing, design, history, playwriting, acting, improvisation, and technical theatre. With graduates performing on and off-Broadway, many have won prestigious awards. Study abroad includes the British American Drama Academy, London, CIEE, Buenos Aires, and C.V. Starr, Chile.

Chapman University (private, Orange, CA)

Though not in the top ten theatre programs, they do have a top-five film program that uses its available actors for the numerous films it produces. Chapman offers an incredibly versatile program with an excellent dance program and renowned music faculty. The campus is compact with multiple theatres and movie studios within a block of one another. Chapman's 1,000-seat Musco Center for the Arts, built in 2016, is a dream performance location for a small school or, frankly, any school. Only 14 students are accepted in theatre each year, making it very competitive. Students can get a BFA in Screen Acting with on-camera experience starting as a freshman. Chapman also offers a BFA in Theatre Performance, BA in Theatre, and a Musical Theatre Minor.

Texas State University (public, San Marcos, TX)

With relationships with summer stock theatres nationwide, students gain significant experience. Furthermore, Texas State provides audition support and training for students after graduation. Nearly all of their graduates are working professionally in theatre, film, or television. A casting director at Telsey Casting produces the senior showcase in New York City. The university produces two musicals and 9 – 12 plays as well as other performance opportunities. Training is extensive with one-on-one coaching, weekly voice lessons, individual musical director sessions, and private work sessions, in acting and musical theatre. One reviewer exclaimed, "San Marcos has become a mecca for musicals."

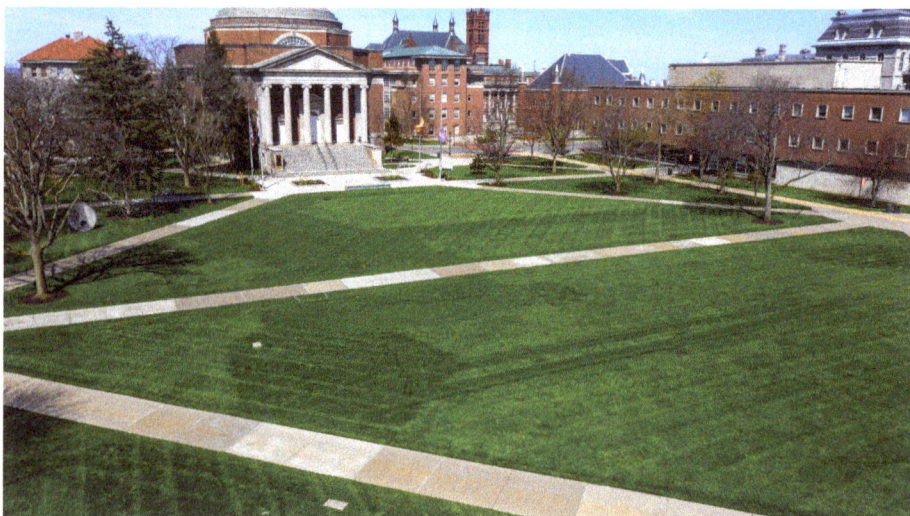

The Many Roads to Theatre Success

While about a quarter of the Tony Award winners never attended college, this was, in part, because in the middle of the last century, wars prevented many people from attending. Furthermore, many famous actors served in the U.S. military.

An abbreviated list of veterans who became successful actors includes Alan Alda, Sunny Anderson, Bea Arthur, Harry Belafonte, Tony Bennett, Charles Bronson, Mel Brooks, Drew Carey, Kirk Douglas, Adam Driver, Robert Duvall, Clint Eastwood, Morgan Freeman, Gene Hackman, MC Hammer, Zulay Henao, Bob Hope, Ice-T, James Earl Jones, Buster Keaton, Harvey Keitel, Steve McQueen, Audie Murphy, Paul Newman, David Niven, Chuck Norris, Jack Palance, Sidney Poitier, Elvis Presley, Robin Quivers, Rob Riggle, Jason Robards, Tom Selleck, Sinbad, Robert Stack, Jimmy Stewart, and Oliver Stone.

Also, to show you that there are many roads to success, here are the top Tony Award winners and the colleges they attended. Some of the schools in which these actors went to were smaller programs where they gained a broader or more extensive liberal arts education.

Note that Juilliard is listed numerous times. Students who study acting can also study voice and dance. Very successful actors and actresses attended Juilliard and gained valuable skills that they later applied to the shows in which they appeared.

TONY AWARD FOR BEST MALE ACTOR IN A MUSICAL OR PLAY

Frank A. Langella, Jr. – 7 nominations, 4 wins – Syracuse University

Boyd Payne Gaines – 5 nominations, 4 wins – Juilliard

Nathan Lane - 6 nominations, 3 wins – did not attend college

Mark Rylance – 5 nominations, 3 wins – Did not attend college

Kevin Kline – 4 nominations, 3 wins –University of Indiana, Bloomington

Zero Mostel – 4 nominations, 3 wins – City College of New York, New York University

Hinton Battle – 3 nominations, 3 wins – did not attend college

Christopher Plummer – 7 nominations, 2 wins – did not attend college

John Lithgow – 6 nominations, 2 wins – Harvard University, London Academy of Music and Dramatic Art

Michael Cerveris – 6 nominations, 2 wins – Yale University

George Hearn – 5 nominations, 2 wins – Rhodes College

George Rose – 5 nominations, 2 wins – Oxford University

John Cullum -– 5 nominations, 2 wins – University of Tennessee

Robert Morse – 5 nominations, 2 wins – did not attend college

Christian Borle – 4 nominations, 2 wins – Carnegie Mellon University

James Earl Jones – 4 nominations, 2 wins – University of Michigan

Norbert Leo Butz – 4 nominations, 2 wins – Webster University, University of Alabama

Richard Kiley – 4 nominations, 2 wins – Loyola University Chicago, Chicago's Barnum Dramatic School

Al Pacino – 3 nominations, 2 wins – Actors Studio

David Burns – 3 nominations, 2 wins – did not attend college

David Wayne – 3 nominations, 2 wins – Western Michigan University

Fredric March – 3 nominations, 2 wins – University of Wisconsin, Madison

Judd Hirsch – 3 nominations, 2 wins – City College of New York, American Academy of Dramatic Arts

Matthew Broderick – 3 nominations, 2 wins – HB Studio

Phil Silvers – 3 nominations, 2 wins – did not attend college

Rex Harrison – 3 nominations, 2 wins – Liverpool College

Robert Preston – 3 nominations, 2 wins – did not go to college

Stephen Spinella – 3 nominations, 2 wins – University of Arizona, New York University

Walter Matthau – 3 nominations, 2 wins – did not attend college

Alan Bates – 2 nominations, 2 wins – Royal Academy of Dramatic Art

Brian Dennehy – 2 nominations, 2 wins – Columbia University

Bryan Cranston – 2 nominations, 2 wins – Los Angeles Valley College

Harvey Fierstein – 2 nominations, 2 wins – Pratt Institute

Hiram Sherman – 2 nominations, 2 wins – did not attend college

James Naughton – 2 nominations, 2 wins – Brown University, Yale University

Jonathan Pryce – 2 nominations, 2 wins – Royal Academy of Dramatic Art

Jose Ferrer – 2 nominations, 2 wins – Princeton University

Russell Nype – 2 nominations, 2 wins – Lake Forest College

Tommy Tune – 2 nominations, 2 wins – Lon Morris College, University of Texas, Austin, University of Houston

Jason Robards – 8 nominations, 1 win – American Academy of Dramatic Arts

Brian Bedford – 7 nominations, 1 win – Royal Academy of Dramatic Art

Danny Burstein – 7 nominations, 1 win – City University of New York, UCSD

Philip Bosco – 6 nominations, 1 win – Catholic University

Brian F. O'Bryrne – 5 nominations, 1 win – Trinity College, Dublin

Hume Cronyn – 5 nominations, 1 win – Ridley College, McGill University

Jim Dale – 5 nominations, 1 win – did not attend college

TONY AWARD FOR BEST FEMALE ACTOR IN A MUSICAL OR PLAY

Audra McDonald – 9 nominations, 6 wins – Juilliard

Julie Harris – 10 nominations, 5 wins – Yale University

Angela Lansbury – 7 nominations, 5 wins – did not attend college

Gwen Verdon – 6 nominations, 4 wins – did not attend college

Zoe Caldwell – 4 nominations, 4 wins – did not attend college

Irene Worth – 5 nominations, 3 wins – UCLA

Jessica Tandy – 5 nominations, 3 wins – did not attend college

Glenn Close – 4 nominations, 3 wins – The College of William and Mary

Mary Martin – 4 nominations, 3 wins – did not attend college

Shirley Booth – 3 nominations, 3 wins – did not attend college

Chita Rivera – 10 nominations, 2 wins – did not attend college

Colleen Dewhurst - 8 nominations, 2 wins – Milwaukee-Downer College

Bernadette Peters - 7 nominations, 2 wins – did not attend college

Frances Sternhagen - 7 nominations, 2 wins – Vassar College, Catholic University

Patti LuPone - 7 nominations, 2 wins – Juilliard

Andrea Martin - 6 nominations, 2 wins – Emerson College

Laurie Metcalf - 6 nominations, 2 wins – Illinois State University

Maureen Stapleton - 6 nominations, 2 wins – did not attend college

Sutton Foster - 6 nominations, 2 wins – Carnegie Mellon University

Cherry Jones - 5 nominations, 2 wins – Carnegie Mellon University

Donna Murphy - 5 nominations, 2 wins – New York University

Swoosie Kurtz - 5 nominations, 2 wins – University of Southern California, London Academy of Music and Dramatic Art

Christine Ebersole - 4 nominations, 2 wins – MacMurray College, American Academy of Dramatic Arts

Cynthia Nixon - 4 nominations, 2 wins – Barnard College

Judith Ivey - 4 nominations, 2 wins – Illinois State University

Judy Kaye - 4 nominations, 2 wins – UCLA

Margaret Leighton - 4 nominations, 2 wins – did not attend college

Mary-Louise Parker - 4 nominations, 2 wins – University of North Carolina School of the Arts

Anne Bancroft - 3 nominations, 2 wins – HB Studio, American Academy of Dramatic Arts, Actors Studio

Helen Gallagher - 3 nominations, 2 wins – did not attend college

Helen Hayes - 3 nominations, 2 wins – did not attend college

Jennifer Ehle - 3 nominations, 2 wins – University of North Carolina School of the Arts, University of London

Judith Light - 3 nominations, 2 wins – Carnegie Mellon University

Liza Minnelli - 3 nominations, 2 wins – did not attend college

Viola Davis - 3 nominations, 2 wins – Rhode Island College, Juilliard

Bebe Neuwirth - 2 nominations, 2 wins – Juilliard

Christine Baranski - 2 nominations, 2 wins – Juilliard

Katie Finneran - 2 nominations, 2 wins – Carnegie Mellon University, HB Studio

Lauren Bacall - 2 nominations, 2 wins – did not attend college

Sandy Dennis - 2 nominations, 2 wins – Nebraska Wesleyan University, University of Nebraska, HB Studio

Tammy Grimes - 2 nominations, 2 wins – Stephens College

Uta Hagen - 2 nominations, 2 wins – Royal Academy of Dramatic Art, University of Wisconsin–Madison

Rosemary Harris- 9 nominations, 1 win – Royal Academy of Dramatic Art

Jane Alexander - 8 nominations, 1 win – Sarah Lawrence College, University of Edinburgh

Stockard Channing - 8 nominations, 1 win – Radcliffe/Harvard University, HB Studio

Kelli O'Hara - 7 nominations, 1 win – Oklahoma City University

Linda Lavin - 6 nominations, 1 win – College of William and Mary

Glenda Jackson - 5 nominations, 1 win – Royal Academy of Dramatic Art

Laura Benanti - 5 nominations, 1 win – did not attend college

Marian Seides - 5 nominations, 1 win – did not attend college

CHAPTER 6

WHAT IS THE DIFFERENCE BETWEEN AN AA, AS, BA, BS, BFA, AND MFA?

"How could we explain that standing on a stage and speaking someone else's words as if they are your own is less an act of bravery than a desperate lunge at mutual understanding? An attempt to forge that tenuous link between speaker and listener and communicate something, anything, of substance."

– **M.L. Rio,** *If We Were Villains*

UNDERGRADUATE AND GRADUATE DEGREES

AA – Associate of Arts – 2-year degree

AS – Associate of Science – 2-year degree

BA – Bachelor of Arts – 4-year degree

BS – Bachelor of Science – 4-year degree

BFA – Bachelor of Fine Arts – 4-year degree with most classes focused on art

MFA – Master of Fine Arts – 1-2-year degree earned after the BA, BS, or BFA

Basically, BA and BS degrees are degrees that typically offer a liberal arts foundation along with a major or concentration in a specific subject. Meanwhile, a BFA is considered a professional arts-focused degree with fewer courses in English, science, math, social science, and the humanities. Thus, the BFA is a specialist qualification in the arts. A BA or BS degree in acting, theatre arts, or musical arts is also valuable. The BFA is more focused on the specific area of art you choose.

The BA and BS degrees include significantly more liberal arts classes and thus are more general degrees. However, the intention of the BFA degree is for students to pursue an arts-focused curriculum, and thus there are fewer general subject courses.

Finally, while many AA or AS degrees are focused on providing technical or professional skills for acting, music, or dance, an AA or AS in these areas are often interchangeable. Similarly, a BA or BS in theatre-oriented degrees are often interchangeable. However, a BFA may be seen as different since there is typically more coursework focused on your specific pursuit, and thus, you may have more technical experiences and knowledge than someone who has a BA or BS.

AA – ASSOCIATE OF ARTS

The Associate of Arts degree is typically a 2-year general studies degree offered online or in-person by a community college. However, some universities offer AA degrees as well. The Associate of Arts degree focused on liberal arts courses often has no barrier to entry, meaning that students can enter most AA programs with a high school diploma or the equivalent. Some students take a longer or shorter time to complete the AA based upon their skills upon entering the program, certainty about the direction they are heading, and the transfer requirements for the program they desire. For example, students majoring in business may have additional business, communication, accounting, and economics requirements and need to create an academic plan early in their program to finish in two years.

AS – ASSOCIATE OF SCIENCE

The Associate of Science degree is very similar to the AA. However, the AS degree frequently emphasizes science and math and often has additional requirements.

BA – BACHELOR OF ARTS

The Bachelor of Arts degree is typically a 4-year degree offered online or in-person by a college or university. However, a few community colleges offer BA degrees as well. Some students complete their BA in fewer years depending upon AP/IB credit, dual enrollment in high school, and summer/intersession classes. College programs have stricter or less stringent requirements depending upon the school. The Bachelor of Arts degree frequently requires students to take lower-division (first and second year) liberal arts courses before taking specialized courses focused around a major or concentration in their third and fourth years. Some students take a longer or shorter time to complete their BA based upon their skills upon entering the program, certainty about the direction they are heading, and their chosen major. According to the National Center for Educational Statistics, college advisors aid students in finishing "on time" though less than half of all students in the United States who start a BA program do not finish their degree in four years.[1]

---

1   IEC NCES, "Digest of Education Statistics, Table 326.10," IES NCES, n.d., https://nces.ed.gov/programs/digest/d20/tables/dt20_326.10.asp?referer=raceindica.asp

BS – BACHELOR OF SCIENCE

The Bachelor of Science degree is very similar to the BA. However, the BS degree frequently emphasizes science and math and often has additional requirements.[2]

BFA – BACHELOR OF FINE ARTS

The Bachelor of Fine Arts is a 4-year college degree focusing on the arts. BFA students are often not required to take as many English, science, math, social science, and humanities courses. However, they must still complete roughly the same number of credits as a person who earns a BA or BS, and the courses are not necessarily easier. BFA students frequently take general art requirements to lay a foundation in drawing, graphic design, and courses in their specialty area during their first two years, along with basic writing and quantitative skill-building.

BFA students are traditionally art-in-practice students who learn the technical craft of their art form while putting in enormous numbers of hours practicing their skill doing assignments and participating in internships and experiential learning. Students who know that they want a future in the arts often finds this avenue perfectly tailored for their pursuits. However, students who change their minds and transfer to a university in another degree program may require an additional year to make up for coursework they have not completed.

MFA – MASTER OF FINE ARTS

The Master of Fine Arts is a graduate degree for students who have completed their BA, BS, or BFA. This degree takes one to two years depending upon the program, coursework, and experiential component, which may be a capstone, practicum, internship, or thesis. While there are also MA and MS degrees, many art students who continue to earn their master's degree in the arts chose to focus on their field of interest. The MFA is an intensive immersion into a higher level of skill-building. However, students who graduate with an MFA have a broader range of talents and experiences than those who earn their bachelor's degrees. While admission into these programs is generally selective, with planning, preparation, and a good portfolio, there are options for you to pursue your interests.

---

2   IEC NCES, "Digest of Education Statistics, Table 326.10," IES NCES, n.d., https://nces.ed.gov/programs/digest/d20/tables/dt20_326.10.asp?referer=raceindica.asp

THE SEVEN MAJOR DIFFERENCES BETWEEN THE ASSOCIATE, BACHELORS, AND MASTER'S DEGREES

1. Starting Point
2. Academic Discipline
3. Time to Completion
4. Location of the Education
5. Educational Costs
6. Earning Power
7. Professional Opportunities

STARTING POINT

Most students who begin with an Associate of Arts (AA) or Associate of Science (AS) have no college credits. Starting from scratch with their college education, they accumulate their 60+ units beginning from this community college starting point. While most students earn AA or AS degrees at a community college, some earn this degree at a 4-year college or university.

The AA or AS is either a terminal degree, meaning that the student will not continue on with their bachelor's degree or just a steppingstone to their BA, BS, or BFA. The difference between the associate's and bachelor's degrees is just the starting point.

The starting point for students who pursue a bachelor's degree may be farther along the traditional 4-year pathway. Meanwhile, the starting point for the master's degree (MA, MS, or MFA) begins after obtaining a bachelor's degree.

ACADEMIC DISCIPLINE

Every degree encompasses different requirements. Requirements for the AA differ from an AS. Similarly, the requirements for the BA, BS, and BFA also differ. With two additional years of coursework, the BA, BS, and BFA are more thorough. The MA, MS, and MFA build upon the bachelor's degree and even deeper. Theatre arts students will not take the same classes as musical theatre, though a few may overlap. Though both are behind-the-scenes players in the dramatic arts, the essential skills for each career area are distinct; course requirements are also unique.

Furthermore, with the myriad of combinations, it is rare that any two undergraduate students have the same exact classes in the same exact order. Since the requirements for a chemistry degree are not the same as for biology and technical theatre differs from acting or musical theatre, the various degrees not only include a different number of credits but different types of classes and program specifications.

TIME TO COMPLETION

Associate of Arts (AA) and Associate of Science (AS) degrees typically take two years, while most BA, BS, and BFA degrees are 4-year programs, depending upon full-time or part-time status. Students who transfer in credits or earn credits otherwise can reduce their time to completion.

Some students may choose to extend their education in acting, theatre arts, or musical theatre by earning a second bachelor's degree in another field. By cross-training in directing or dramaturgy, students open more doors. Additionally, a degree in business on the bachelor's level or Master's in Business Administration (MBA) may lead to alternative leadership positions.

Time in college can be reduced. Some students enter a BA, BS, or BFA program having already completed college credits because they were dual-enrolled or they took college classes directly through a college or university ahead of time. Some students have taken AP/IB tests from taking higher-level tests while in high school and earned qualifying scores to be granted credits by the college or university. Other ways students can enter at a different starting point are with credit-by-exam, CLEP tests, experiential credits, and those granted in the military.

Colleges and universities are keenly aware of the challenges students face today with work, illness, and family responsibilities. Thus, many schools of higher education offer flexible enrollment with opportunities for part-time, evening, weekend, and online classes.

LOCATION OF THE EDUCATION

The AA and AS are earned at colleges that grant 2-year degrees. The location may be at a local community college or a university. BA, BS, and BFA programs are offered at a 4-year college or university. However, with online classes, students have the flexibility to take classes from colleges farther away as well. Thus, the location in which a typical student studies is not as set as it once was. Nevertheless, the in-person internships are often situated in corporate hubs and thus require grounding to a specific location.

EDUCATIONAL COSTS

Since the AA or AS requires a shorter amount of time and is typically completed at a lower-cost community college, the cost for an associate's degree is typically less than a bachelor's degree. Master's degree programs cost more per credit but take less time than a bachelor's degree.

On the other hand, many students can obtain financial aid in the form of grants, loans, and both merit and need-based scholarships. This aid can pay for school and reduce debt after college.

EARNING POWER

Students with more education can earn more. According to the 2019 National Center for Educational Statistics (NCES) data for the median person,[3]

Master's Degree or Higher - $70,000

Bachelor's Degree - $55,700

Associate's Degree - $43,300

High School - $35,000

Of course, there is a wide range in annual salaries from those who have consistent work and are paid six-digit or seven-digit salaries to those who work one or two paid shows per year and earn less than $20,000. Thus, the average seems low when the variation is huge.

---

3   IES NCES, "Annual Earnings by Educational Attainment," IEC NCES, May 2021, https://nces.ed.gov/programs/coe/indicator/cba

PROFESSIONAL OPPORTUNITIES

Earning a BA, BS, or BFA opens more doors than an AA or AS. Similarly, an MA, MS, or MFA opens more doors than a BA, BS, or BFA. Baccalaureate and master's degrees require more training. You can obtain this training through workshops or studio classes, but with a scholarship to pay for college, you might find that the training and opportunities are worth your time. Besides, you will gain additional skills that could prove valuable in your future.

CHAPTER 7

COLLEGE ADMISSIONS: APPLICATIONS, ESSAYS, RECOMMENDATIONS, AND SCHOLARSHIPS

"Some may say a life in the theatre can ruin you. I say it was my salvation. In the days when walking down the street or by a playground might leave me with a bloody nose or a hurled insult that hurt even more, the theatre was my refuge, my shelter."

– Jim Provenzano, Finding Tulsa

With amazing faculty, excellent facilities, and easy access to Broadway, NYU stands as one of the premier schools for musical theatre. Just a few of NYU's talented alumni are Broadway musical theatre actors, directors, designers, artisans, and crew including – drumroll – Jordan Allen-Dutton, Jessica Almasy, Deborah Aquila, Hilary Austin, De'Adre Aziza, Alec Baldwin, David Bernon, Rachel Bloom, Travis Boatright, Salty Brine, Jere Burns, Adam Butterfield, Evan Cabinet, Kimberly Chatterjee, Ben Chavez, Rachel Chavkin, Mia Cook, Ismael Cruz Cordova, Bryan Dechart, Mark Dobrow, Kathryn Erbe, Raul Esparza, Jack Falahee, Andrew Farmer, Cory Fitzgerald, Thais Francis, Meghan Gaber, Lady Gaga, Gina Gershon, Clark Gregg, Arjun Gupta, Lisa Gay Hamilton, Alex Hawthorn, Ben Heller, Courtney Hoffman, Philip Seymour Hoffman, Christine Hope, Bryce Dallas Howard, Timothy Huang, Tina Huang, Felicity Huffman, Richie Jackson, Nikki M. James, Dan Jinks, Kristen Johnston, Lauren Keating, Stephanie Kurtzuba, John Lavelle, Sarah Rose Leonard, Justin Levine, Lex Liang, Amy Lipitz, Zoe Lister-Jones, Katie Lowes, Claire Marberg, Ken Marino, Jesse L. Martin, Mary McCann, Andrew McCarthy, Jonathan McCrory, Jesse Metcalfe, Dimitri Moise, Donna Murphy, Elizabeth Olsen, Haley Joel Osment, Yianni Papadimos, Bill Paxton, Sam Pinkleton, David Pittu, Jayson Prim, Anthony Rapp, Joe Regalbuto, Jason Ritter, Gina Rodriguez, Steve Rosen, Adam Sandler, Julie Schubert, Molly Shannon, Jason Sherwood, Gary Solomon, Paul Sparks, Bobby Steggert, Rachel Sterner, Ali Stroker, Rachel Sussman, Sarah Sutherland, Franklin Swann, Shaina Taub, Miles Teller, Bernie Telsey, Maura Tierney, Olivia Washington, Katherine Waterston, Erik Weiner, Kate Whoriskey, Casey Wilson, Chandra Wilson, and Zachary Zirlin.

NYU Tisch: BFA in Drama (conservatory training)

- Collaborative Arts
- Dance
- Drama
- Open Arts
- Performance Studies

Cinema Studies

Rita & Burton Goldberg Department of Dramatic Writing

Undergraduate Film & Television

NYU Tisch Drama combines rigorous conservatory training with NYU's academic studies in the humanities and social sciences and the whole of New York's wide-ranging theatre and film opportunities. Students combine performance, creativity, artistry, and intellectualism. Tisch's studio system offers a unique approach to conservatory training and the totality of theatre arts. You will learn to think broadly, pursue your craft creatively, tell stories, and ask questions. Moreover, you will be fully prepared for professional opportunities with lifelong connections.

NYU Steinhardt, BM (Musical Theatre)	NYU Tisch BFA (Drama)
Music Theatre History I and II	Primary Studio Training (32 credits)
Acting I and II for Singers	Advanced Studio/Internships (16 credits)
Vocal Coaching/Vocal Performance	Theatre Studies/Theatre Production
Music Theatre Workshop	Dramatic Literature
Tap, Jazz, Hip Hop, Music Theatre Dance	Theatre Theory
Vocal Production for Singers	Performance Studies

SCHOLARSHIPS

Nearly every school in the United States offers need-based scholarships. However, most also offer merit scholarships. Many are listed in the profile section. Check it out.

Below are a couple of schools chosen at random to give you a sense of a few of the options listed in the profile section.

Baldwin Wallace University

- BFA Acting; BW School of Humanities

Merit scholarships are offered up to $21,000 per year. Additional monies added to the merit scholarships are offered.

Chapman University

- BA Theatre Studies or Theatre Technology or BFA in Screen Acting or Theatre Performance

First-year scholarships range in amounts up to $36,000 per year. Select admitted students will also be offered institutional awards. These include awards for first-generation and underrepresented students, as well as awards from departments and schools/colleges. The College of Performing Arts (CoPA) has a limited number of Talent Awards for incoming first-year and transfer students. Students must be theatre majors. Consideration is made at the audition/interview and notified afterward.

Columbia College Chicago

- BA/BFA Acting

Students are automatically considered for renewable scholarships upon admission. For need-based scholarship, submit a FAFSA. For talent-based scholarships, submit an audition that demonstrates your best creative work. First-year, international students may be considered for talent-based scholarships.

Florida State University

- BFA Acting, BA Theatre

The School of Theatre awards scholarships to selected incoming and continuing students. BFA students can qualify based on academic ability and potential.

Long Island University Post

- BFA in Theatre Arts

LIU Post awards over $100 million in scholarships & grants each year.

Marymount Manhattan University

- BFA Acting, BFA Musical Theatre
- BA Theatre (Concentrations in performance, directing, producing, management, history, new media, technical design).

Scholarships are available for successful candidates. Consideration for these competitive talent awards is made at the time of the audition. Scholarships are renewable for four years if the student remains academically successful and stays in the program.

Pace University

- BA, BFA Acting, BA Directing, BFA Production & Design, BA Stage Management

Students are considered for need-based scholarships. There are also Dyson College Scholarships specifically for each program. The average non-need-based scholarship awarded to first-year students is $24,996. There is also the Professor Chris Thomas Endowed Scholarship.

Pepperdine University

- BA Theatre Arts, BA Theatre and Screen Arts (Musical Theatre Emphasis)

Merit and need-based scholarships are available for Theatre/Musical Theatre students. Approximately 75% of theatre majors receive scholarships in varying amounts. Students must complete a FAFSA form. The Ubben Endowed Scholarship for Production Design Majors provides $25,000 per year.

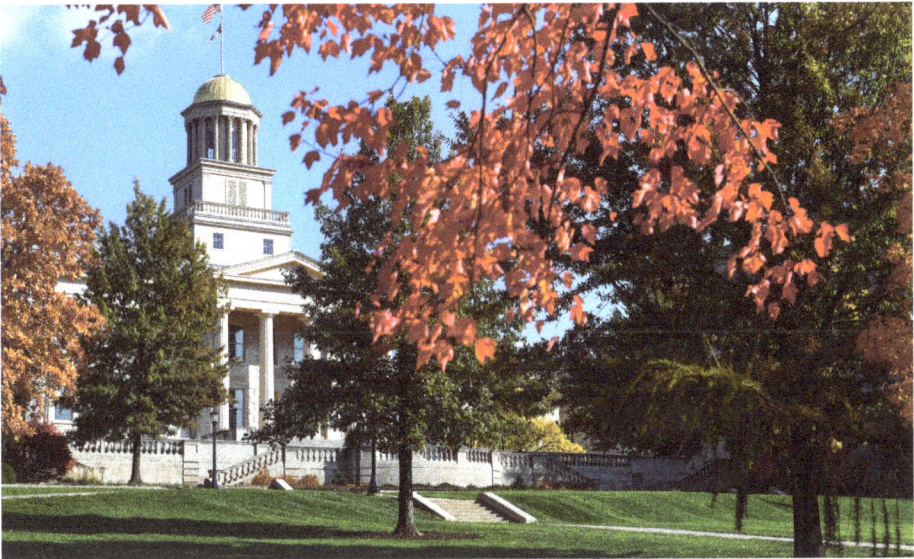

COLLEGE ADMISSIONS:

Success in the Face of Uncertainty

There are no guarantees in college admissions. However, planning is essential for success. The most beneficial advice is to pursue your passions with gusto, train to be the best you can be, take advantage of internships and experiences, and meet lots of people along the way. Remember, "life is a journey, not a destination." Often the journey is more exciting, leading to lessons, friendships, and indelible moments. However, the fact is…in the end, if college is your goal, then you need to know a few action items to remember for success.

Should you worry about grades? Of course. You should also take classes that will challenge you. Colleges pick the best candidates from those who apply. Students must be academically prepared, socially conscious, and talented in a few different areas in which they are passionate (conceptual design, graphic arts, costumes, theater, acting, singing, dance, musical instruments, debate, public speaking, leadership, athletics, community service, computer coding, robotics, construction, etc.).

This selection process is not that much different than companies picking employees. While colleges are more or less competitive, companies may have only one job and fifty resumes. Discover the unique drive and internal motivations within you that make you the very best you can be. Be exceptional at what you choose to do academically, personally, and professionally.

Most of all,

You Do You

TALENT FOCUSED

Not all schools require high grades and test scores. Many are simply interested in selecting students who are the most talented, most driven, and the most willing to be team players on the college campus. Thus, while you should take a solid set of courses and fulfill requirements, only the top schools emphasize completing a challenging curriculum, high grades, and standardized test scores.

FOR HIGHLY SELECTIVE COLLEGES, TALENT IS JUST THE BEGINNING

A few highly selective colleges seek extraordinary talent over academics, but most zero in on a student's challenging courses and high grades. To gain admission into the most highly selective colleges, you must take the most challenging course load you can manage and succeed. Highly selective colleges want disciplined scholars AND remarkably talented students.

Determine what you can handle, knowing that some colleges with extremely competitive admission will only take students who have completed more than ten

AP, IB, or honors classes over the four years, including AP Calculus. AP Statistics is not of equal rigor in their eyes. Why, then, would these most competitive colleges require a class that is beyond the scope of what you need for your major? This situation is the $50,000 question. However, if this seems daunting, remember that most colleges accepting students for artistic fields do not need these types of classes.

College admissions can feel like a rollercoaster of energy and emotion. Creating a portfolio of talent, training, and experience is just the beginning. Meanwhile, some colleges want to see standardized test scores which are aided by practice. Applications and essays may seem easy at first, but managing the various requirements and deadlines can be difficult. Therefore, this application period is a good time to get a calendar and organize your tasks.

STANDARDIZED TESTING

A few schools require testing. Check first. Many colleges are test optional. This means that you are not required to take the SAT or ACT. However, if you do have a good score, it may make all the difference in accepting you. College admissions offices are studying this topic and considering their future policies. Much of their concern began with cancelations worldwide due to the pandemic. Schools did not want to let students into their site who may be infected. In addition, social distancing limited the number of students who could take a test at a site at a time.

Yet, college admissions decisions were once centered around grades and test scores. The change has rattled admissions departments. Meanwhile, colleges proclaim that test-optional truly means that the test is not required, but evidence proves otherwise. Thus, many students are still taking the test and working around the hurdles amid all of the confusion. Competition continues to drive students to present evidence to show that they are worthy candidates.

In the end, colleges need to make a final decision between very good candidates. If one student has a high score, that student may have a higher likelihood of admission depending upon the admissions committee's decision-making process. Data show that students who submitted scores within the college's range or higher were accepted at a higher rate than those without a score. Some schools are test blind in that they say that they do not consider your scores. A few of these colleges still provide a place for you to input your scores, thus, they are not truly blind. Nevertheless, this decision is yours. If the school does not require an admissions test, then you can choose to take the test. If your academics are solid and you are willing to prepare, you should take the test.

APPLYING EARLY

Early Action (EA), Restricted Early Action (REA), and Early Decision (ED)

With low acceptance rates, the chance to get more scholarship money, and chaos surrounding the cancellations and changes in AP, IB, SAT, and ACT testing, students clamor to apply early to schools. In addition, applications to top schools increased during the pandemic, resulting in colleges making difficult admissions decisions in their quest to build a diverse, talented, and engaged class of students. Furthermore, students applying early have access to many more scholarship options. This confluence sent students in droves to apply early and this trend is likely to continue.

In Early Action (EA), Restricted Early Action (REA), and Early Decision (ED), students apply in late summer or early fall to college and generally find out around winter break, though some decisions come out earlier and a few arrive later. This advantage not only gives students the chance for more scholarship money in some cases but the benefit of finding out early reduces the tension of the long waiting period to find out about Regular Decision schools.

Early Action (EA) and Restricted Early Action (REA) are different. In restricted early action, a limitation is placed on either how many or what colleges you can apply to simultaneously. Many REA schools do not allow students to apply to other early action schools, though some will allow students to apply EA to public colleges. In addition, some schools like Georgetown will allow students to apply EA elsewhere but not apply to a binding Early Decision (ED) program where the student commits to attending if they are accepted. However, most EA schools do not have these restrictions, and some students apply to a handful of EA schools during the Admissions process.

Early Decision (ED) is a binding agreement between the student and college with signatures from the student's parents and the high school. Each of these parties acknowledges and agrees that, if granted admission, they will attend. There are incentives. Frequently, acceptance rates are higher with ED. Also, at some schools, a large percentage of their class is filled with students who profess their unequivocal love for their dream school. Students who know they have a top choice school, have the necessary admissions requirements, and are committed to accepting the binding agreement to attend, should apply ED.

COMMON APPLICATION, COALITION APPLICATION, OR COLLEGE-SPECIFIC APPLICATION

Every college's process is unique. However, there are a few commonalities. In 2022, approximately 900 colleges used the Common App; about 150 colleges used the Coalition Application. A few used both. The University of California system has its own application as do the California State Universities and the Texas schools. The Common App and Coalition App may be started early. In your junior year, consider getting a head start on reviewing what is required. The college-specific questions may change each year. However, the basic application is generally the same and can be created ahead of time. At the end of July, make a copy of everything you have completed just in case.

In August, most admissions applications are open and ready for you to dive into the college-specific questions. Some schools admit on a rolling basis. 'Rolling' means that periodically, after all of the materials are received, the admissions committee determines who they will accept, and they send the notification right away. Many students are accepted as early as August. The thrill of acceptance cannot be overstated.

Complete the application fully. Think carefully about optional sections. Typically, they offer you the chance to provide the school with just the right cherry on top of the ice cream sundae. If you have absolutely nothing to say, then leave it blank. There are often required essays on the main Common App and the supplemental applications for each school. Some include scholarship essays. Start early.

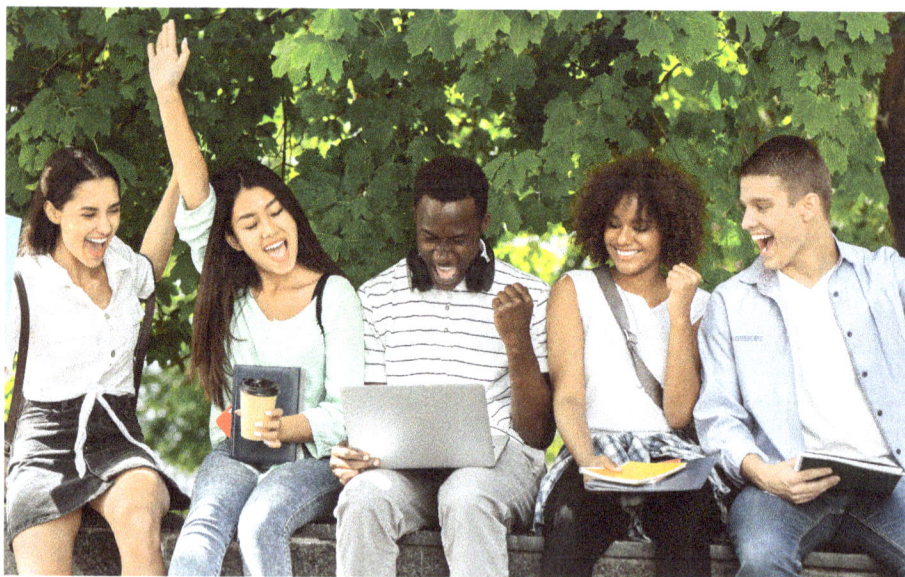

DECISIONS, DECISIONS: WAITING FOR A RESPONSE

The period between submitting your application and getting your results may not require a tremendous amount of work, but it does require patience and diligence. First, most schools will send you a link to a portal where you will check your results, though the most important reason for checking every couple of weeks is to ensure that they are not missing something or have not offered you the chance to apply for an extra scholarship. Check your portal regularly. Otherwise, read the correspondence that the school may send through your e-mail.

Waiting is difficult. This is a tough period because students want to know. However, on the portal, the college typically lists the date they will send out the results. You will find out soon.

CELEBRATING ACCEPTANCES AND DEALING WITH REJECTION

Acceptance is not guaranteed. The probabilities are low at the most highly selective schools. However, you just need to work to have what it takes and give this commitment all you have.

When you find out the results, you will celebrate your acceptances. Congratulations! These go on your list of wins. Check your financial aid and scholarship package. Money is often an important factor in making your decision. Consider visiting the school. Many students apply by only looking at pictures and profiles on a website or book. There is nothing that replaces the actual visit. After all, you will be spending a few years there.

However, you may not be accepted everywhere you apply. The pandemic's uncertainty added more question marks to an already complicated set of admissions processes. The buzzword for the 2020s is resilience. It is never easy to be rejected. However, rejection happens, and you will survive this. Note that many colleges still accept applications in April, May, and June. Look up those colleges if you did not get accepted or if you want to see what other schools might be good options for you. You will be surprised to see the colleges on the list.

WAITLISTS: THE ART OF WAITING

Confirm immediately if you are given a waitlist spot and still want to attend. There is often a deadline, and you do not want to miss this. If you are no longer interested or have selected another school, go into the portal and turn down the offer. Someone else is bound to be thrilled by your anonymous gift.

Next, if you are highly interested, find the location on the portal or site designated by the college to update them on what you have done – accomplishments, awards, extra class, honors, art, shows, or films. You only want to add what they have not yet seen, but if you have taken the initiative to do something more than what you originally stated on the application, by all means, tell them. You could just wait for their decision, but you are better off being proactive and showing that you really want to be at their school.

Students do get off of the waitlists at most schools. Meanwhile, you will have to deposit somewhere else before the May 1st deadline. Stay hopeful. This next year will be a significant step along your journey. Relax!

DETERMINING FINANCIAL AID

You do not need to complete the FAFSA (Free Application for Federal Student Aid) or CSS Profile (College Scholarship Service) if you do not need aid. However, a handful of schools want to see one or both of these forms to obtain scholarships. Check now since there are deadlines.

If you completed the FAFSA (and CSS profile, if required), the financial aid package you receive would be viewable on your portal. The college will delineate the amounts you will receive for grants, loans, and work-study. Some students turn down work-study, but I caution against that. There are jobs on campus where you conduct research, work with a professor, work in the library, or assist an athletic team. Some of these jobs pay well, and you might have even done them as a volunteer.

If your financial situation has changed since you applied, you may be able to renegotiate the amount they offered.

CHOOSING THE RIGHT SCHOOL FOR YOU

Once you have acceptances, you need to make a decision. With the turmoil of the pandemic, disruption in clubs, sports, and experiential activities, and serious family health concerns, access to some opportunities has been non-existent. Most training and practice have been virtual. Furthermore, few students have traveled to visit colleges due to the crisis. However, with college costs for four years around $300,000 at some schools, college is the most significant investment some families will ever make. Furthermore, student loans can saddle a student in debt for a decade or more.

Financial decisions are key. However, there are many variables in deciding which school to choose. Will I be able to afford my education? Will classes be online or in-person? Will I be able to continue my training? Will I get to visit the colleges first? Can I live through the repercussions of stressful decision-making? Should I defer my admissions and take a year off?

Once you make your decision, focus on your future. What is trending? What do people want? How can you deliver? What will be the most fulfilling for you?

You've Got This!

CHAPTER 8

THEATRE: SUPPLEMENTAL MATERIALS, AUDITIONS, AND OTHER REQUIREMENTS

"The gift of human beings is that we have the power of empathy."

– Meryl Streep

At the top schools like New York University, Juilliard, Carnegie Mellon, University of Michigan, a BFA in theatre is one of the most intense and most demanding degrees students can earn in college. Mastering dramatic roles, theatre arts, and related studies require students to be on the ball, multitalented, and extremely focused. Students must be literally and figuratively brilliant and unstoppable. With that kind of multitasking intensity and vigorous competition, admissions officers and program directors are as interested in the applicant's personality as they are in their talent. As a result, after prescreening, most of the student candidates who audition are either extremely talented or show significant potential.

THOUSANDS OF APPLICANTS – MULTITUDES OF ROADS

The number of applicants is astounding. Schools like Carnegie Mellon University often have 2,000 to 2,500 applicants for 12 – 14 spots. CMU is not alone. Other schools like the University of Michigan, UCLA, USC, NYU, and Northwestern University also have tremendously high numbers of applications.

The process is daunting. Of course, students will apply to 10-20 schools, but that takes a ton of dedicated time and money for coaching, preparation, application fees, and travel to auditions. Other options that may not require prescreening include the pursuit of degrees in writing, theatre studies, or another area of your interest.

Although BFA training is often exceptional and the contacts made through the faculty, alumni, and NYC showcases are valuable, being cast in a play or film is more about whether your talent, look, and personality fit the production. Thus, a BFA is helpful but not necessary. Many outstanding performers never went to college or studied in a completely different degree area. However, if you have a passion to perform and train for your own enjoyment, commitment, and desire, you could land a fabulous part. A bachelor's degree may also come in handy down the line.

You only have to read a few blogs or threads on *Broadway World* or other sites to grasp the stories of students who discussed their journey, found their niche, or decided their pathway in theatre. As Euclid once said, "There is no royal road." The journey from trainee to the stage takes mental and physical stamina with ups and downs. Even so, anything is possible.

DEFYING GRAVITY

In 2015, more than 73,000 people worked in live performance venues in the United States. Unfortunately, this number dropped to less than 54,000 in 2021. The drop of approximately 20,000 jobs, a function of quarantines and the pandemic, marked a sad period in our history. However, if the enthusiastic reactions of audiences who attended the theatre in 2022 are any indication, new shows will be added, and the excitement will return. Old and new actors will take to the stage, and patrons will buy tickets for shows. Undoubtedly, playwrights wrote exciting new plays during the pandemic with upbeat, contemporary themes to bring more people out for a wonderful, impassioned show.

Normal may not happen until 2025, but the 20,000 jobs will return, and possibly new theatre venues will also open. People want to feel empowered again. Theatres offer a rare boundless space for actors and patrons alike. Limitless dreams can come true and regular people can defy gravity as Glinda and Elphaba sing, "There's no fight we cannot win. Just you and I, defying gravity."

PRESCREENS AND AUDITIONS

The first entry point for most theatre programs is the prescreen. BFA programs require prescreening to determine each applicant's skill level and compare students to select the best ones they feel are moldable. Prescreens also eliminate about half of the applicants who do not have the adequate mix of required skills.

There is not one standard prescreen process. Unfortunately, each school is somewhat different. While some of the requirements are listed in the profile section of this book, there is limited space. Below you will find the prescreen and audition requirements for three schools with three different processes in more detail. Be sure to check the website for greater detail and any changes. Note: NYU has multiple options with different requirements.

UNIVERSITY OF SOUTHERN CALIFORNIA
SCHOOL OF DRAMATIC ARTS (SDA)

BFA in Acting for Stage, Screen, and New Media

Initial Application/Prescreen

- Submit the Common Application with USC-specific supplemental essays. List BFA in Acting for Stage, Screen, and New Media was your first choice. You are encouraged to choose BA in Theatre as your second choice.

- Submit SDA SlideRoom Application which opens in September. This includes (1) headshot, (2) performance resume, (3) three images, each with a caption, to reveal what is important to you, (4) artistic review fee.

- Letter of Recommendation from a drama teacher/coach.

- Essay questions – prompts posted in SlideRoom

- Self-Intro Video, sharing more about you and your interests.

Prescreen Monologue Requirement (SlideRoom Submission)

- Two separately filmed monologues from published plays (no longer than 90 seconds) are required – one classical (written before 1900) and one contemporary (written after 1900). These should be memorized and performed in the context of the entire play.

- Film with a clear image and audio. These do not need to be professionally filmed, but each should be well-lit with few background distractions. Do not wear a costume or use an accent or dialect.

- Include a slate with your name, play's title, and playwright's name.

Callback Weekend – All applicants will receive an application update in January regarding callback audition/interview.

NEW YORK UNIVERSITY TISCH DRAMA
BFA in Drama

Initial Application/Prescreen

- Submit the Common Application with NYU's supplemental essay as soon as you know you want to apply since there are fewer slots available as the deadline approaches. Note recommended deadlines for Tisch are approximately 15 – 30 days before NYU's published deadline.

- Two to four days after submission, you will receive an e-mail from NYU with a personalized link to the Drama Artistic Review.

- Schedule your artistic review and submit required materials, including (1) headshot, (2) resume, (3) information about your monologues, songs, or portfolios, (4) answers to questions, (5) media portfolio, and (6) artistic review fee.

Acting Artistic Review

- Your artistic review will be conducted with one evaluator in the room for each applicant.

- Two contrasting monologues from published plays (no longer than 90 seconds) are required – one classical (written before 1900) and one contemporary (written after 1900).

- Do not choose a musical, film, television script, or original material. Choose material in your age range.

- Do not wear a costume, use a prop, or use an accent or dialect.

Conversation – Interviewees will converse with the evaluator after presenting the monologues. The interviewer wants to get to know you as a person.

Session Times – Your audition is approximately 3.5 hours. You will have either a morning or an afternoon. All candidates will check-in at the same time (9:00 am for morning auditions; 2:00 pm for afternoon auditions)

CARNEGIE MELLON UNIVERSITY SCHOOL OF DRAMA
BFA in Acting

Initial Application/Prescreen

- Submit the Common Application with CMU-specific supplemental essays and recommendations.

- Submit supplemental materials for the prescreen through Acceptd. Instructions are provided in the site. You must complete the prescreening process in order to be invited to an audition or interview.

Audition

- Dates to register for your audition or interview open in the fall through the Acceptd portal by invitation only following the prescreen process.
- Appointments are available on a first-come, first-served basis. Apply Early!
- Acting auditions will be held in January and February.

SIX SUGGESTIONS TO CREATE YOUR VIDEOS

The following suggestions may help you set up your home "studio" for filming your monologues.

1. Find a creative space where you have freedom of movement without impediments or distractions.
2. Ensure your camera is placed at eye level to record naturally as others see you. You might use a tripod, bookcase, stack of books on a desk, or stand that is 60 – 70 inches high.
3. Solid-colored walls are ideal to avoid visual distractions considering your possible clashes with your outfit and desire to focus on your performance.
4. Check the lighting. Adequate lighting is important for reviewers to see you clearly. Lamps and windows behind you are likely to cast a shadow over your face. Thus, it is best for the lighting to emanate from behind your recording device to provide lighting to your face.
5. Place the microphone near you, so the sound of your voice reaches the recording device in a natural way.
6. Only perform Shakespeare if you feel comfortable. You can find other monologue options before 1900 in the public domain. Shakespeare is a common choice. With seasoned performers, this choice of a monologue is often very well done.

OTHER PRESCREEN AND AUDITION METHODS

Some colleges use institution-specific platforms and methods to upload content and audition candidates for their programs. Nevertheless, while colleges may not have students post their videos on YouTube, SlideRoom, or Acceptd, they often require the same types of monologues prepared in the same way. This uniformity aids in simplifying the process. However, a few schools do not participate in similar prescreening processes since they look for unique elements in their candidates.

Best wishes to each of you as you prepare your prescreen and audition materials.

CHAPTER 9

COSTUME DESIGN: DEGREES AND REQUIREMENTS

"Theatre is a voyage into the archives of the human imagination"

– Natasha Tsakos

Costume design requires more than envisioning and drawing a costume. Costume designers must be skilled seamstresses and stitchers. Becoming an expert in sewing is a must. Most costume design programs are rigorous. Furthermore, pattern making requires mathematical skills as well as graphic design to layout and replicate patterns for various sizes. Costume design school will teach the workflow, production patterns, construction techniques, and finishing methodologies used in the industry.

Thus, the first three necessary skills are centered around creativity, drawing, and sewing. However, college degrees in costume design teach much more. Some of those skills include manually working with a life fit model, specialized cutting techniques with different kinds of scissors and hand stitching types for seams, hems, and crafting.

Costume design programs will teach you skills for stage and film like breaking down characters from a script and conceptualizing their identities by developing a look book using mood boards, color stories, and illustrations. Creativity and ingenuity provide the fit within the historical period, theme, and emotional context. This entails stretching your mind by watching shows of all types and imagining what you would do to change the audience's feeling through the character's costume.

Keep a small notebook with you to jot down inspiration as you witness it throughout your experiences.

At the beginning of the inspiration for this book, the plan was to only include profiles of schools for acting. However, there is so much more to theatre and film. Thus, while only this book started with profiles of the top twenty schools, more were added to include schools with diverse opportunities. Thus, the profile section includes 74 schools. Nevertheless, some schools rank high on every list. Here is one of those lists.

According to the *Hollywood Reporter*, the top ten schools for Costume Design are:

1. California Institute of the Arts (CalArts)
2. Carnegie Mellon School of Drama
3. NYU Tisch School of the Arts
4. Savannah College of Art and Design (SCAD)
5. UCLA School of Theater, Film, and Television
6. The University of Missouri – Kansas City (UMKC)

7. Wimbledon College of Arts, University of the Arts London (UAL)
8. University of North Carolina School of the Arts (UNSCA)
9. USC School of Dramatic Arts
10. Yale School of Drama

FAMOUS COSTUME DESIGNERS

Edith Head: won 8 Academy Awards; 35 nominations
    College: BA University of California, Berkeley in French;
        MA Stanford University in Roman Languages

Milena Canonero: won 4 Academy Awards; 9 nominations
    Studied art, design history, and costume design in Genoa

Colleen Atwood: won 4 Academy Awards; 12 nominations
    College: Cornish College of the Arts in Painting

Irene Sharaff: won 5 Academy Awards; 15 nominations
    College: Parsons School of Design
           Art Students League of New York
           Académie de la Grande Chaumière in Paris

Charles Le Maire: won 3 Academy Awards; 13 nominations

Sandy Powell: won 3 Academy Awards; 15 nominations
    College: Central School of Art and Design in Theatre Design

Dorothy Jeakins: won 3 Academy Awards; 12 nominations
     College: Otis College of Art and Design

Anthony Powell: won 3 Academy Awards; 6 nominations
     College: Central School of Art and Design

TONY AWARD NOMINATED COSTUME DESIGNERS FOR A MUSICAL (2010 – 2020)

Greg Barnes for *Follies* (2012), *Kinky Boots* (2013), *Something Rotten!* (2015), *Tuck Everlasting* (2016), *Mean Girls* (2018)

Tim Chappel for *Priscilla, Queen of the Desert* (2011)

Linda Cho for *A Gentleman's Guide to Love and Murde*r (2014), *Anastasia* (2017)

Bob Crowley for *An American in Paris* (2015)

Marina Draghici for *Fela!* (2010)

Lizzy Gardiner for *Priscilla, Queen of the Desert* (2011)

Rob Howell for *Matilda the Musical* (2013)

Eiko Ishioka for *Spider-Man: Turn Off the Dark* (2012)

Michael Krass for *Hadestown* (2019)

Dominique Lemieux for *Pippin* (2013)

William Ivey Long for *Rogers and Hammerstein's Cinderella* (2013), *Bullets Over Broadway* (2014), *On the Twentieth Century* (2015), *Beetlejuice* (2019), *Tootsie* (2019)

Santo Loquasto for *Hello Dolly!* (2017)

Jeff Mahshie for *She Loves Me* (2016)

Bob Mackie for *The Cher Show* (2019)

Martin Pakledinaz for *Anything Goes* (2011), *Nice Work If You Can Get It* (2012)

Arianne Phillips for *Hedwig and the Angry Inch* (2014)

Clint Ramos for *Once on This Island* (2018)

Emily Rebholz for *Jagged Little Pill* (2020)

Ann Roth for *The Book of Mormon* (2011), *Shuffle Along* (2016), *Carousel* (2018),

ESosa for *Porgy and Bess* (2012)

Paul Tazewell for *Memphis* (2010), *Hamilton* (2016), *Ain't Too Proud* (2019)

Mark Thompson for *Tina* (2020)

Isabel Toledo for *After Midnight* (2014)

Matthew Wright for *La Cage aux Folles* (2010)

Paloma Young for *Natasha, Pierre & The Great Comet of 1812* (2017)

David Zinn for *SpongeBob SquarePants* (2018)

Catherine Zuber for *How to Succeed in Business Without Really Trying* (2011), *The King and I* (2015), *War Paint* (2017), *My Fair Lady* (2018), *Moulin Rouge!* (2020)

TONY AWARD **NOMINATED COSTUME DESIGNERS FOR A PLAY** (2010 – 2020)

Dede Ayite for *Slave Play* (2020), *A Soldier's Play* (2020)

Bob Crowley for *The Audience* (2015), *The Inheritance* (2020)

Johnson Fensom for *Farinelli and the King* (2018)

Nicky Gillibrand for *Angels in America* (2018)

Soutra Gilmour for *Cyrano de Bergerac* (2013)

Jess Goldstein for *The Merchant of Venice* (2011)

Jane Greenwood for *Act One* (2014), *You Can't Take It with You* (2015), *Long Day's Journey into Night* (2016), Little Foxes (2017)

Desmond Heeley for *The Importance of Being Earnest* (2011)

Susan Hilferty for *Present Laughter* (2017)

Rob Howell for *The Ferryman* (2019)

Toni-Leslie James for *Jitney* (2017), *Bernhardt/Hamlet* (2019)

Michael Krass for *Machinal* (2014), *Noises Off* (2016)

Katrina Lindsay for *Harry Potter and the Cursed Child* (2018)

William Ivey Long for *Don't Dress for Dinner* (2012)

Christopher Oram for *Wolf Hall Parts One & Two* (2015)

Martin Pakledinaz for *Lend Me a Tenor* (2010)

Clint Ramos for *Eclipsed* (2016), *Torch Song* (2019), *The Rose Tattoo* (2020)

Constanza Romero for *Fences* (2010)

Ann Roth for *The Nance* (2013), *Three Tall Women* (2018), *The Iceman Cometh* (2018), *To Kill a Mockingbird* (2019), *Gary: A Sequel to Titus Andronicus* (2019)

Rita Ryack for *Casa Valentina* (2014)

Tom Scutt for *King Charles III* (2016)

Paul Tazewell for *A Streetcar Named Desire* (2012), *Hamilton* (2016), *Ain't Too Proud* (2019)

Mark Thompson for *La Bete* (2011), *One Man, Two Guvnors* (2012)

Jenny Tiramani for *Twelfth Night* (2014)

Albert Wolsky for *The Heiress* (2013)

Paloma Young for *Peter and the Starcatcher* (2012)

David Zinn for *In the Next Room (or The Vibrator Play)* (2010), *Airline Highway* (2015), *A Doll's House, Part 2* (2017)

Catherine Zuber for *The Royal Family* (2010), *Born Yesterday* (2011), *Golden Boy* (2013)

CHAPTER 10

TECHNICAL THEATRE: DEGREES AND REQUIREMENTS

"If there is only shadow on a theatre stage, that play will be boring; if there is only light on a theatre stage, that play will be boring! What makes the play interesting is the struggle of shadows and lights with each other!"

– Mehmet Murat Ildan

Great singers hypnotize. Talented dancers dazzle. Captivating actors mesmerize. Performers come to life in an impressive backdrop as singers, dancers, and actors enthrall audiences. With the stage set, actors appear, adorned in detailed costume designs. The visual spectacle appears centerstage with simple sets like "Music and the Mirror" in *A Chorus Line* or more complex designs like the barricade of chairs, tables, and boxes in *Les Misérables*.

Yet, the designs are just part of the work of technical theatre, which most people involved call a grueling and exhausting job. Celebrating afterward behind the curtains, the crew, wiped out, cheer for a job well down, while the singers, dancers, and actors take their bows to the audience. What draws students to technical theatre is the overwhelming sense of accomplishment the stage crew feels when the show is over and they hear the resounding reverberation of clapping and cheering from the crowd. Most say that nothing is more rewarding.

Nevertheless, mishaps occasionaly occur, like missing a stair and grabbing a ladder for mercy, hammering a nail partway into a finger, or barely getting a set out of the way before the curtains go up. Outside of the minor challenges and drops of spilled blood, most crew members keep going. First aid knowledge is a must. Keep soap, warm water, alcohol wipe, cotton ball, and sterilized tweezers or a needle handy to remove the occasional splinter. Fortunately, accidents are not common – it's all in a day's work.

Digital skills are enhanced and developed in a technical theatre program. Graphic design using Adobe Creative Cloud (Photoshop, Illustrator, InDesign, Premiere Pro, Acrobat, etc.) is one area of study. However, additional skills are required in order to create scale models, renderings, scale construction drawings, and the like. It could also include AutoCAD, 3DS Max, Revit, or Sketchup.

According to *College Raptor*, in 2022 the top ten technical theatre programs are:

1. University of North Carolina School of the Arts (UNSCA)
2. California Institute of the Arts (CalArts)
3. SUNY Purchase College
4. Savannah College of Art and Design (SCAD)
5. University of Cincinnati
6. University of Arizona
7. Boston University
8. Cornish College of the Arts
9. DePaul University
10. Emerson College

While this list may have one school higher or lower each year, this list is a good start and there a few dozen more that I have profiled in the back of this book.

TONY AWARD WINNERS FOR BEST SCENIC DESIGN IN A MUSICAL (2010-2020)

Christine Jones for *American Idiot* (2010)

Scott Pask for *The Book of Mormon* (2011)

Bob Crowley for *Once* (2012)

Rob Howell for *Matilda the Musical* (2013)

Christopher Barreca for *Rocky the Musical* (2014)

Bob Crowley & 59 Productions for *An American in Paris* (2015)

David Rockwell for *She Loves Me* (2016)

Mimi Lien for *Natasha, Pierre & The Great Comet of 1812* (2017)

David Zinn for *SpongeBob Square Pants* (2018)

Rachel Hauck for *Hadestown* (2019)

Derek McLane for *Moulin Rouge!* (2020)

TONY AWARD WINNERS FOR BEST SCENIC DESIGN IN A PLAY (2010-2020)

Christopher Oram for *Red* (2010)

Rae Smith for *War Horse* (2011)

Donyale Werle for *Peter and the Starcatcher* (2012)

John Lee Beatty for *The Nance* (2013)

Beowulf Boritt for *Act One* (2014)

Bunny Christie and Finn Ross for *The Curious Incident of the Dog in the Night-Time* (2015)

David Zinn for *The Humans* (2016)

Nigel Hook for *The Play That Goes Wrong* (2017)

Christine Jones for *Harry Potter and the Cursed Child* (2018)

Rob Howell for *The Ferryman* (2019), *A Christmas Carol* (2020)

CHAPTER 11

POST-PANDEMIC EMPLOYMENT OUTLOOK: STATISTICS AND ECONOMIC PROJECTIONS

"The curtain rises even on an actor's worst day."

– Stewart Stafford

ECONOMIC OUTLOOK FOR THEATRE, MUSICAL THEATRE, AND THE PERFORMING ARTS

A ctors portray characters in all forms of media, stages, and venues, interpreting a script to entertain or inform. According to the *Occupational Outlook Handbook*, most actors struggle to find steady work and often have long periods of unemployment between roles, often holding other jobs to make a living. Some actors teach classes, sing, dance, work as "extras", do voiceover/narration for animated feature stories, audiobooks, or electronic media.

In acting, there are typically more applicants than positions. With the volume of people choosing this direction, acting spots tend to go to those whose talent and experience fit the company's needs. Also, the more competitive markets, like New York City, will require additional skills and extraordinary ambition. On the Texas Shakespeare Festival site where you are to upload your headshot and resume, Artistic Director, Meaghan Simpson's note to actors states,

> At this time, we have closed our online submissions for the TSF 2022 season. I want to say thank-you for the time and effort you put into learning a new monologue, stacking books under your iPhone, or perfecting the ideal 32-bar cutting. The energy and devotion to your craft is incredible and admirable.

> Each year, we receive approximately 1500 submissions to fill 22 tracks in our summer acting company. Suffice it to say, the odds are not in your favor. That said, we promise to view your audition and to contact you to inform you of your status once the casting process has completed.

With those odds, it is easy to get discouraged. Do not let the number of people applying for undergraduate or graduate degree programs or an internship or a job stop you. If acting is the field you want to pursue, pave the road in front of you and drive. An internship or apprenticeship or two would not hurt you in your pursuit. Although most internships are unpaid, you will find that most applicants will have one or more.

If you are serious, you can make a fantastic career out of your pursuit. Initiative-taking persistence, talent, creativity, and moxie can get you into your desired college program and career. You may have to start at the very bottom of the ladder, but you can climb the rungs methodically one by one.

Acting companies want to know the work ethic, personality, and professionalism of the employees they choose. An internship allows you to get to know their corporate climate better and allows them to get to know you better too. Thus, many companies hire the interns they feel are the best fit rather than choosing candidates from the piles of resumes, headshots, and audition tapes that have been submitted.

Education unlocks doors. In the dramatic arts, this is also true. Persistence and showmanship are invaluable tools. Your education, highlighted on your resume, can move your audition materials to the top of the pile.

Those who perform on stage do so on Broadway, Off-Broadway, and in touring companies, summer stock, and resident companies. Approximately two-thirds of all actors are men with 23% LGBTQ+. Nearly 60% are White, 15.6% Hispanic, 13.9% African American, and 6% Asian. The average age of employed actors is 37 years old.

ECONOMIC OUTLOOK FOR ACTORS

Bureau of Labor Statistics – Actors

2020 Median Pay: $21.88 per hour

Bachelor's Degree: Theatre, Drama, Musical Theatre

Number of Jobs in 2020: 51,600

Job Growth: 32% Increase (much higher than average)

Location of Most Positions: New York and Los Angeles

According to the Bureau of Labor Statistics, the growth rate of 32% for acting is much higher than the average for jobs in the United States. Furthermore, the growth in jobs from 2020 – 2030 is expected to be 16,700 new jobs in theatre, film, television, and other performing arts media. Work assignments tend to be short contract work. As for education,

Master's Degree – 6%

Bachelor's Degree – 61%

Associate's Degree – 12%

HS Diploma – 16%

Another degree/certificate – 5%

Actors with a bachelor's degree or higher earn on average approximately $13,000 per year more. Most actors live in New York or Los Angeles.

Alternative jobs related to acting:

Actor	Host
Anchor	Lighting Technicians
Audio Engineer	Magician
Audition Coach	Makeup Artists
Background Actor	Marketing
Bartending	Modeling
Carpenter	Musical Theatre
Cast Member	Painter
Catering	Personal Assistant
Character Performer	Production Studios
Comedian	Promo Work
Company Manager	Scare Actor
Costume Assistant	Scenic Carpenter
Crafts Technician	Seamstress
Debate Teacher	Set Dresser
Drama Coach	Stage Crew
Dramaturg	Stitcher
Entertainer	Stunt Double
First Hand	Teacher

Theatre

Theatre Arts Educator

Theatre Camp Counselor

Theme Parks

Trade Shows

Video Editor

Voice Actor

Voice-Over Artist

Wardrobe

Whatever direction you pursue, if you lay a foundation, undaunted by the competition, and are unafraid of starting at the bottom, you will do fine. Hard work and creativity go a long way in this industry. Start by getting a solid education.

MANAGEMENT AND EMPLOYEE RETENTION

Skills to Know: *Management, Human Resources, Social Consciousness, Ethics*

One of the most significant challenges facing the years from 2022 - 2030 will be locating and retaining talent. The pandemic slowed education and learning with online classes, reduced access to faculty/advising, limited access to labs, inability to attend workshops, retail closures, and fewer conferences, meetings, and shows. Health concerns rose to the top of importance as did financial stress, job uncertainty, and social consciousness. Many students chose to work rather than study and start online stores when they could not access locations for community service or continue with their sport, instrument, or hobbies. With the changes in lifestyle and fears about health, safety, and wellness, many bright and talented students developed a fearless sense of autonomy and independence, while for others, the necessary skills ordinarily developed in school were fraught by limitations.

Finding talent within the changing hiring atmosphere will require new skills to retain staff. Employees are increasingly looking elsewhere for a better opportunity. This development will require managers to earn and harness employee trust and loyalty.

The digital workforce has also placed demands on human resources. While many companies want their employees to work in-person, the convenience of working at home and the drudgery of commuting to work have created an environment where employees seek greater flexibility. Changes are coming. The employee talent challenge is likely to create a more global workforce where companies look for less expensive online talent from a pool of eager workers in other countries.

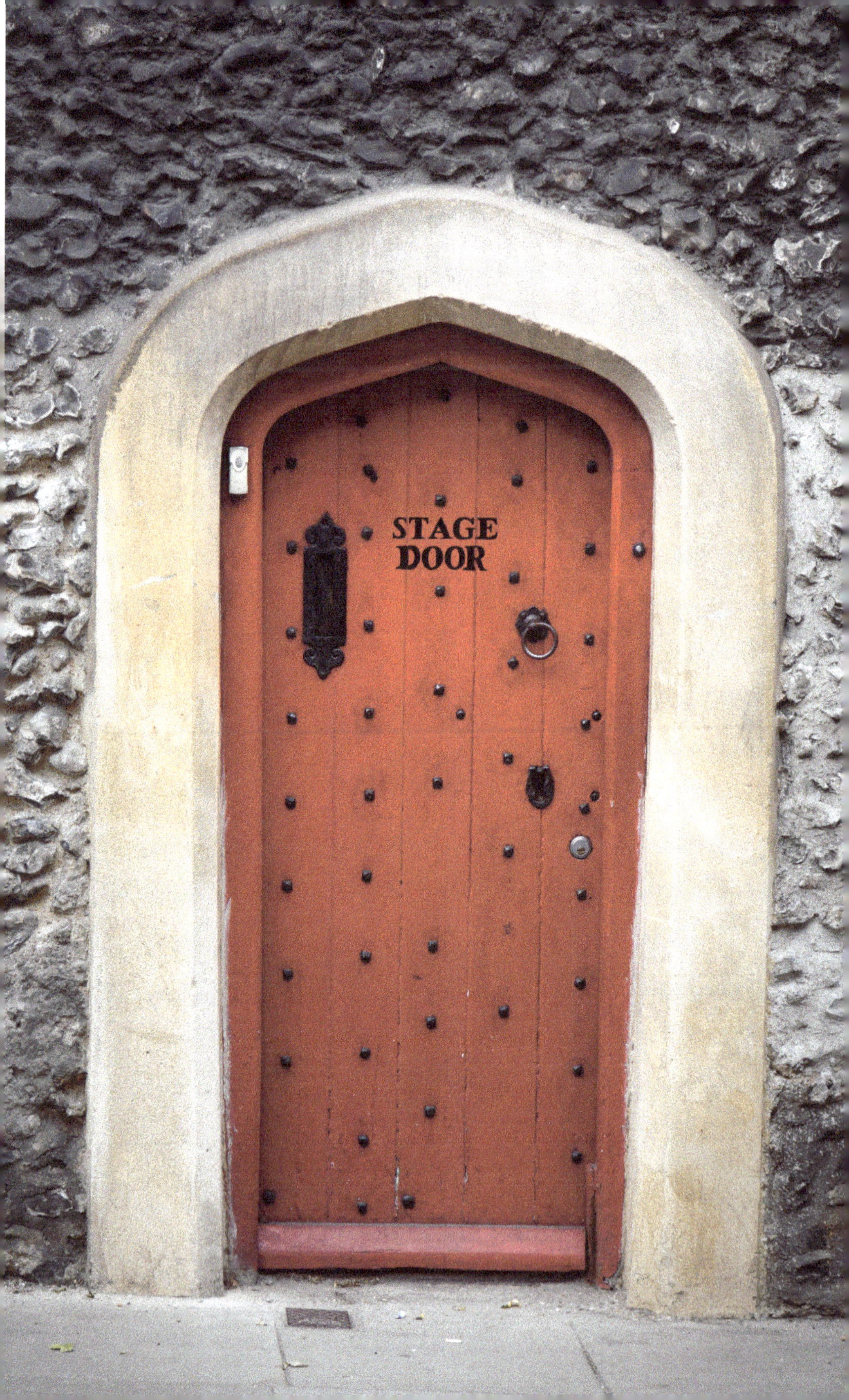
STAGE
DOOR

CHAPTER 12

NEXT STEPS: PREPARATION AND REAL-WORLD SKILLS

"Acting is half shame, half glory. Shame at exhibiting yourself, glory when you can forget yourself."

– John Gielgud

While you do not need a college education, a Bachelor of Fine Arts from a respected school certainly helps you get noticed. Connections through your professors, classmates, and alumni are excellent ways to discover opportunities. Performances in school, out of school, in the summer, or through social media can help you get noticed. Also, throughout your varied experiences, you will meet other actors who can recommend you or let you know of auditions, even some that are not publicly announced. Many schools have a senior showcase in front of agents and casting directors where you can put your best foot forward.

Exposure to agents and industry professionals helps. Interacting with people online or in-person allows you to maintain those connections. You could wait for the phone to ring or for you to be discovered, however, you will have to be out and about for that to happen. Some pine away hoping to be signed or reading scripts deciding which would be a perfect fit. However, the reason why so many actors work in New York restaurants is to get out and see what is happening outside of their apartment.

BOLD NETWORKING

Networking takes social skills and a bit of moxie. From elevator speeches and restaurant encounters to auditions, masterclasses, and workshops, your job is to find a way to get in front of people. How can you be recognized? Meet people, hand out your resume, give them your business card, ask for their business card, follow up, ask if you can call or meet them, even when the instance may be uncomfortable. Stay in touch with people you meet, even if it is just happenstance or serendipity. Keep a log with each person's phone, e-mail, identifying information, and both date and location where you met. You never know when you will need it.

If you meet people professionally at a masterclass or workshop, even if you do not exchange information, you will recognize them. They may recognize you in a future event too. Keep training. You should always want to improve no matter how good you are, though you should not train just for the sake of meeting people. Your focus will not be on improvement and you may appear insincere. However, this forum can allow others to see you too. Big-ticket training does not always mean better trainers or opportunities. See shows, film premieres, and engage in all things theatre.

STAY IN TOUCH

Do not annoy busy people, but you can keep in touch every couple of months. Communicating more frequently is overwhelming. However, life is long, and people who grow with their craft in this industry, transitioning through career phases of their life often perform until they are in their 60s and 70s. In this industry, contacts are important in all phases of your career.

Also, do not be surprised. Many go-getters auditioning with you could become lifelong colleagues and friends and may also turn out to be very successful. People tend to only want to stay in touch with the "important" people. Note: your contemporaries or peers are important people...although possibly not yet. Remember that as you form your lists of contacts, you are likely to stay in touch with them throughout your career.

Be audacious, while also being authentic. Networking can sometimes appear fake or forced, as if you are going out on a hunt to find people for your own benefit. Worse, the act of networking in theatre can reach the verge of stalking as a young actor follows an agent or casting director to connect. The mental image this type of 'networking' conjures up the image of people congregating at stage doors, smiling broadly and blatantly flirting.

Friendships and mutual support of allies can be enormously helpful, 20,000 or even 200,000 followers on your website does not mean you are popular. However, you can have unexpected meaningful exchanges if you get out and live life. I once had a fascinating and memorable conversation with Matthew Perry in Palm Desert, CA for more than an hour where we talked about life, culture, and world affairs. I was not trying to network, nor was he, and we did not exchange information. We live in very different worlds. Nevertheless, there are times when deeply moving, casual conversations in non-professional settings could also turn into connections.

Do not lose touch with people or burn bridges along the way. This industry is not that big, and you will continually see movers and shakers on all levels of the acting and performance world. You never know. They may contact you to collaborate one day or meet for coffee at an event. Networking is a two-way street, and the best networkers know this.

"In all the universe nothing remains permanent and unchanged but the spirit."

- Anton Chekhov, "The Seagull", The Plays of Checkhov (1895).

"There is nothing either good or bad, but thinking makes it so."

- William Shakespeare, Hamlet, 1603.

COLLEGE AND CAREER CENTERS

Although college theatre managers, program directors, and conservatory coordinators often do what they can to help you get acting roles, summer stock opportunities, and auditions, you might also go to your campus career center. They often have interesting prospects that you might not get elsewhere. There may be a specific career liaison for the dramatic arts.

Connect with them for help in your search process. Besides, you might just want to get a related job that utilizes your presentation skills. Companies that hold tradeshows often hire theatre majors. Marketing companies also appreciate people who can tell more about their products. These jobs may not be your ideal, but sometimes you just need a position to earn money and get yourself on your feet. Career center coordinators often have excellent ideas.

Furthermore, they can assist you with creating a professional resume and cover letters for specific industries that are different from the ones you have for acting, voice, or dance. They may also connect you with past graduates in the industry who make excellent connections. Some of them may have been in your program and have been through the ropes, know a few people, and may be able to get you an interview or invite you to an industry event. Any contact may be able to get your foot into the door or a job to make money in the meantime.

LINKEDIN

LinkedIn is especially helpful for career searches. You can find numerous influential contacts on LinkedIn. After each audition, connect with each person you met on LinkedIn. Keep a contact list of individuals you know in the theatre and performing arts world. Do not constantly try to connect with people you do not really know. However, if you have made the connection, occasionally keep in touch.

While some LinkedIn message boxes may be full and you may not get a reply, you can try. Occasionally, you hit on a lucky break. Though I do not have time to communicate with everyone, I have connected with some of my most inspiring authors, advisors, and intellectual leaders through LinkedIn.

FINALLY

Most people are willing to help you. Five percent will not. Thus, you have a 19 out of 20 chance of interacting with decent people who have the time and will give you advice. Don't lose faith in humanity just because you run into a few people who are too busy to stop for you or are too self-absorbed that they cannot answer your question.

- Work ethic is everything.
- Excellence is expected.
- Learn what you do not know on your own time.
- Come to work prepared.
- Take constructive criticism well.
- Keep your cool under pressure.
- Avoid being timid.
- Stay on task.
- Come early.
- Stay late.
- Take your work seriously.
- Do more than expected.
- Read your e-mail/texts after hours in case something is important.
- Ask questions. No question is too stupid.
- Maintain a clean workspace.
- Dress and act professionally.
- Don't gossip or complain.
- Avoid frustrating your phenomenally busy supervisor.
- Be straightforward, and don't beat around the bush.

You've Got This!

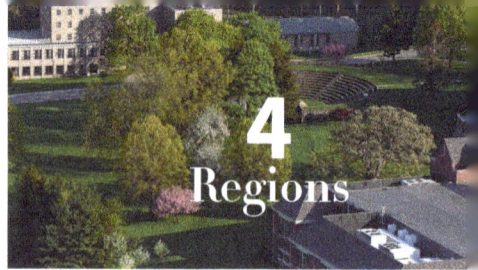

4
Regions

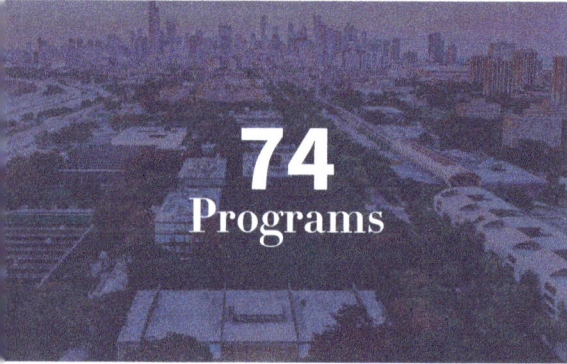

74
Programs

COLLEGE PROFILES AND REQUIREMENTS

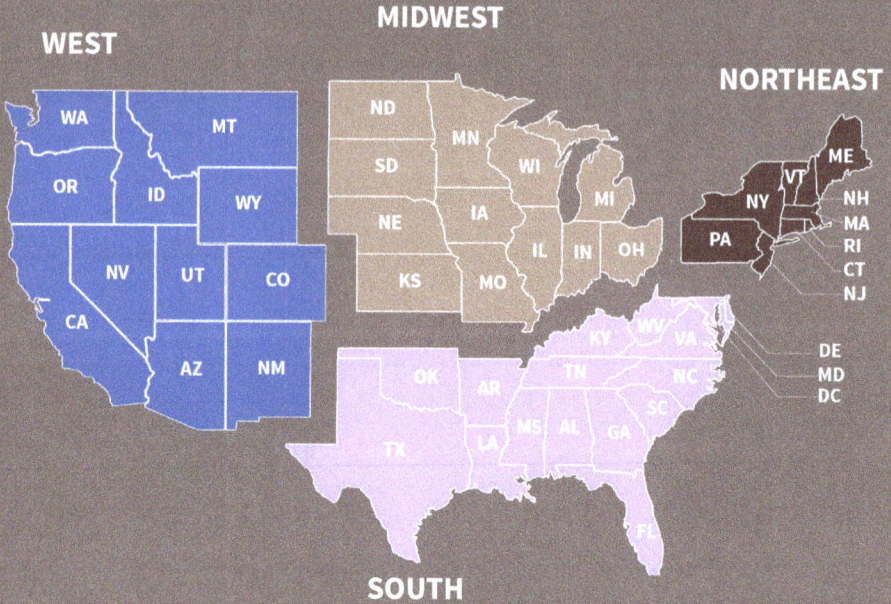

WEST

MIDWEST

NORTHEAST

SOUTH

PROGRAMS BY REGION
U.S. CENSUS BUREAU CLASSIFICATIONS

REGION 1 – NORTHEAST

Connecticut, Maine, Massachusetts, New Hampshire, New Jersey, New York, Pennsylvania, Rhode Island, and Vermont

REGION 2 – MIDWEST

Illinois, Indiana, Iowa, Kansas, Michigan, Minnesota, Missouri, Nebraska, North Dakota, Ohio, South Dakota, and Wisconsin

REGION 3 – SOUTH

Alabama, Arkansas, Delaware, District of Columbia, Florida, Georgia, Kentucky, Louisiana, Maryland, Mississippi, North Carolina, Oklahoma, South Carolina, Tennessee, Texas, Virginia, and West Virginia

REGION 4 – WEST

Alaska, Arizona, California, Colorado, Hawaii, Idaho, Montana, Nevada, New Mexico, Oregon, Utah, Washington, and Wyoming

LIST OF THEATRE AND DRAMATIC ARTS PROGRAMS

T he programs listed in the following pages include top theatre programs. In addition, this book also lists the top musical theatre, costume design, and technical theatre programs. Many students interested in theatre are also interested in the artistic side of dance, voice, costume design, and theatre arts.

Thus, this book aims to provide you with a more comprehensive set of lists so that you can explore your options. Keep the book handy. Even after you begin college, you may find the additional programs in the back are helpful for connections or summer programs.

Creating lists is often tedious and cumbersome. These lists were gathered to help you with this task. Acceptance rates for theatre programs were often unavailable. Thus, university acceptance rates were provided.

These descriptions of the college programs, tuition, requirements, and deadlines are accurate as of March 2022. The requirements may have changed somewhat by the time you purchase this book, but this information is a great place to start!

Note: To simplify the text and fit information into the charts and descriptions, abbreviations were used as well as shortened sentences and acronyms. Also, note that theater and theatre are spelled differently depending upon the school or program. While "theatre" was used throughout the text, if a school or program used 'theater', we attempted to leave that name as they chose.

CONNECTICUT

MAINE

MASSACHUSETTS

NEW HAMPSHIRE

NEW JERSEY

NEW YORK

PENNSYLVANIA

RHODE ISLAND

VERMONT

CHAPTER 13

REGION ONE

NORTHEAST

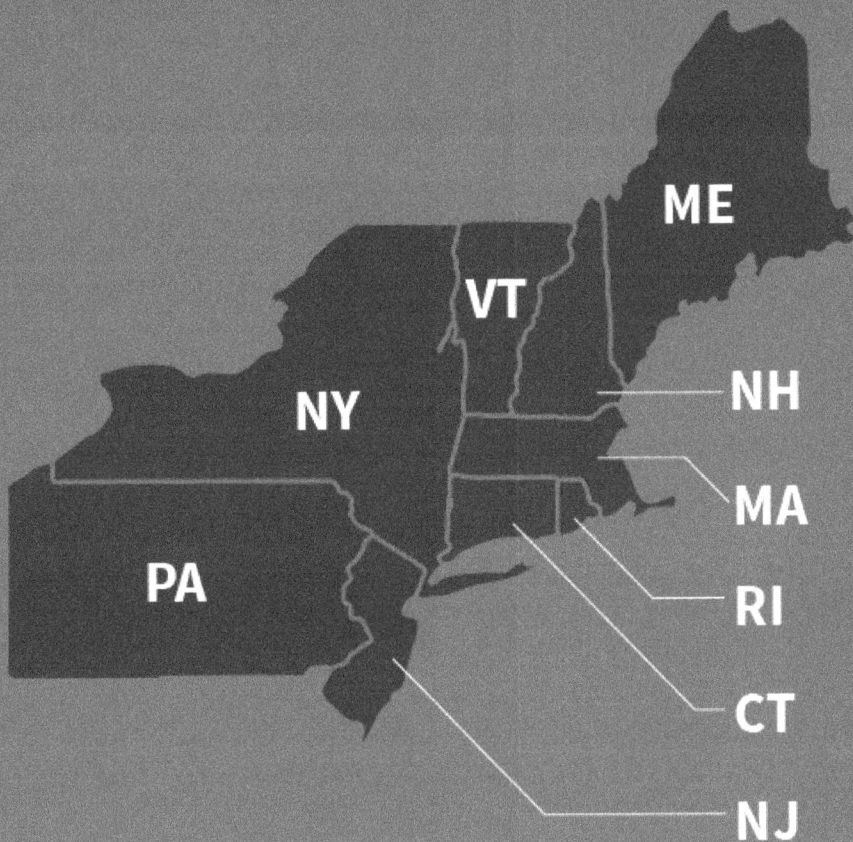

25 *Programs* | 9 *States*

THEATRE PROGRAMS

School	Avg. GPA, SAT Evidence Based Reading and Writing (ERW), SAT Math (M), and ACT Composite (C) Early Decision (ED): Yes/No	Admission Statistics	Program(s) See website for additional options.	Artistic Review Required (Req.)
University of Connecticut (UConn) 802 Bolton Rd., Unit-1127, Storrs, CT 06269	GPA: N/A SAT (ERW): 580-680 SAT (M): 590-710 ACT (C): 27-32 ED: No	Overall College Admit Rate: 56% Undergrad Enrollment: 18,917 Total Enrollment: 27,215	BA Theatre Studies BFA Acting Degrees Awarded in the Program(s): 25	BA Theatre Studies No portfolio req. BFA Acting Audition req.
Wesleyan University 275 Washington Terrace, Middletown, CT 06459	GPA: N/A SAT (ERW): 670-750 SAT (M): 670-770 ACT (C): 31-34 *Test-optional ED: Yes	Overall College Admit Rate: 21% Undergrad Enrollment: 2,852 Total Enrollment: 3,053	BA Theater Degrees Awarded in the Program(s): 14	None req.
Yale University 38 Hillhouse Avenue, New Haven, CT 06520	GPA: N/A SAT (ERW): 720-780 SAT (M): 740-800 ACT (C): 33-35 ED: No	Overall College Admit Rate: 7% Undergrad Enrollment: 4,664 Total Enrollment: 12,060	BA Theater Studies Degrees Awarded in the Program(s): 10	None req.
Boston University 233 Bay State Road, Boston, MA 02215	GPA: 3.76 SAT (ERW): 640-720 SAT (M): 670-780 ACT (C): 30-34 ED: Yes	Overall College Admit Rate: 20% Undergrad Enrollment: 16,872 Total Enrollment: 32,718	BFA Acting, Concentration: Music Theatre BFA Theatre Arts— Performance Degrees Awarded in the Program(s): 37	Audition req.

School	Avg. GPA, SAT Evidence Based Reading and Writing (ERW), SAT Math (M), and ACT Composite (C) Early Decision (ED): Yes/No	Admission Statistics	Program(s) *See website for additional options.*	Artistic Review Required (Req.)
Emerson College 120 Boylston Street Boston, MA 02116	GPA: 3.5 SAT (ERW): 610-690 SAT (M): 580-690 ACT (C): 27-31 *Test-optional ED: Yes	Overall College Admit Rate: 41% Undergrad Enrollment: 3,708 Total Enrollment: 5,115	BFA Theatre BFA Theatre & Performance BFA Acting BFA Comedic Arts BFA Musical Theatre BFA Theatre Education & Performance Degrees Awarded in the Program(s): 87	BFA Comedic Arts Portfolio req. BFA Musical Theatre Prescreen req. BFA Acting; BFA Theatre & Performance; BFA Musical Theatre; BFA Theatre Education & Performance Audition req.
University of Massachusetts at Amherst 181 Presidents Dr., Amherst, MA 01003	GPA: 3.99 SAT (ERW): 620-710 SAT (M): 630-750 ACT (C): 28-33 ED: No	Overall College Admit Rate: 66% Undergrad Enrollment: 24,231 Total Enrollment: 32,045	BA Theater Degrees Awarded in the Program(s): 28	None req.
Montclair State University 1 Normal Ave., Montclair, NJ 07043	GPA: N/A SAT (ERW): 500-600 SAT (M): 510-610 ACT (C): 21-28 *Test-optional ED: No	Overall College Admit Rate: 86% Undergrad Enrollment: 16,093 Total Enrollment: 20,744	BA Theatre Studies BFA Theatre BFA Musical Theatre Degrees Awarded in the Program(s): 71	BFA Theatre, concentration: Acting; BFA Musical Theatre Prescreen and audition req.

NORTHEAST

THEATRE PROGRAMS

School	Avg. GPA, SAT Evidence Based Reading and Writing (ERW), SAT Math (M), and ACT Composite (C) Early Decision (ED): Yes/No	Admission Statistics	Program(s) *See website for additional options.*	Artistic Review Required (Req.)
Rutgers, The State University of New Jersey 100 Sutphen Road, Piscataway, NJ 08854	GPA: N/A SAT (ERW): 580-680 SAT (M): 600-730 ACT (C): 25-32 ED: No	Overall College Admit Rate: 67% Undergrad Enrollment: 35,844 Total Enrollment: 50,411	BA Theater BFA Theater Degrees Awarded in the Program(s): 34	BFA Theatre, concentration: Acting Audition req.
Barnard College 3009 Broadway, New York, NY 10027	GPA: N/A SAT (ERW): 680-747.5 SAT (M): 670-770 ACT (C): 31-34 ED: Yes	Overall College Admit Rate: 14% Undergrad Enrollment: 2,744 Total Enrollment: 2,744	BA Drama and Theatre Arts Degrees Awarded in the Program(s): 8	None req.
Fordham University 441 E. Fordham Rd., Bronx, NY 10458	GPA: 3.64 SAT (ERW): 620-700 SAT (M): 620-740 ACT (C): 28-32 ED: Yes	Overall College Admit Rate: 46% Undergrad Enrollment: 9,767 Total Enrollment: 16,972	BA Theatre Degrees Awarded in the Program(s): 31	BA Theatre, concentration: Performance Audition req.
Ithaca College 953 Danby Road, Ithaca, NY 14850	GPA: N/A SAT (ERW): 600-680 SAT (M): 580-670 ACT (C): 27-31 *Test-optional ED: Yes	Overall College Admit Rate: 78% Undergrad Enrollment: 4,818 Total Enrollment: 5,239	BA Theatre Studies BFA Acting BFA Musical Theatre Degrees Awarded in the Program(s): 64	BFA Musical Theater Prescreen and audition req.

School	Avg. GPA, SAT Evidence Based Reading and Writing (ERW), SAT Math (M), and ACT Composite (C) Early Decision (ED): Yes/No	Admission Statistics	Program(s) *See website for additional options.*	Artistic Review Required (Req.)
Long Island University (LIU) 720 Northern Blvd., Brookville, NY 11548	GPA: N/A SAT (ERW): 540-640 SAT (M): 540-650 ACT (C): 22-29 ED: No	Overall College Admit Rate: 85% Undergrad Enrollment: 10,403 Total Enrollment: 15,066	BA in Theatre Arts BFA Theatre Arts Degrees Awarded in the Program(s): 28	All programs Portfolio req. BFA Theatre Arts, concentration: Musical Theatre Audition req.
Marymount Manhattan College 221 E 71st St, New York, NY 10021	GPA: N/A SAT (ERW): 500-580 SAT (M): 460-620 ACT (C): 20-28 *Test-optional ED: Yes	Overall College Admit Rate: 88% Undergrad Enrollment: 1,722 Total Enrollment: 1,722	BFA Acting BFA Musical Theatre BA Theatre Studies Degrees Awarded in the Program(s): 122	BFA Acting; BFA Musical Theatre Audition req.
New York University (NYU) 27 West 4th Street, New York, NY 10014	GPA: 3.71 SAT (ERW): 670-740 SAT (M): 700-800 ACT (C): 31-34 ED: Yes	Overall College Admit Rate: 21% Undergrad Enrollment: 27,444 Total Enrollment: 52,775	BA Performance Studies BFA Drama Degrees Awarded in the Program(s): 358	BA Performance Studies; Portfolio req. BFA Drama, concentrations: Acting, Musical Theatre, and Directing Audition req.

NORTHEAST

THEATRE PROGRAMS

School	Avg. GPA, SAT Evidence Based Reading and Writing (ERW), SAT Math (M), and ACT Composite (C) Early Decision (ED): Yes/No	Admission Statistics	Program(s) *See website for additional options.*	Artistic Review Required (Req.)
Pace University 1 Pace Plaza, New York, NY 10038	GPA: N/A SAT (ERW): 540-630 SAT (M): 520-610 ACT (C): 22-28 *Test-optional ED: Yes	Overall College Admit Rate: 83% Undergrad Enrollment: 7,994 Total Enrollment: 12,835	BA Acting BFA Acting BFA Musical Theater Degrees Awarded in the Program(s): 159	BA Acting; BFA Acting; BFA Musical Theater; Prescreen req. BA Acting; BFA Acting; BFA Musical Theater Audition req.
Skidmore College 815 N. Broadway, Saratoga Springs, NY 12866	GPA: N/A SAT (ERW): 630-720 SAT (M): 640-720 ACT (C): 29-33 ED: Yes	Overall College Admit Rate: 31% Undergrad Enrollment: 2,686 Total Enrollment: 2,686	BS Theater Degrees Awarded in the Program(s): 13	None req.
State University of New York at Binghamton 4400 Vestal Pkwy E, Binghamton, NY 13902	GPA: N/A SAT (ERW): 640-710 SAT (M): 640-710 (ERW) 650-740 ACT (C): 29-32 ED: No	Overall College Admit Rate: 43% Undergrad Enrollment: 14,333 Total Enrollment: 18,148	BA Theatre Degrees Awarded in the Program(s): 23	None req.

School	Avg. GPA, SAT Evidence Based Reading and Writing (ERW), SAT Math (M), and ACT Composite (C) Early Decision (ED): Yes/No	Admission Statistics	Program(s) See website for additional options.	Artistic Review Required (Req.)
Syracuse University 401 University Place, Syracuse, NY 13244-2130	GPA: 3.67 SAT (ERW): N/A SAT (M): N/A ACT (C): N/A ED: Yes	Overall College Admit Rate: 69% Undergrad Enrollment: 14,479 Total Enrollment: 21,322	BS Drama BFA Acting: Actor-Singer Track BFA Musical Theater Degrees Awarded in the Program(s): 69	BFA Acting; BFA Musical Theater Prescreen and audition req.
The Juilliard School 60 Lincoln Center Plaza, New York, NY 10023	GPA: N/A SAT (ERW): N/A SAT (M): N/A ACT (C): N/A *Test-optional ED: No	Overall College Admit Rate: 67% Undergrad Enrollment: 589 Total Enrollment: 961	BFA Acting Degrees Awarded in the Program(s): 9	Prescreen and audition req.
University at Buffalo 285 Alumni Arena, North Campus, Buffalo, New York 14260	GPA: 3.7 SAT (ERW): 560-640 SAT (M): 580-670 ACT (C): 23-29 ED: No	Overall College Admit Rate: 37% Undergrad Enrollment: 22,306 Total Enrollment: 32,347	BA Theatre BFA Theatre BFA Music Theatre Degrees Awarded in the Program(s): 25	BFA Theatre, concentration: Performance; BFA Music Theatre Audition req.

NORTHEAST

THEATRE PROGRAMS

School	Avg. GPA, SAT Evidence Based Reading and Writing (ERW), SAT Math (M), and ACT Composite (C) Early Decision (ED): Yes/No	Admission Statistics	Program(s) *See website for additional options.*	Artistic Review Required (Req.)
Vassar College 124 Raymond Avenue, Poughkeepsie, NY 12604	GPA: N/A SAT (ERW): 680-750 SAT (M): 680-770 ACT (C): 32-34 ED: Yes	Overall College Admit Rate: 25% Undergrad Enrollment: 2435 Total Enrollment: 2435	BA Drama Degrees Awarded in the Program(s): 28	None req.
Carnegie Mellon University 5000 Forbes Avenue, Pittsburgh, PA 15213	GPA: 3.85 SAT (ERW): 700-760 SAT (M): 760-800 ACT (C): 33-35 ED: Yes	Overall College Admit Rate: 17% Undergrad Enrollment: 7,073 Total Enrollment: 14,189	BFA Drama Degrees Awarded in the Program(s): 73	BFA Drama, options: Acting and Music Theater Prescreen req. BFA Drama, options: Directing, Acting and Music Theater Audition req.
Pennsylvania State University 201 Shields Building, University Park, PA 16802	GPA: N/A SAT (ERW): 580-670 SAT (M): 580-700 ACT (C): 25-30 ED: No	Overall College Admit Rate: 49% Undergrad Enrollment: 40,639 Total Enrollment: 47,223	BA Theatre BFA Theatre BFA Acting BFA Musical Theatre Degrees Awarded in the Program(s): N/A	BA Theatre; BFA Theatre Portfolio req. BFA Acting; BFA Musical Theatre Prescreen and audition req.

School	Avg. GPA, SAT Evidence Based Reading and Writing (ERW), SAT Math (M), and ACT Composite (C) Early Decision (ED): Yes/No	Admission Statistics	Program(s) *See website for additional options.*	Artistic Review Required (Req.)
University of the Arts (UArts) 320 S. Broad St., Philadelphia, PA 19102	GPA: N/A SAT (ERW): N/A SAT (M): N/A ACT (C): N/A *Test-optional ED: No	Overall College Admit Rate: 76% Undergrad Enrollment: 1,380 Total Enrollment: 1,530	BFA Acting BA Musical Theater Degrees Awarded in the Program(s): 66	Audition req.
Middlebury College 131 South Main Street, Middlebury, VT 05753	GPA: N/A SAT (ERW): 670-750 SAT (M): 670-770 ACT (C): 31-34 ED: Yes	Overall College Admit Rate: 22% Undergrad Enrollment: 2,580 Total Enrollment: 2,666	BA Theatre Degrees Awarded in the Program(s): 8	None req.

NORTHEAST

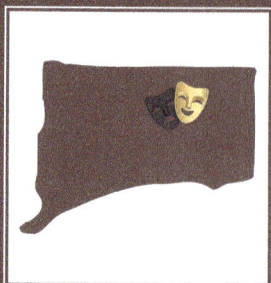

CONNECTICUT

MAINE

MASSACHUSETTS

NEW HAMPSHIRE

NEW JERSEY

NEW YORK

PENNSYLVANIA

RHODE ISLAND

VERMONT

UNIVERSITY OF CONNECTICUT (UCONN)

Address: 802 Bolton Rd., Unit-1127, Storrs, CT 06269
Website: *https://drama.uconn.edu/programs/*
Contact: *https://drama.uconn.edu/overview/contact/*
Phone: (860) 486-2281
Email: dramaoffice@uconn.edu

COST OF ATTENDANCE:

In-State Tuition & Fees: $15,030 | **Additional Expenses:** $16,752
Total: $31,782

New England Tuition & Fees: $24,048 | **Additional Expenses:** $16,752
Total: $40,800

Out-of-State Tuition & Fees: $37,698 | **Additional Expenses:** $16,752
Total: $54,450

Financial Aid: https://financialaid.uconn.edu/

ADDITIONAL INFORMATION:

Available Degree(s)

- BA Theatre Studies, areas of concentration: Dramaturgy, Playwriting, Directing, Theatre Management, and Stage Management
- BFA Acting

Artistic Review Requirement

After submission of University application, submit additional materials for Acting, Design & Technology, and Theatre Studies to SlideRoom. A portfolio is required for Theatrical Design & Technology. An audition is required for Acting and Puppet Arts. There is a Priority Deadline for Merit Scholarship & Honors Consideration.

Scholarships Offered

First-year applicants are automatically considered for most merit scholarships offered at the University of Connecticut. The Nutmeg and Day of Pride scholarships require a school counselor nomination.

Special Opportunities

Located near New York City, students have access to some of the best regional theatres in the country and receive free tickets to shows. An academic connection to the Metropolitan Opera Hartford Stage and TheatreWorks offer internships and chances to see free performances. Students may also enjoy study abroad opportunities at Bournemouth University College of the Arts and London University Wimbledon College of the Arts in the UK. Last, the Ballard Institute and Museum of Puppetry hosts a collection of over 3,000 puppets.

Notable Alumni

Jennifer Barnhart, Chris Barreca, Thomas Brazzle, Jackie Burns, Greg Fuscaldo, Bobby Moynihan, and Dan Rousseau

WESLEYAN UNIVERSITY

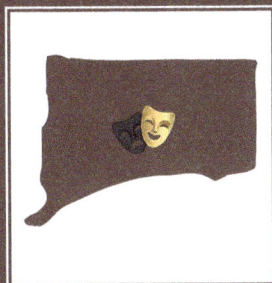

Address: 275 Washington Terrace, Middletown, CT 06459
Website: *https://www.wesleyan.edu/theater/*
Contact: *https://www.wesleyan.edu/about/contactus.html*
Phone: (860) 685-2961
Email: admission@wesleyan.edu

COST OF ATTENDANCE:

Tuition & Fees: $61,449 | **Additional Expenses:** $20,496
Total: $81,945

Financial Aid: https://www.wesleyan.edu/finaid/index.html

ADDITIONAL INFORMATION:

Available Degree(s)

- BA Theater

Artistic Review Requirement

Portfolios or auditions are not required for admission to Wesleyan. Supplemental material is optional. Declaration to become a Theater major is usually made in the second semester of the sophomore year.

Scholarships Offered

Aid is typically need-based at Wesleyan University. However, students may apply to fellowships, scholarships, and internships. In addition, the university has the Three-Year Option, an initiative to help students plan to complete their degree in three years, thus saving 20% of the total degree cost.

Special Opportunities

Theater students are encouraged to spend a semester at British American Drama Academy and Moscow Art Theatre. The Theater Department awards the Rachel Henderson Theater Prize, Outreach and Community Service Prize, and the J.Peter Adler Memorial Fund.

Notable Alumni

David Babcock, Julia Barclay, Nick Benacerraf, David Bickford, Chloe Brown, Daniel Cantor, Jonathan Cardone, William Christopher, Dana Delany, Alek Lev, Lin-Manuel Miranda, Roderick Murray, Matthew Penn, Jessica Phillippi, Lisa Anne Porter, Michael Rau, Bradley Whitford, and Frank Wood

CONNECTICUT

MAINE

MASSACHUSETTS

NEW HAMPSHIRE

NEW JERSEY

NEW YORK

PENNSYLVANIA

RHODE ISLAND

VERMONT

NORTHEAST

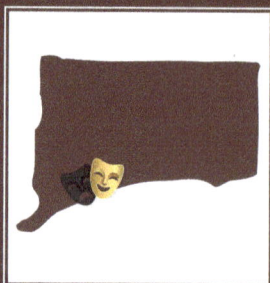

YALE UNIVERSITY

Address: 220 York Street, Room 102, New Haven, CT 06511
Website: *https://theaterstudies.yale.edu/*
Contact: *https://theaterstudies.yale.edu/about/contact-us*
Phone: (203) 432-1310
Email: student.questions@yale.edu

COST OF ATTENDANCE:

Tuition & Fees: $59,950 | **Additional Expenses:** $21,625
Total: $81,575

Financial Aid: https://www.yale.edu/admissions/financial-aid

ADDITIONAL INFORMATION:

Available Degree(s)

- BA Theater Studies

Artistic Review Requirement

No audition is required for undergraduate Theatre Studies at Yale. After admission, make an appointment with the Director of Undergraduate Studies to take the first-year Survey of Theater and Drama (THST 110 and 111).

Scholarships Offered

Yale scholarships are grants that are solely need-based. Merit-based scholarships are funded by external organizations or private companies.

Special Opportunities

All students must complete a senior project requirement. Seniors may direct or design a theatrical production, write a musical/play, create a documentary, perform a role, or participate in many other theater-based activities to satisfy this requirement.

Notable Alumni

Roberto Aguirre-Sacasa, Angela Bassett, Lewis Black, Dick Cavett, Patricia Clarkson, David Clennon, Enrico Colantoni, Polly Draper, Charles S. Dutton, Paul Giamatti, David Grier, Ernie Hudson, David Henry Hwang, Jane Kaczmarek, Robert Klein, Sanaa Lathan, Delbert Mann, Tarell Alvin McCraney, Frances McDormand, Lynn Nottage, Lupita Nyong'o, Paul Newman, Alan Rosenberg, Live Schreiber, Tony Shalhoub, Roger L. Simon, Robin Strasser, Meryl Streep, John Turturro, Joan Van Ark, Courtney B. Vance, Sigourney Weaver, Henry Winkler, and Jeff Yagher

BOSTON UNIVERSITY

Address: 855 Commonwealth Avenue, Boston, MA 02215
Website: *https://www.bu.edu/cfa/academics/find-a-degreeprogram/school-of-theatre/theatre-arts/*
Contact: *https://www.bu.edu/cfa/aboutcfa/contact/*
Phone: (617) 353-3350
Email: cfastu@bu.edu

COST OF ATTENDANCE:

Tuition & Fees: $58,560 | **Additional Expenses:** $21,046
Total: $79,606

Financial Aid: http://www.bu.edu/finaid/

ADDITIONAL INFORMATION:

Available Degree(s)

- BFA Acting, concentration: Music Theatre
- BFA Theatre Arts—Performance
- BFA Theatre Arts—Design & Production

Artistic Review Requirement
Artistic Review for BU's School of Theatre was virtual through AuditionRoom for 2022 admissions. Live-virtual appointments are made through Acceptd (1,000-1,300 applicants, first-year class 40-45 students).

Scholarships Offered
Boston University offers merit-based and need-based aid to all incoming students. Some of the merit scholarships for incoming students include the Trustee Scholarship (full tuition and fees), the Presidential Scholarship ($25,000 annually), the National Merit Scholarship (for National Merit finalists, valued at $25,000 per year), among many others. Need-based aid may come from the BU Grant, the BU Community Service Award, the Charles River Housing Grant, the Richard D. Cohen Scholarship (need and merit-based), or the Alumni Council Scholarship ($2,500).

Special Opportunities
The School of Theatre requires that BFA performance majors spend one semester studying abroad. They have established, "conservatory-style, studio-specific training semester programs in London, England… as well as in Arezzo Italy." Students are not limited to these two programs, they may also study abroad anywhere in the world.

Notable Alumni
Jason Alexander, Bob Avian, Noah Bean, Reed Birney, Sara Chase, Michael Chiklis, Alessandro Colla, Geena Davis, Emily Deschanel, Olympia Dukakis, Faye Dunaway, Dan Fogler, David Garrison, Ginnifer Goodwin, Abraham Higginbotham, Greg Hildreth, Russel Hornsby, Brooke Karzen, Craig Lucas, Julianne Moore, Nina Tassler, Marisa Tomei, Baron Vaughn, and Alfre Woodardl

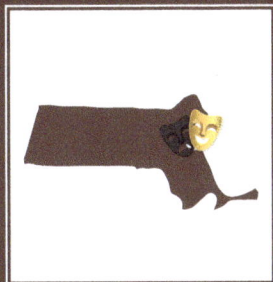

CONNECTICUT

MAINE

MASSACHUSETTS

NEW HAMPSHIRE

NEW JERSEY

NEW YORK

PENNSYLVANIA

RHODE ISLAND

VERMONT

NORTHEAST

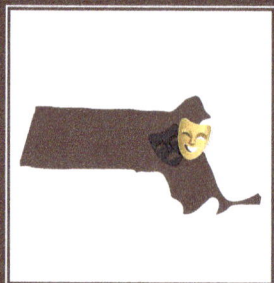

CONNECTICUT

MAINE

MASSACHUSETTS

NEW HAMPSHIRE

NEW JERSEY

NEW YORK

PENNSYLVANIA

RHODE ISLAND

VERMONT

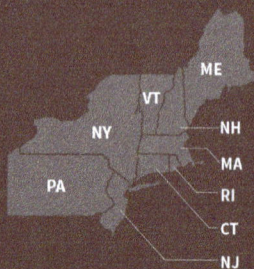

EMERSON COLLEGE

Address: 120 Boylston Street, Boston, MA 02116
Website: *https://www.emerson.edu/programs*
Contact: *https://www.emerson.edu/contact*
Phone: (617) 824-8500
Email: admission@emerson.edu

COST OF ATTENDANCE:

Tuition & Fees: $51,264 | **Additional Expenses:** $24,788
Total: $76,052

Financial Aid: https://www.emerson.edu/admissions-aid/
undergraduate-admission/financial-aid-scholarships

ADDITIONAL INFORMATION:

Available Degree(s)

- BFA Theatre
- BFA Theatre & Performance
- BFA Acting
- BFA Comedic Arts
- BFA Musical Theatre
- BFA Theatre Education & Performance

Artistic Review Requirement

A creative sample is required for Comedic Arts and should be submitted to the Emerson Application Portal. Emerson participates in Musical Theater Common Prescreen. Acceptd is used for submitting Artistic Application and scheduling and completing auditions and interviews.

Scholarships Offered

The Trustees Scholarship is awarded to students who are accepted into the Honors Program. The award amount is $28,000 per year. An Honors Program essay is required with the admission application for consideration. The Aspire Scholarship is a merit-based award valued at $20,000 annually. The Trailblazer Scholarship awards $15,000 annually. The Aspire and Trailblazer scholarships do not require a separate application.

Special Opportunities

The student-to-teacher ratio at Emerson College is 14:1. This means students have individualized support as they progress in their programs. Furthermore, Emerson College has a producing laboratory, the Emerson Stage. Students in a design program focused exclusively on undergraduates will have unique access to performance and production spaces including five theatres.

Notable Alumni

Kevin Bright, Joseph Leo Bwarie, Eric Falconer, Denis Leary, Jay Leno, Pierce Lyden, Quinn Marcus, Andrea Martin, Matt McGorry, Carl Menninger, Maria Menounos, Betsy Morgan, Sarah Nicklin, Chrystee Pharris, Jon Prescott, Chris Romano, Hartley Sawyer, Mark Hsu Syers, Michael Grant Terry, Justin Willman, and Henry Winkler

UNIVERSITY OF MASSACHUSETTS AT AMHERST

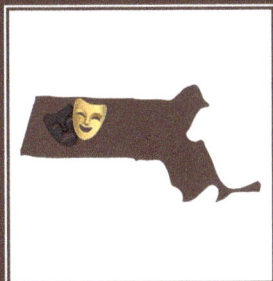

Address: 181 Presidents Dr., Amherst, MA 01003
Website: *https://www.umass.edu/theater/undergraduate-theater*
Contact: *https://www.umass.edu/admissions/undergraduate-admissions/connect*
Phone: (413) 545-0222
Email: mail@admissions.umass.edu

COST OF ATTENDANCE:

In-State Tuition & Fees: 16,834 | **Additional Expenses:** 14,644
Total: 31,478

Out-of-State Tuition & Fees: 38,053 | **Additional Expenses:** 14,644
Total: 52,697

Financial Aid: https://www.umass.edu/admissions/undergraduate-admissions/costs-aid/financial-aid

ADDITIONAL INFORMATION:

Available Degree(s)

- BA Theater, concentrations: Dramaturgy; Performance; Design, Technology, and Management

Artistic Review Requirement

There is no artistic review requirement. All UMass students in good standing are welcome to declare their major in Theater, advisely no later than their sophomore year.

Scholarships Offered

All students are automatically considered for merit-based and need-based scholarships. Furthermore, students who qualify for honors receive additional scholarships.

Special Opportunities

Although students choose one concentration, they can take classes in all three areas. Students leave the program well-rounded in all aspects of theatre. Furthermore, students may earn a multicultural theatre certificate to learn more about representation in the field and how theatre is explored globally.

Notable Alumni

Paul Jens Adolphson, Melanie Armer, Ifa Bayeza, Toby Vera Bercovici, Denis Berfield, Ethan Berube, Jeannie-Marie Brown, Nefertiti Burton, James Busker, Robin Carus, Lisa Channer, Constance Condgon, Rob Corddry, Jane Cox, Heather Crocker Aleunack, Jeffrey Donovan, Katy Geraghty, Richard Gere, Michael Haley, Jujubee, Bill Pullman, Keisha Tucker, and Lawrence Wilker

CONNECTICUT

MAINE

MASSACHUSETTS

NEW HAMPSHIRE

NEW JERSEY

NEW YORK

PENNSYLVANIA

RHODE ISLAND

VERMONT

NORTHEAST

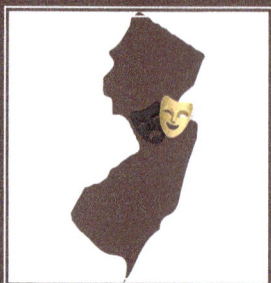

CONNECTICUT

MAINE

MASSACHUSETTS

NEW HAMPSHIRE

NEW JERSEY

NEW YORK

PENNSYLVANIA

RHODE ISLAND

VERMONT

MONTCLAIR STATE UNIVERSITY

Address: 1 Normal Ave., Montclair, NJ 07043
Website: *https://www.montclair.edu/theatre-and-dance/*
Contact: *https://www.montclair.edu/about-montclair/contact-us/*
Phone: (973) 655-4000
Email: msuadm@montclair.edu

COST OF ATTENDANCE:

In-State Tuition & Fees: $13,298 | **Additional Expenses:** $21,100
Total: $34,398

Out-of-State Tuition & Fees: $21,417 | **Additional Expenses:** $21,100
Total: $42,517

Financial Aid: https://www.montclair.edu/admissions/cost-and-financial-aid/affordability/

ADDITIONAL INFORMATION:

Available Degree(s)

- BA Theatre Studies, concentration: Teacher Education
- BFA Musical Theatre
- BFA Theatre, concentrations: Acting; Design, Technology, and Management

Artistic Review Requirement

Auditions take place in person or via Zoom. A pre-screen is not required for applicants auditioning via Zoom or through a partner organization.

Scholarships Offered

The Presidential Scholars Program is available to NJ high school students with a 3.5+ GPA. The award for this scholarship is $20,000. The National Student Scholarship offers in-state tuition to out-of-state students who have a 3.0+ GPA.

Special Opportunities

Montclair State offers a dual, Bachelor/Master of Arts (BA/MA) in Theatre Studies. This opportunity allows students to directly earn their graduate-level degree at Montclair.

Notable Alumni

Erick Avari, Stephen Bienskie, Kevin Carolan, Gerard McIntyre, Wilson Mendietta, Allison Strong, Michele Tauber, and Stuart Zagnit

RUTGERS, THE STATE UNIVERSITY OF NEW JERSEY

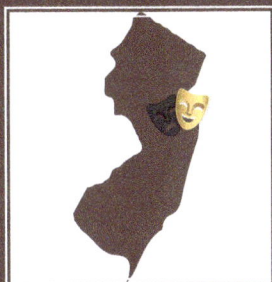

Address: 2 Chapel Drive, New Brunswick, NJ 08901
Website: *https://www.masongross.rutgers.edu/degrees-programs/theater/programs/*
Contact: *https://www.masongross.rutgers.edu/admissions/contact*
Phone: (848) 932-5241
Email: admissions@ugadm.rutgers.edu

COST OF ATTENDANCE:

In-State Tuition & Fees: $16,010 | **Additional Expenses:** $20,257 **Total:** $36,267

Out-of-State Tuition & Fees: $33,082 | **Additional Expenses:** $20,769 **Total:** $53,851

Financial Aid: https://financialaid.rutgers.edu/

ADDITIONAL INFORMATION:

Available Degree(s)

- BA Theater
- BFA Theater, concentrations: Acting; Production; Design
- Production, areas of study:
  - Technical Direction
  - Stage Management
  - Costume Technology
- Design, areas of study:
  - Scenic Design
  - Lighting Design
  - Costume Design

Artistic Review Requirement

BFA Theater applicants are required to complete a talent assessment through the Mason Gross supplemental application.

Scholarships Offered

Scholarships are awarded on a rolling basis, based on fund availability.The Mason Gross School of the Arts also awards merit scholarships to students.

Special Opportunities

All theater students with a concentration in design spend the fall semester of their third year in London at Shakespeare's Globe. The Costume Technology students also spend the semester studying with designers in London.

Notable Alumni

Mary Howard, Keith Sonnier, Ray Stark

CONNECTICUT

MAINE

MASSACHUSETTS

NEW HAMPSHIRE

NEW JERSEY

NEW YORK

PENNSYLVANIA

RHODE ISLAND

VERMONT

NORTHEAST

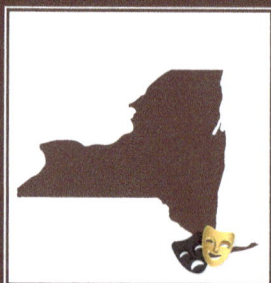

CONNECTICUT

MAINE

MASSACHUSETTS

NEW HAMPSHIRE

NEW JERSEY

NEW YORK

PENNSYLVANIA

RHODE ISLAND

VERMONT

BARNARD COLLEGE

Address: 3009 Broadway, New York, NY 10027
Website: *https://theatre.barnard.edu/*
Contact: *https://theatre.barnard.edu/contact-0*
Phone: (212) 854-2015
Email: admissions@barnard.edu

COST OF ATTENDANCE:

Tuition & Fees: $60,087 | **Additional Expenses:** $21,006
Total: $81,093

Financial Aid: https://barnard.edu/finaid

ADDITIONAL INFORMATION:

Available Degree(s):

- BA Drama and Theatre Arts, areas of concentration: Drama and Theatre Studies; Dramaturgy; Playwriting; Acting; Directing; Stage & Production Management; Design

Artistic Review Requirement

Barnard students may declare their major during the first or second year. There is no artistic review requirement.

Scholarships Offered

Barnard College offers need-based grants. They do not offer merit-based institutional scholarships. Students are encouraged to apply for outside scholarships.

Special Opportunities

Barnard College is a part of Columbia University. However, they have their own curriculum requirements, admissions processes, and financial aid processes. Students can take classes and participate in each other's events/clubs at either campus.

Notable Alumni

Clara Bryant, Jill Eikenberry, Denise Faye, Greta Gerwig, Lauren Graham, Mozhan Mamo, Kelly McCreary, Cynthia Nixon, Chelsea Peretti, Lee Remick, Ariane Rinehart, Joan Rivers, Frankie Shaw, Vinessa Shaw, Ebonie Smith, Leslie Stefanson, Zuzanna Szadkowski, and Jane Wyatt

FORDHAM UNIVERSITY

Address: 113 W. 60th St. New York, NY, 10023
Website: *https://www.fordham.edu/info/21304/theatre/*
Contact: *https://www.fordham.edu/info/20880/about/1767/contact_the_lincoln_center_campus/*
Phone: (718) 817-4000
Email: enroll@fordham.edu

COST OF ATTENDANCE:

Tuition & Fees: $56,131 | **Additional Expenses:** $24,855
Total: $80,986

Financial Aid: https://www.fordham.edu/info/20069/undergraduate_financial_aid

ADDITIONAL INFORMATION:

Available Degree(s)

- BA Theatre, concentrations: Playwriting; Directing; Performance; Design & Production

Artistic Review Requirement

The BA Theatre, concentrations in Design & Production, Playwriting, and Directing all require an interview. An audition is required only for the Performance concentration. Writing samples are required for the playwriting track. An optional portfolio review is available for the Directing track.

Scholarships Offered

The Fordham Theatre Scholarship is based on merit and need. The award ranges from $7,000 to full tuition. In addition, the Excellence in Theatre Scholarship is for the top two theatre student admits. This award varies based on financial aid, but intends to cover the full tuition cost and room & board. The Presidential Scholarship is gifted to students who rank in the top 1-2% of their graduating class. This award is given to 20 students per year. The award is full tuition and fees each year. For students staying in on-campus housing, the Cunniffe Presidential Scholarship covers the cost of housing. Furthermore, the Dean's Scholarship is for entering freshmen based on high academic performance and an SAT score of 1490+. The award for this scholarship is at least $20,000.

Students who demonstrate high academic performance and leadership who did not receive the Presidential or Dean's scholarships may be eligible for the Loyola Scholarship.

Special Opportunities

Theatre majors typically intern at theatre, film, and television companies. Most often, students are hired by an organization upon graduation. Internships have occurred at Cherry Lane Theatre, Disney, Saturday Night Live, CNN, The Tony Awards, and more.

Notable Alumni

Michelle Selene Ang, Patricia Clarkson, Tommy Dorfman, Peter Gil-Sheridan, Morgan Gould, John Johnson, Benjamin Hickey, Christopher Larkin, R.J. Roster, and Denzel Washington

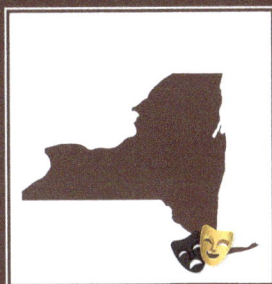

CONNECTICUT

MAINE

MASSACHUSETTS

NEW HAMPSHIRE

NEW JERSEY

NEW YORK

PENNSYLVANIA

RHODE ISLAND

VERMONT

NORTHEAST

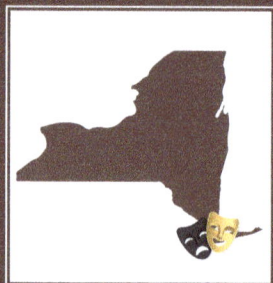

CONNECTICUT

MAINE

MASSACHUSETTS

NEW HAMPSHIRE

NEW JERSEY

NEW YORK

PENNSYLVANIA

RHODE ISLAND

VERMONT

ITHACA COLLEGE

Address: 953 Danby Road, Ithaca, NY 14850
Website: *https://www.ithaca.edu/academics/school-humanities-and-sciences/theatre-arts*
Contact: *https://www.ithaca.edu/contact/*
Phone: (607) 274-3124
Email: admission@ithaca.edu

COST OF ATTENDANCE:

Tuition & Fees: $48,126 | **Additional Expenses:** $19,564
Total: $67,690

Financial Aid: https://www.ithaca.edu/tuition-financial-aid

ADDITIONAL INFORMATION:

Available Degree(s)

- BA Theatre Studies
- BFA Acting
- BFA Musical Theatre

Artistic Review Requirement

After applying to Ithaca College, applicants to the Department of Theatre Arts are required to upload artistic review materials to Acceptd.

Scholarships Offered

No separate application is necessary for merit-based scholarships at Ithaca College. The Ithaca College Merit Scholarship provides up to $2,000 to students who listed Ithaca College as their first-choice institution to the National Merit Scholarship Corporation program. The Ithaca Leadership Scholar Program Award gives students $7,000 based on demonstrated leadership and superior academic performance. In addition, the Martin Luther King Scholar Program is for first year students who demonstrate academic talent, community service, and "embody the ideas of Martin Luther King, Jr.". This award is valued at a minimum of $25,000.

Special Opportunities

Students may attend a field studies trip to New York City to connect with alumni and professionals in the entertainment business. Additionally, many students study abroad for one semester at Ithaca College's London Center.

Notable Alumni

Jerad Bortz, Kerry Butler, Matt Cavenaugh, Michelle Federer, Ben Feldman, Jeremy Jordan, Megan Ort, Caesar Samayoa, Q. Smith, and Aaron Tveit

THE JUILLIARD SCHOOL

Address: 60 Lincoln Center Plaza, New York, NY 10023
Website: *https://www.juilliard.edu/drama*
Contact: *https://www.juilliard.edu/admissions/connect-us*
Phone: (212) 799-5000
Email: admissions@juilliard.edu

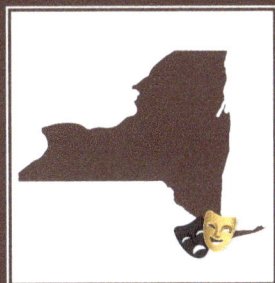

COST OF ATTENDANCE:

Tuition & Fees: $51,230 | **Additional Expenses:** $22,714
Total: $73,944

Financial Aid: https://www.juilliard.edu/campus-life/financial-aid

ADDITIONAL INFORMATION:

Available Degree(s)

- BFA Acting

Artistic Review Requirement

Applicants who currently live outside of the US and Canada are required to do a pre-screen regardless of citizenship status or permanent address. Pre-screens are optional for applicants living in Alaska, Hawaii, Puerto Rico, US Virgin Islands, or Canada.

Scholarships Offered

Juilliard Scholarship award amounts vary based on individual need and merit. According to Juilliard, approximately 85% of their students receive institutional aid. Applicants are encouraged to use the net price calculator for estimating potential aid amount.

Special Opportunities

Students do not audition for roles in school productions but are cast by faculty. In their first and second years, roles are assigned to serve the needs of individual students. Students participate in a different play each quarter. In the fall of the third year, students have 2 performance opportunities. In the spring, they participate in a musical cabaret and a heightened-language play. By the fourth year, students participate in Playwrights Festival workshops.

Notable Alumni

Michael Arden, Christine Baranski, Andre Braugher, Danielle Brooks, Jessica Chastain, Keith David, Viola Davis, Adam Driver, Maya Hawke, Glenn Howerton, Gillian Jacobs, Peter Jacobson, Val Kilmer, Laura Linney, Patti LuPone, Elizabeth Marvel, Audra McDonald, Elizabeth McGovern, James Marsters, Tim Blake Nelson, Lee Pace, Wendell Pierce, Sara Ramirez, Christopher Reeve, Ving Rhames, Phillipa Soo, Kevin Spacey, Michael Stuhlbarg, Leslie Uggams, Michael Urie, Benjamin Walker, Samira Wiley, and Robin Williams

CONNECTICUT

MAINE

MASSACHUSETTS

NEW HAMPSHIRE

NEW JERSEY

NEW YORK

PENNSYLVANIA

RHODE ISLAND

VERMONT

NORTHEAST

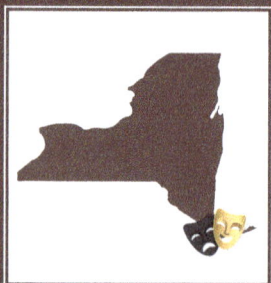

CONNECTICUT

MAINE

MASSACHUSETTS

NEW HAMPSHIRE

NEW JERSEY

NEW YORK

PENNSYLVANIA

RHODE ISLAND

VERMONT

LONG ISLAND UNIVERSITY (LIU)

Address: 720 Northern Blvd., Brookville, NY 11548
Website: *https://liu.edu/post/academics/School-of-Performing-Arts/programs*
Contact: *https://apply.liu.edu/form/inquiry.aspx?id=1*
Phone: (516) 299-2900
Email: post-enroll@liu.edu

COST OF ATTENDANCE

Tuition & Fees: $37,926 | **Additional Expenses:** $22,535
Total: 60,461

Financial Aid: https://liu.edu/enrollment-services/financial-aid

ADDITIONAL INFORMATION:

Available Degree(s)

- BA in Theatre Arts
- BFA Theatre Arts, concentrations: Acting; Musical Theatre

Artistic Review Requirement

Applicants in acting require an audition and interview either on campus by appointment or through the National Unified Auditions. Students must fill out the Audition Form. Prepare two short contrasting contemporary monologues in English from published plays. Headshot and resume required. Production and design students should bring a portfolio of their recent work. Video auditions are also available through Acceptd.

Scholarships Offered

LIU Post awards over $100 million in scholarships & grants each year.

Special Opportunities

Rigorous grounding in history, literature, theories, and methodologies of Suzuki, Stanislavsky, Chekhov, and Linklater techniques, and work with professional musicians, actors, and playwrights. Taught by professional theatre artists and coordinated with the Post Theatre Company, students develop a riveting stage presence, dynamic physicality, emotional authenticity, and a commanding voice. Individual and ensemble training in stage, television, and film acting. The program culminates with a senior showcase before agents, managers, and directors in New York City. Students intern on and off-campus and travel to festivals in the U.S. and abroad.

Notable Alumni

Ed Lauter, Dina Meyer, Nicholas Pileggi, Michael Tucci, and Denise Vasi

MARYMOUNT MANHATTAN COLLEGE

Address: 221 East 71st Street New York, NY 10021
Website: *https://www.mmm.edu/departments/theatre-arts/programs/*
Contact: *https://www.mmm.edu/admissions/contact-us/*
Phone: (212) 517-0430
Email: admissions@mmm.edu

COST OF ATTENDANCE:

Tuition & Fees: $37,410 | **Additional Expenses:** $26,400
Total: $63,810

Financial Aid: https://www.mmm.edu/admissions-and-aid/cost-and-financial-aid/

ADDITIONAL INFORMATION:

Available Degree(s)
- BFA Acting
- BFA Musical Theatre
- BA Theatre, concentrations: Performance; Directing; Producing & Management; History; New Media; Design & Technology

Artistic Review Requirement
Candidates participate in an acting class, vocal exercises, improvisation, and theatre games. Candidates perform one contemporary monologue for the theatre faculty. BFA candidates will submit a portfolio and interview with the Resident Designer/Technical Director. Applicants to the Theatre History and Performance Texts as well as Theatre and New Media programs can submit a secondary application to be considered for a Competitive Theatre Scholarship.

Scholarships Offered
Scholarships are available for successful candidates. Consideration for these competitive talent awards is made at the time of the audition. Scholarships are renewable for four years if the student remains academically successful and stays in the program.

Special Opportunities
MMC's BFA in Acting offers close, tight-knit relationships with faculty and studio trainers. Students gain intensive training and performance skills while researching and performing complex characters with script analysis and character development. Given MMC's location, students often get free tickets to Broadway and Off-Broadway shows and gain professional internships in casting offices and theatre companies. Study abroad opportunities at institutes such as the Kingston University London are available via CIEE and CCIS. Students can minor in Drama Therapy and Arts Management.

Notable Alumni
Annaleigh Ashford, Candace Bailey, Maddie Baillio, Laverne Cox, Alexandra Daddario, Abby Elliott, Spencer Grammar, Mimi Imfurst, Moire Kelly, Erik Palladino, Andrew Rannells, Melissa Rauch, Emmy Raver-Lampman, Alexander Skarsgard, Paige Spara, Chris Stafford, Tika Sumpter, Vanessa Trump, Jenna Ushkowitz, and Adrienna Warren

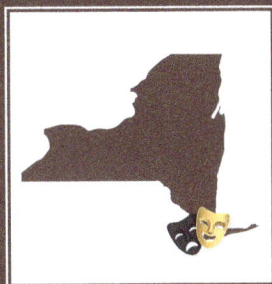

CONNECTICUT

MAINE

MASSACHUSETTS

NEW HAMPSHIRE

NEW JERSEY

NEW YORK

PENNSYLVANIA

RHODE ISLAND

VERMONT

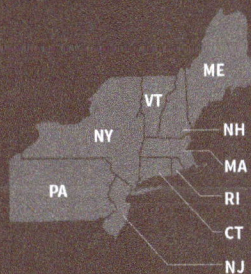

NORTHEAST

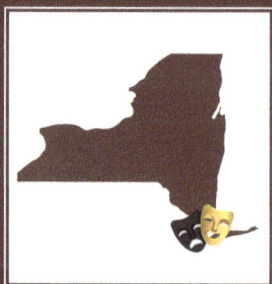

CONNECTICUT

MAINE

MASSACHUSETTS

NEW HAMPSHIRE

NEW JERSEY

NEW YORK

PENNSYLVANIA

RHODE ISLAND

VERMONT

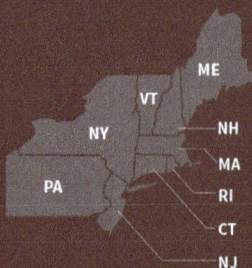

NEW YORK UNIVERSITY

Address: 27 West 4th Street, New York, NY 10014
Website: *https://tisch.nyu.edu/drama*
Contact: *https://tisch.nyu.edu/admissions/contact-admissions*
Phone: (212) 998-1900
Email: admissions@nyu.edu

COST OF ATTENDANCE:

Tuition & Fees: $56,500 | **Additional Expenses:** $24,378
Total: $80,878

Financial Aid: https://tisch.nyu.edu/admissions/financial-aid

ADDITIONAL INFORMATION:

Available Degree(s)

- BFA Drama, concentrations: Acting; Musical Theatre; Directing; Production & Design

Artistic Review Requirement

A personalized link to the Drama Artistic Review portal will be sent after submission of the Common Application. For more information, visit: https://tisch.nyu.edu/admissions/undergraduate-admissions

Scholarships Offered

NYU offers various need-based and/or merit-based scholarships to students in any major. Some examples include the AnBryce Scholarships (GPA 3.5+), the Martin Luther King, Jr., Scholarships, and several others. NYU Tisch recommends students apply for outside funding. The Tisch Scholarship Guide is a resource that includes various scholarship opportunities.

Special Opportunities

Once accepted, students are placed into one of 8 studios to start their intensive conservatory training. This lasts for two years. Studio placement is up to the department, not the applicant. The eight studios are:

- Stella Adler Studio of Acting
- Atlantic Acting School
- Experimental Theatre Wing
- The Meisner Studio
- New Studio on Broadway
- Playwrights Horizons Theater School
- Production & Design Studio
- Lee Strasberg Theatre Institute

Notable Alumni

Jelani Alladin, Woody Allen, Rachel Bloom, Kristen Bell, Alec Baldwin, Dakota Fanning, Lady Gaga, Matthew Gray Gubler, Anne Hathaway, Adam Jacobs, Angelina Jolie, Nikki M. James, Denis Jones, Moisés Kaufman, Camila Mendes, Idina Menzel, Matthew Morrison, Javier Muñoz, Donna Murphy, Elizabeth Olsen, Mary-Kate Olsen, Anthony Rapp, Meg Ryan, Martin Scorsese, Philip Seymour, M. Night Shyamalan, Ali Stroker, Shaina Taub, and Brandon Uranowitz

PACE UNIVERSITY

Address: 1 Pace Plaza, New York, NY 10038
Website: *http://performingarts.pace.edu/*
Contact: *https://www.pace.edu/contact-us*
Phone: (800) 874-7223
Email: undergradadmission@pace.edu

COST OF ATTENDANCE:

Tuition & Fees: $53,940 | **Additional Expenses:** $23,174
Total: $77,114

Financial Aid: https://www.pace.edu/financial-aid/

ADDITIONAL INFORMATION:

Available Degree(s)

- BA Acting
- BFA Acting
- BFA Musical Theater

Artistic Review Requirement

Applicants to all programs are required to submit prescreen materials via Acceptd and will be notified if a callback interview/audition is given.

Scholarships Offered

Students are considered for need-based scholarships. There are also Dyson College Scholarships specifically for each program. The average non-need-based scholarship awarded to first-year students is $24,996. There is also the Professor Chris Thomas Endowed Scholarship.

Special Opportunities

Pace offers conservatory-style focused training. BFA Acting students perform in a scene festival during spring of freshman year. Pace offers a highly-individualized International Performance Ensemble which creates and produces new work starting in the first year with possible international travel. Students organize a senior showcase for agents, directors, managers, and designers from NYC and LA.

Notable Alumni

Ailee, Michelle Borth, Trevor Braun, Kate Bristol, Bradley Cooper, Paul Dano, Dominique Fishback, Jordan Scott Gilbert, Matthew Humphreys, Tommy Nelson, Vincent Pastore, Diana Scarwid, Rafael L. Silva, and Glenn Taranto

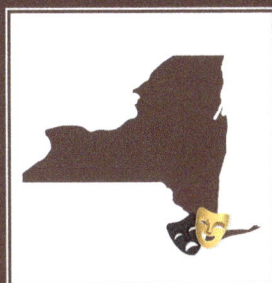

CONNECTICUT

MAINE

MASSACHUSETTS

NEW HAMPSHIRE

NEW JERSEY

NEW YORK

PENNSYLVANIA

RHODE ISLAND

VERMONT

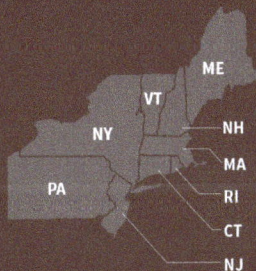

NORTHEAST

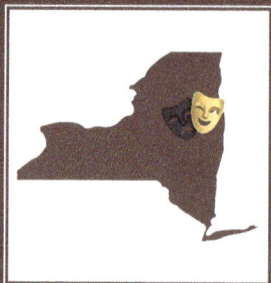

CONNECTICUT

MAINE

MASSACHUSETTS

NEW HAMPSHIRE

NEW JERSEY

NEW YORK

PENNSYLVANIA

RHODE ISLAND

VERMONT

SKIDMORE COLLEGE

Address: 815 N. Broadway, Saratoga Springs, NY 12866
Website: *https://theater.skidmore.edu/*
Contact: *https://www.skidmore.edu/about/contacts.php*
Phone: (518) 580-5570
Email: admissions@skidmore.edu

COST OF ATTENDANCE:

Tuition & Fees: $60,302 | **Additional Expenses:** $16,068
Total: $76,370

Financial Aid: https://www.skidmore.edu/financialaid/

ADDITIONAL INFORMATION:

Available Degree(s)

- BS Theater, concentrations: Acting; Directing; Design and Technical Theater

Artistic Review Requirement

There is no artistic review requirement.

Scholarships Offered

Student aid at Skidmore is all need-based, besides a music scholarship and a scholarship for students excelling in the sciences or math.

Special Opportunities

Students are strongly encouraged to participate in a professional internship while they are enrolled in the program. Students may earn academic credit while they are interning.

Notable Alumni

Zazie Beetz, Jon Bernthal, and Michael Zegen

STATE UNIVERSITY OF NEW YORK AT BINGHAMTON

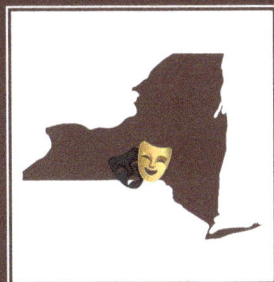

Address: 4400 Vestal Pkwy E, Binghamton, NY 13902
Website: *https://www.binghamton.edu/theatre/undergraduate/index.html*
Contact: *https://www.binghamton.edu/theatre/contact/*
Phone: (607) 777-2567
Email: theatre@binghamton.edu

COST OF ATTENDANCE:

In-State Tuition & Fees: $10,556 | **Additional Expenses:** $19,228
Total: $29,784

Out-of-State Tuition & Fees: $28,396 | **Additional Expenses:** $19,428
Total: $47,824

Financial Aid: https://www.binghamton.edu/financial-aid/

ADDITIONAL INFORMATION:

Available Degree(s)

- BA Theatre, concentrations: Acting; Directing; Design/Technical

Artistic Review Requirement

No artistic review is required. However, applicants to Acting and Design/Technical Concentrations have the option to submit a special talent, which does not affect their intended major.

Scholarships Offered

All students are considered for the President's, Provost's, and Dean's Scholarships. There are also departmental scholarships: The John and Vi Bielenberg Theatre Scholarship is awarded to a sophomore or junior majoring in Theater with exceptional promise in technical theater. The Solomon Israel Theatre Arts Scholarship is awarded to a Theatre major from a metropolitan New York area with proven financial need.

Special Opportunities

Each year, the Department of Theatre gives awards carrying modest financial stipends to students. The Summer Scholars and Artists Program supports original research or creative projects of students in all academic disciplines through a stipend.Additionally, there is an accelerated degree program which allows students to complete a BA and a MPA in Public Administration in 5 years.

Notable Alumni

William Baldwin, Neil Berg, Stephanie Courtney, Todd Lituchy, and Madeleine Smithberg

CONNECTICUT

MAINE

MASSACHUSETTS

NEW HAMPSHIRE

NEW JERSEY

NEW YORK

PENNSYLVANIA

RHODE ISLAND

VERMONT

NORTHEAST

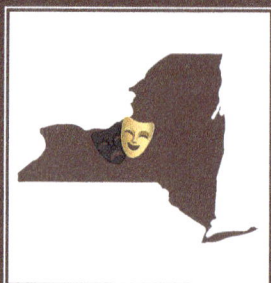

CONNECTICUT

MAINE

MASSACHUSETTS

NEW HAMPSHIRE

NEW JERSEY

NEW YORK

PENNSYLVANIA

RHODE ISLAND

VERMONT

SYRACUSE UNIVERSITY

Address: 202 Crouse College, Syracuse, NY 13244
Website: *https://vpa.syr.edu/academics/drama/*
Contact: *https://vpa.syr.edu/academics/drama/contact/*
Phone: (315) 443-2769
Email: admissu@syr.edu

COST OF ATTENDANCE:

Tuition & Fees: $57,591 | **Additional Expenses:** $44,448.8
Total: $80,039.80

Financial Aid: https://www.syracuse.edu/admissions/cost-and-aid/

ADDITIONAL INFORMATION:

Available Degree(s)

- BS Drama, tracks: Playwriting; Directing; Theater Management
- BFA Acting, track: Actor-Singer
- BFA Musical Theater

Artistic Review Requirement

Applicants to the Acting and Musical Theater programs are required to submit a prescreen audition via Acceptd. There are special requirements for applicants who wish to be considered for both programs. Theater Management, Stage Management, and Theater Design and Technology applicants are required to submit their portfolio via SlideRoom and schedule a virtual or in-person interview.

Scholarships Offered

Syracuse University offers various merit-based and need-based scholarships and grants. The 1870 Scholarship covers full tuition for the full length of the undergraduate program. Artistic Scholarships are awarded to students based on talent and a maintained cumulative GPA of 2.75+. The Distinguished Drama Performance Award offers $10,000 annually. The Distinguished Art Portfolio Award offers $10,000 awards annually.

Special Opportunities

The Tepper Semester allows students in Theater to work with professional artists in New York City. Students interested in a longer-term introduction to Los Angeles may participate in Summer in LA, a six-week, two-course experience that includes a professional internship and a series of workshops and master classes.

Theater Design and Technology majors and Stage Management majors may spend a semester in London through an exchange program with Rose Bruford College. Drama majors have the opportunity to study abroad in Florence, London, Madrid, and Graz, Austria.

Notable Alumni

Darryl Bell, Dick Clark, Taye Diggs, Peter Falk, Vera Farmiga, Frank Langella, Neal McDonough, Jessie Mueller, Patti Murin, Julia Murney, Suzanne Pleshette, Kevin Michael Richardson, Joan Schirle, Aaron Sorkin, Jerry Stiller, Arielle Tepper, Peter Weller, Vanessa Williams, and Josh Young

UNIVERSITY AT BUFFALO

Address: 285 Alumni Arena, North Campus, Buffalo, New York 14260
Website: *https://arts-sciences.buffalo.edu/theatre-dance/ undergraduate/overview.html*
Contact: *https://arts-sciences.buffalo.edu/theatre-dance/about/ contact-us.html*
Phone: (716) 645-6897
Email: td-theatredance@buffalo.edu

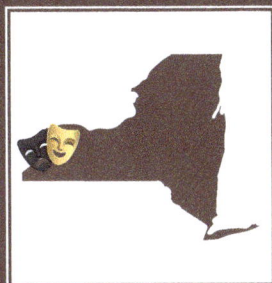

COST OF ATTENDANCE

In-State Tuition & Fees: $7,270 | **Additional Expenses:** $39,066
Total: $46,336

Out-of-State Tuition & Fees: $24,740.00 | **Additional Expenses:** $4126
Total: $28,866

Financial Aid: https://financialaid.buffalo.edu/

ADDITIONAL INFORMATION:

Available Degree(s)

- BA Theatre
- BFA Theatre, concentrations: Performance; Design & Technology
- BFA Music Theatre

Artistic Review Requirement

Theatre Performance and Music Theatre applicants are required to submit an audition video and attend an audition. Theatre Design and Technology applicants are required to submit a portfolio and attend an interview.

Scholarships Offered

University at Buffalo offers various merit-based and need-based scholarships and grants including the Presidential Scholarship and the Provost Scholarship.

Special Opportunities

Through the International Artistic & Cultural Exchange Program, Theatre Performance students may participate in the winter UK Culture & Performance Appreciation in London program, summer Ireland: Plays and Places program, Canada Performing Arts Experiential Research Program, and immersive spring break at the American Shakespeare Center. Theatre students may also study abroad in England, Australia and Italy.

Notable Alumni

Thomas Curley, Brad Grey, and Harvey Weinstein

CONNECTICUT

MAINE

MASSACHUSETTS

NEW HAMPSHIRE

NEW JERSEY

NEW YORK

PENNSYLVANIA

RHODE ISLAND

VERMONT

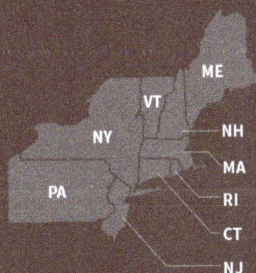

NORTHEAST

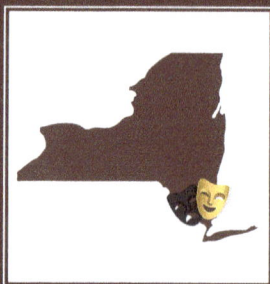

CONNECTICUT

MAINE

MASSACHUSETTS

NEW HAMPSHIRE

NEW JERSEY

NEW YORK

PENNSYLVANIA

RHODE ISLAND

VERMONT

VASSAR COLLEGE

Address: 124 Raymond Avenue, Poughkeepsie, NY 12604
Website: *https://drama.vassar.edu/*
Contact: *https://www.vassar.edu/admissions/contact/*
Phone: (845) 437-7300
Email: admissions@vassar.edu

COST OF ATTENDANCE:

Tuition & Fees: $62,870 | **Additional Expenses:** $20,210
Total: $83,080

Financial Aid: https://studentfinancialservices.vassar.edu/

ADDITIONAL INFORMATION:

Available Degree(s)

- BA Drama

Artistic Review Requirement

There is no artistic review requirement.

Scholarships Offered

Vassar College funds "come from Vassar's endowment, money raised by Vassar alumnae/i clubs, and gifts from friends of the college". Students are urged to apply to external scholarship opportunities.

Special Opportunities

First-year students interested in a Drama major enroll in introductory courses during their first year at the college: Drama 102 Introduction to Theater-Making and Drama 103 Introduction to Stagecraft. Students must be enrolled in Drama courses to audition for department major productions, though department sponsored workshops and extracurricular theatrical activities that are open to all students.

Notable Alumni

Dan Bucatinsky, Erin Daniels, Hope Davis, Jane Fonda, Lecy Goranson, Kerri Green, Grace Gummer, Anne Hathaway, Brooke Hayward, Sakina Jaffrey, Shaha King, Lisa Kudrow, Marguerite Moreau, Alysia Reiner, Erica Schmidt, Frances Sternhagen, Meryl Streep, Jonathan Tenny, and Lisa Zane

CARNEGIE MELLON UNIVERSITY

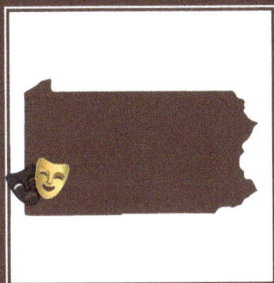

Address: 5000 Forbes Avenue, Pittsburgh, PA 15213
Website: *https://www.drama.cmu.edu/*
Contact: *https://www.drama.cmu.edu/about/contact/*
Phone: (412) 268-2082
Email: admission@andrew.cmu.edu

COST OF ATTENDANCE:

Tuition & Fees: $57,560 | **Additional Expenses:** $19,914
Total: $77,474

Financial Aid: https://www.cmu.edu/admission/aid-affordability/types-of-aid

ADDITIONAL INFORMATION:

Available Degree(s)

- BFA Drama, options: Dramaturgy; Acting; Music Theater; Directing; Stage & Production Management; Production Technology; Sound Design; Scenic Design; Lighting Design; Costume Design

Artistic Review Requirement

Applicants interested in the Music Theater and Acting Options should submit a prescreen for the Music Theater Option, which will fulfill the prescreen requirements of both programs. Applicants to Stage and Production Management, Production Technology, and all Design Options are required to submit a portfolio before being invited to an interview. Those materials should all be submitted via Acceptd. Directing applicants are required to submit an audition video, a statement, and a sample before the interview.

Scholarships Offered

CMU offers a need-based grant and endowed scholarships. The Presidential and Carnegie Scholarship programs are only available to returning students.

Special Opportunities

All Drama students may participate in various showcases and performances including Dance/Light, Playground (a 3-day performance festival), the Visiting Artists Program, and the School of Drama Showcase. CMU's School of Drama offers exchange programs at the National School of Drama in India and the Royal Conservatoire of Scotland. Acting and Music Theater students have the opportunity to study at London's Drama Centre, Moscow Art Theatre, and other schools in France, South Africa, China and South Korea.

Notable Alumni

Christian Borle, Eduardo Castro, Ted Danson, Cote de Pablo, Peggy Eisenhauer, Barbara Feldon, Sutton Foster, Josh Gad, Jeff Goldblum, Megan Hilty, Peter Hylenski, Cherry Jones, Jack Klugman, Kara Lindsay, Aaron Staton, Telly Leung, Joe Manganiello, Leslie Odom, Jr., Pablo Schreiber, Tamara Tunie, and John Wells

CONNECTICUT

MAINE

MASSACHUSETTS

NEW HAMPSHIRE

NEW JERSEY

NEW YORK

PENNSYLVANIA

RHODE ISLAND

VERMONT

NORTHEAST

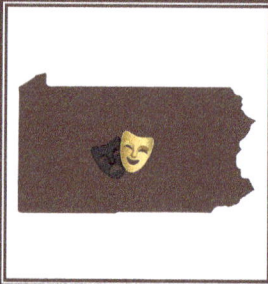

CONNECTICUT

MAINE

MASSACHUSETTS

NEW HAMPSHIRE

NEW JERSEY

NEW YORK

PENNSYLVANIA

RHODE ISLAND

VERMONT

PENNSYLVANIA STATE UNIVERSITY

Address: 201 Shields Building, University Park, PA 16802
Website: *https://theatre.psu.edu/*
Contact: *https://admissions.psu.edu/contact/*
Phone: (814) 865-5471
Email: admissions@psu.edu

COST OF ATTENDANCE:

In-State Tuition & Fees: $18,898 | **Additional Expenses:** $14,158
Total: $33,056

Out-of-State Tuition & Fees: $36,476 | **Additional Expenses:** $14,158
Total: $50,634

Financial Aid: https://studentaid.psu.edu/

ADDITIONAL INFORMATION:

Available Degree(s)

- BA Theatre
- BFA Theatre, options: Design & Technology;
- BFA Theatre, specializations: Costume Design; Lighting Design; Scenic Design; Sound Design; Technical Direction; Stage Management
- BFA Acting
- BFA Musical Theatre

Artistic Review Requirement

A prescreen and audition and prescreen are required for Acting and Musical Theater applicants, while a portfolio is required for BA Theatre and BFA Theatre. Acceptd is used for submitting prescreen materials and portfolios.

Scholarships Offered

Penn State offers various university scholarships including the Discover Penn State Award ($6,000-7,000 annually) and the Provost's Award ($5,000-7,000 annually) as well as campus and college scholarships.

Special Opportunities

Acting students train with British faculty at Theatre Academy London during the spring semester of their third year. Musical Theatre students will benefit from trips to NYC, the Musical Theatre Wellness Center, and the New Musicals Initiative, where Tony, Grammy, Obie winning writers are commissioned to write for the students. Students working toward a B.F.A. in Theatre will have access to state-of-the-art theater facilities, among which the Lightning Lab is one of the most advanced and well-equipped labs of its kind in the country. Theatre students may study abroad in Edinburgh.

Notable Alumni

John Aniston, Caroline Bowman, Ty Burrell, Patrick Fabian, Carrie Fishbein, Jeremy Greenbaum, Carly Hughes, Nathan Lucrezio, Rick Lyon, Oliver Smith, Emma Stratton, and Natalie Weiss

UNIVERSITY OF THE ARTS (UARTS)

Address: 320 S. Broad St., Philadelphia, PA 19102
Website: *https://www.uarts.edu/academics/undergraduate-programs*
Contact: *https://www.uarts.edu/about/contact-us*
Phone: (800) 616-2787
Email: admissions@uarts.edu

COST OF ATTENDANCE:

Tuition & Fees: $48,350 | **Additional Expenses:** $21,644
Total: $69,994

Financial Aid: https://www.uarts.edu/tuition-and-financial-aid

ADDITIONAL INFORMATION:

Available Degree(s)

- BFA Acting
- BA Musical Theater

Artistic Review Requirement

Audition is required for Acting and Musical Theater applicants, while portfolio and interview are required for admissions to the Design and Technology and Directing, Playwriting, and Production programs. UArts offers in-person and virtual interviews/auditions as well as asynchronous artistic review, for which Acceptd is used. Applicants can request a preliminary portfolio review with an admissions counselor. UArts also participates in National Portfolio Day.

Scholarships Offered

All applicants including international students are automatically considered for numerous scholarships. Scholarships dedicated to the Ira Brind School of Theater Arts include the Ira Brind Scholarship and the Jac and Miriam Striezheff Lewis Scholarship.

Special Opportunities

UArts offers pre-college Summer Institute and Saturday School in Acting, Music, Design, and Theater.

Notable Alumni

Sarah Bolt, Elana Boulos, Jennifer Childs, Rory Donovan, Jacob Jarrett, Aimé Donna Kelly, Jillian Keys, Elaina Di Monaco, Brad Pouliot, Matteo Scammell, and Lucas Steele

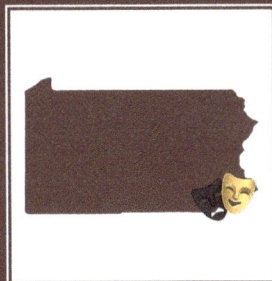

CONNECTICUT

MAINE

MASSACHUSETTS

NEW HAMPSHIRE

NEW JERSEY

NEW YORK

PENNSYLVANIA

RHODE ISLAND

VERMONT

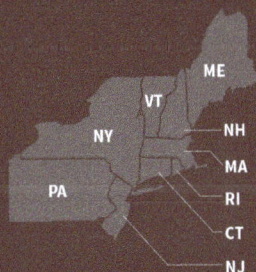

NORTHEAST

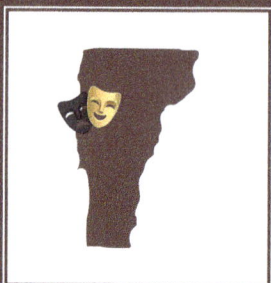

CONNECTICUT

MAINE

MASSACHUSETTS

NEW HAMPSHIRE

NEW JERSEY

NEW YORK

PENNSYLVANIA

RHODE ISLAND

VERMONT

MIDDLEBURY COLLEGE

Address: 131 South Main Street, Middlebury, VT 05753
Website: *http://www.middlebury.edu/academics/thea*
Contact: *https://www.middlebury.edu/college/admissions/contact*
Phone: (802) 443-3000
Email: admissions@middlebury.edu

COST OF ATTENDANCE:

Tuition & Fees: $59,330 | **Additional Expenses:** $19,250
Total: $78,580

Financial Aid: http://www.middlebury.edu/offices/support/sfs

ADDITIONAL INFORMATION:

Available Degree(s)

- BA Theatre

Artistic Review Requirement

Applicants may submit optional arts supplements using SlideRoom.

Scholarships Offered

Merit scholarships are not offered at Middlebury College. All institutional financial assistance is need-based. According to Middlebury College, the average grant is $52,000.

Special Opportunities

Middlebury College's affiliation with the Potomac Theatre Project offers students opportunities to work in NYC in the summer.

Notable Alumni

Rob Ackerman, Anna Belknap, Vanessa Branch, Roscoe Lee Brown, William Burden, Jeffrey Bushell, Kristen Connolly, James Cromwell, Sam Daly, Malaya Drew, Even Ensler, Lucy Faust, Cassidy Freeman, Warren Frost, Rich Gallup, Rebecca Gilman, William Blake Herron, Jason Mantzoukas, Emily McLaughlin, Dan O'Brien, Amanda Peterson, Rodney Rothman, Shawn Ryan, Jessica St. Clair, Angus Sutherland, Jake Weber, and Julia Whelan

CHAPTER 14

REGION TWO

MIDWEST

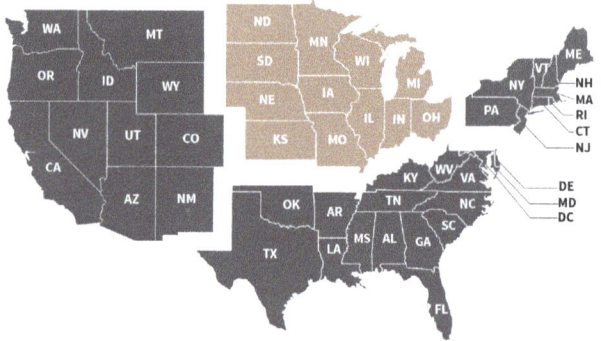

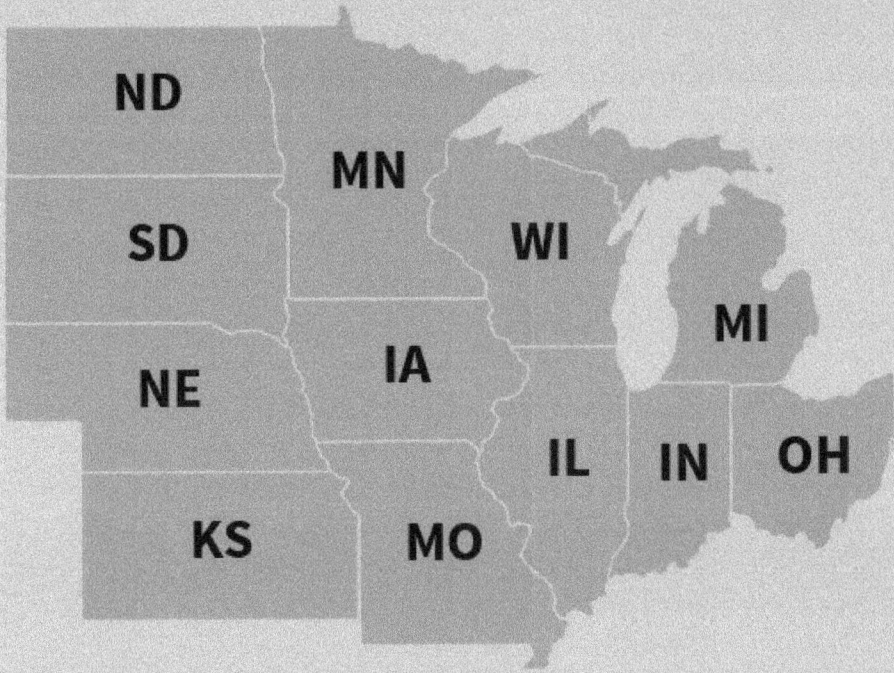

21 *Programs* | **12** *States*

1. *IL - Columbia College Chicago*
2. *IL – DePaul University*
3. *IL - Northwestern University*
4. *IL - University of Chicago*
5. *IL - University of Illinois Urbana-Champaign (UIUC)*
6. *IN - Ball State University*
7. *IN - Indiana University Bloomington*
8. *IN - Purdue University*
9. *IN - University of Evansville*
10. *IN - University of Notre Dame*
11. *KS - Wichita State University*
12. *MI - University of Michigan*
13. *MN - University of Minnesota*
14. *MO - College of the Ozarks*
15. *MO - Missouri State University*
16. *MO - University of Missouri*
17. *OH - Baldwin Wallace University*
18. *OH - Kent State University*
19. *OH - Kenyon College*
20. *OH - Ohio State University*
21. *WI - University of Wisconsin*

THEATRE PROGRAMS

School	Avg. GPA, SAT Evidence Based Reading and Writing (ERW), SAT Math (M), and ACT Composite (C) Early Decision (ED): Yes/No	Admission Statistics	Program(s) See website for additional options.	Artistic Review Required (Req.)
Columbia College Chicago 600 S Michigan Ave, Chicago, IL 60605	GPA: N/A SAT (ERW): N/A* SAT (M): N/A* ACT (C): N/A* *Test-optional ED: Yes	Overall College Admit Rate: 90% Undergrad Enrollment: 6,542 Total Enrollment: 6,769	BA Theatre BA Acting BFA Acting BA Musical Theatre BFA Musical Theatre Performance BA Comedy Writing and Performance Degrees Awarded in the Program(s): 16	All BA programs are portfolio-optional BFA Acting and BFA Musical Theatre Performance Prescreen and audition req.
DePaul University 2350 N. Racine Ave., Chicago, IL 60614	GPA: 3.8 SAT (ERW): 530-640 SAT (M): 530-640 ACT (C): N/A ED: No	Overall College Admit Rate: 70% Undergrad Enrollment: 14,145 Total Enrollment: 21,922	BFA Theatre Arts BFA Comedy Arts BFA Acting Degrees Awarded in the Program(s): 64	BFA Theatre Arts Interview req. BFA Comedy Arts Prescreen and interview req. BFA Acting Prescreen and audition req.
Northwestern University 633 Clark St, Evanston, IL 60208	GPA: N/A SAT (ERW): 700-760 SAT (M): 730-790 ACT (C): 33-35 ED: No	Overall College Admit Rate: 9% Undergrad Enrollment: 8,194 Total Enrollment: 22,072	BA Performance Studies BA Theatre Degrees Awarded in the Program(s): 93	BA Theatre, area of study: Music Theatre Supplement optional No other req. for other programs

THEATRE PROGRAMS

School	Avg. GPA, SAT Evidence Based Reading and Writing (ERW), SAT Math (M), and ACT Composite (C) Early Decision (ED): Yes/No	Admission Statistics	Program(s) See website for additional options.	Artistic Review Required (Req.)
University of Chicago 915 E 60th St., Chicago, IL 60637	GPA: N/A SAT (ERW): 730-770 SAT (M): 770-800 ACT (C): 34-35 ED: Yes	Overall College Admit Rate: 7% Undergrad Enrollment: 7,550 Total Enrollment: 18,405	BA Theater and Performance Studies Degrees Awarded in the Program(s): 5	Portfolio optional
University of Illinois Urbana-Champaign (UIUC) 901 West Illinois Street, Urbana, IL 61801	GPA: N/A SAT (ERW): 590-700 SAT (M): 620-770 ACT (C): 27-33 ED: Yes	Overall College Admit Rate: 50% Undergrad Enrollment: 34,559 Total Enrollment: 56,257	BFA Theatre Degrees Awarded in the Program(s): 32	Audition req.
Ball State University 2000 W University Ave, Muncie, IN 47306	GPA: 3.52 SAT (ERW): N/A* SAT (M): N/A* ACT (C): N/A* *Test-optional ED: No	Overall College Admit Rate: 69% Undergrad Enrollment: 15,780 Total Enrollment: 21,597	BFA Theatre Degrees Awarded in the Program(s): 70	Audition req.
Indiana University Bloomington 107 S. Indiana Avenue, Bloomington, IN 47405	GPA: 3.74 SAT (ERW): 580-700 SAT (M): 560-680 ACT (C): 26-32 ED: No	Overall College Admit Rate: 85% Undergrad Enrollment: 34,253 Total Enrollment: 45,328	BA Theatre and Drama BFA Musical Theatre Degrees Awarded in the Program(s): 20	BA Theatre and Drama None req. BFA Musical Theatre Prescreen and audition req.

MIDWEST

THEATRE PROGRAMS

School	Avg. GPA, SAT Evidence Based Reading and Writing (ERW), SAT Math (M), and ACT Composite (C) Early Decision (ED): Yes/No	Admission Statistics	Program(s) See website for additional options.	Artistic Review Required (Req.)
Purdue University Purdue University, West Lafayette, IN 47907	GPA: 3.67 SAT (ERW): 590-690 SAT (M): 600-740 ACT (C): 25-33 ED: No	Overall College Admit Rate: 67% Undergrad Enrollment: 34,920 Total Enrollment: 45,869	BA Theatre Degrees Awarded in the Program(s): 8	None req.
University of Evansville 1800 Lincoln Ave, Evansville, IN 47722	GPA: N/A SAT (ERW): N/A* SAT (M): N/A* ACT (C): N/A* *Test-optional ED: Yes	Overall College Admit Rate: 64% Undergrad Enrollment: 2,041 Total Enrollment: 2,323	BFA Theatre Performance BS Theatre Performance Degrees Awarded in the Program(s): 17	Audition and interview req.
University of Notre Dame University of Notre Dame, Notre Dame, IN 46556	GPA: N/A SAT (ERW): 690-760 SAT (M): 710-790 ACT (C): 32-35 ED: Yes	Overall College Admit Rate: 19% Undergrad Enrollment: 8,874 Total Enrollment: 12,809	BA Film, Television, and Theatre, concentration: Theatre Degrees Awarded in the Program(s): 41	None req.
Wichita State University 1845 Fairmount St, Wichita, KS 67260	GPA: 3.51 SAT (ERW): 510-630 SAT (M): 520-630 ACT (C): 20-27 ED: No	Overall College Admit Rate: 55% Undergrad Enrollment: 12,406 Total Enrollment: 15,550	BA Theatre BFA Theatre Performance Degrees Awarded in the Program(s): N/A	BA Theatre Audition & interview optional, req. for scholarship consideration BFA Theatre Performance Audition & interview req.

THEATRE PROGRAMS

School	Avg. GPA, SAT Evidence Based Reading and Writing (ERW), SAT Math (M), and ACT Composite (C) Early Decision (ED): Yes/No	Admission Statistics	Program(s) See website for additional options.	Artistic Review Required (Req.)
University of Michigan 500 S. State St., Ann Arbor, MI 48109	GPA: 3.87 SAT (ERW): 660-740 SAT (M): 680-780 ACT (C): 31-34 ED: No	Overall College Admit Rate: 26% Undergrad Enrollment: 31,329 Total Enrollment: 47,907	BTA Theatre BFA Interarts Performance BFA Theatre Performance: Acting BFA Musical Theatre Degrees Awarded in the Program(s): 59	BTA Theatre Writing req. BFA Interarts Performance None req. BFA Theatre Performance: Acting and BFA Musical Theatre Prescreen and audition req.
University of Minnesota 330 21st Ave S., Minneapolis, MN 55455	GPA: N/A SAT (ERW): 600-700 SAT (M): 640-760 ACT (C): 25-31 ED: No	Overall College Admit Rate: 70% Undergrad Enrollment: 36,061 Total Enrollment: 52,017	BA Theatre Arts BFA Acting Degrees Awarded in the Program(s): 49	BA Theatre Arts None req. BFA Acting Prescreen and audition req.
College of the Ozarks 100 Opportunity Ave, Point Lookout, MO 65726	GPA: 3.37 SAT (ERW): 470-540 SAT (M): 480-560 ACT (C): 18-23 ED: No	Overall College Admit Rate: 56% Undergrad Enrollment: 836 Total Enrollment: 836	BA Theatre BA/BS Music Theatre Degrees Awarded in the Program(s): 1	None req.

MIDWEST

THEATRE PROGRAMS

School	Avg. GPA, SAT Evidence Based Reading and Writing (ERW), SAT Math (M), and ACT Composite (C) Early Decision (ED): Yes/No	Admission Statistics	Program(s) See website for additional options.	Artistic Review Required (Req.)
Missouri State University 901 S National Ave, Springfield, MO 65897	GPA: 3.73 SAT (ERW): 510-610 SAT (M): 510-610 ACT (C): 21-27 ED: No	Overall College Admit Rate: 19,620 Undergrad Enrollment: Total Enrollment: 23,504	BS Theatre BA Theatre BFA Theatre and Dance BFA Musical Theatre Degrees Awarded in the Program(s): 31	BS/BA Theatre Interview req. BFA Theatre & Dance: Acting and BFA Musical Theatre Audition and interview req.
University of Missouri University of Missouri, Columbia, MO 65211	GPA: N/A SAT (ERW): 560-660 SAT (M): 550-660 ACT (C): 23-29 ED: No	Overall College Admit Rate: 82% Undergrad Enrollment: 23,396 Total Enrollment: 31,103	BA Theatre Degrees Awarded in the Program(s): 11	None req.
Baldwin Wallace University 275 Eastland Rd, Berea, OH 44017	GPA: 3.64 SAT (ERW): 520-640 SAT (M): 520-620 ACT (C): 21-27 ED: No	Overall College Admit Rate: 70% Undergrad Enrollment: 2,860 Total Enrollment: 3,399	BFA Acting BA Theatre BM Music Theatre Degrees Awarded in the Program(s): 27	BFA Acting Audition and interview req. BM Music Theatre Prescreen optional and audition req. BA Theatre None req.

THEATRE PROGRAMS

School	Avg. GPA, SAT Evidence Based Reading and Writing (ERW), SAT Math (M), and ACT Composite (C) Early Decision (ED): Yes/No	Admission Statistics	Program(s) See website for additional options.	Artistic Review Required (Req.)
Kent State University 1325 Theatre Drive, Kent, OH 44242	GPA: 3.61 SAT (ERW): 510-610 SAT (M): 510-600 ACT (C): 20-26 ED: No	Overall College Admit Rate: 84% Undergrad Enrollment: 21,621 Total Enrollment: 26,822	BA Theatre Studies BFA Musical Theatre Degrees Awarded in the Program(s): 59	BA Theatre Studies None req. BFA Musical Theatre Prescreen req. if auditioning virtually, audition req. for all
Kenyon College 103 College Rd, Gambier, OH 43022	GPA: N/A SAT (ERW): 660-730 SAT (M): 620-730 ACT (C): 30-33 ED: Yes	Overall College Admit Rate: 37% Undergrad Enrollment: 1,615 Total Enrollment: 1,615	BA Drama Degrees Awarded in the Program(s): 14	None req.
Ohio State University 1849 Cannon Drive, Columbus, OH 43210	GPA: N/A SAT (ERW): 590-690 SAT (M): 620-740 ACT (C): 26-32 ED: No	Overall College Admit Rate: 87% Undergrad Enrollment: 19,284 Total Enrollment: 25,714	BA Theatre Degrees Awarded in the Program(s): 18	None req.

MIDWEST

THEATRE PROGRAMS

School	Avg. GPA, SAT Evidence Based Reading and Writing (ERW), SAT Math (M), and ACT Composite (C) Early Decision (ED): Yes/No	Admission Statistics	Program(s) See website for additional options.	Artistic Review Required (Req.)
University of Wisconsin 821 University Ave., 6173 Vilas Hall, Madison, WI 53706	GPA: 3.87 SAT (ERW): 610-690 SAT (M): 650-770 ACT (C): 27-32 ED: No	Overall College Admit Rate: 57% Undergrad Enrollment: 32,688 Total Enrollment: 44,640	BS Theatre and Drama Degrees Awarded in the Program(s): 8	None req.

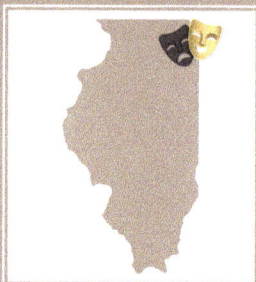

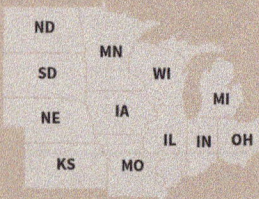

COLUMBIA COLLEGE CHICAGO

Address: 600 S. Michigan Avenue, Chicago, IL 60605
Website: *https://www.colum.edu/academics/fine-and-performing-arts/theatre/majors-and-programs*
Contact: *https://www.colum.edu/contact*
Phone: (312) 369-1000
Email: admissions@colum.edu

COST OF ATTENDANCE:

Tuition & Fees: $35,716 | **Additional Expenses:** $18,000
Total: $53,716

Financial Aid: https://www.colum.edu/columbia-central/where-to-start/index

ADDITIONAL INFORMATION:

Available Degree(s)

- BA Theatre
- BA Acting
- BFA Acting
- BA Musical Theatre
- BFA Musical Theatre Performance
- BA Comedy Writing and Performance

Artistic Review Requirement

Portfolios are optional for all applicants that apply to a BA program at Columbia College Chicago. Applicants are encouraged to submit a portfolio not only for admission to their desired program but also for the Faculty Recognition Award. The BFA Acting and BFA Musical Theatre Performance programs require a prescreen and audition.

Scholarships Offered

Students are automatically considered for renewable scholarships upon admission. For need-based scholarship, submit a FAFSA. For talent-based scholarships, submit an audition that demonstrates your best creative work. First-year, international students may be considered for talent-based scholarships.

Special Opportunities

Columbia College stages 40 productions each year. Students are encouraged to audition as soon as they begin for both musical and non-musical productions. Students also perform in student films, devised production, off-campus productions, and Mainstage productions directly by faculty. Columbia hosts two internship fairs per year from theatres like Steppenwolf, Victory Gardens, and the Goodman. The Getz Theatre Center has four professional-quality stages, a state-of-the-art scene shop, and labs for costume, makeup, prosthetics, and lighting. Minors include Stage Combat, ASL, Theatre Directing, and Live and Performing Arts Management.

Notable Alumni

Scott Adsit, Jeremy Beiler, Aidy Bryant, Harter Clingman, Shantel Cribbs, Dehzad Dabu, Michael George, Calle Johnson, Michael Kuroski, Courtney Mack, Mallory Maedke, Ashley Mondisa , Michelle Monaghan, Tonya Pinkins, Anna D. Shapiro, and Nadine Velazquez

ILLINOIS

INDIANA

IOWA

KANSAS

MICHIGAN

MINNESOTA

MISSOURI

NEBRASKA

NORTH DAKOTA

OHIO

SOUTH DAKOTA

WISCONSIN

DEPAUL UNIVERSITY

Address: 2350 N. Racine Ave., Chicago, IL 60614
Website: *https://theatre.depaul.edu/Pages/default.aspx*
Contact: *https://theatre.depaul.edu/about/Pages/contact-us.aspx*
Phone: (773) 325-7999
Email: theatreadmissions@depaul.edu

COST OF ATTENDANCE:

Tuition & Fees: $42,651 | **Additional Expenses:** $18,759
Total: $61,410

Financial Aid: https://www.depaul.edu/admission-and-aid/
financial-aid/Pages/default.aspx

ADDITIONAL INFORMATION:

Available Degree(s)

- BFA Theatre Arts
- BFA Comedy Arts
- BFA Acting

Artistic Review Requirement

The BFA Acting requires a video prescreen and a callback audition. The prescreen requires 2 monologues, one of which is contemporary. Submit the video prescreen to the Depaul's Portal - Blue Demon Domain. Applicants with a successful prescreen are notified of their callback. The callback is 2-3 hours and is in small group format.

The BFA Comedy Arts requires an interview, resume, writing sample, and a comedic performance video. Last, applicants of the BFA in Theatre Arts can expect an interview with faculty, writing sample, and resume submission.

Scholarships Offered

Students who apply to The Theatre School are automatically considered for the Theatre School Scholarship. Award amounts vary and are determined based on academic qualifications and artistic talent during the entrance audition or interview. All students are considered for the DePaul Freshman Scholarships (award $15,000-$24,000) when they submit their application for admission. Priority consideration for these scholarships are given to those who submit their application by November 15th.

Special Opportunities

DePaul University offers a combined Bachelor's and Master's degree program. Earn your undergraduate degree in The Theatre School and a graduate degree in another DePaul college. Students may complete both degrees in a 4+1 or 4+2 pathway.

Notable Alumni

Lisa Joyce, Kiki Layne, Adam Mayfield, Zak Orth, DeWayne Perkins, Amy Pietz, John C. Reilly, Leonard Roberts, and Lili Taylor

ILLINOIS

INDIANA

IOWA

KANSAS

MICHIGAN

MINNESOTA

MISSOURI

NEBRASKA

NORTH DAKOTA

OHIO

SOUTH DAKOTA

WISCONSIN

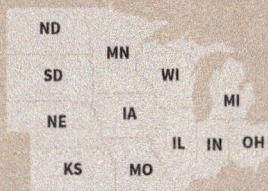

MIDWEST

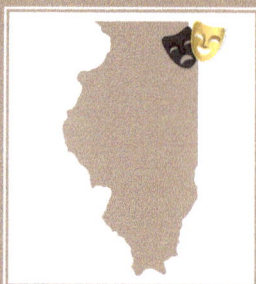

NORTHWESTERN UNIVERSITY

Address: 633 Clark St, Evanston, IL 60208
Website: *https://www.communication.northwestern.edu/ departments/theatre/about*
Contact: *https://www.communication.northwestern.edu/contact*
Phone: (847) 491-3741
Email: dear-soc@northwestern.edu

COST OF ATTENDANCE:

Tuition & Fees: $60,768 | **Additional Expenses:** $23,070
Total: $83,838

Financial Aid: https://undergradaid.northwestern.edu/index.html

ADDITIONAL INFORMATION:

Available Degree(s)

- BA Performance Studies
- BA Theatre, areas of study: Acting; Music Theatre; Playwriting; Design and Stage Management

Artistic Review Requirement

Northwestern University does not require a pre-screen or audition for their BA Theatre nor BA Performance Studies programs. However, applicants interested in the Musical Theatre Certificate may submit an optional Musical Theatre Supplement. Students who are admitted to the Theatre program at Northwestern must undergo an in-person audition for full admittance to the Musical Theatre Certificate Program after beginning their first quarter of study.

Scholarships Offered

The Northwestern University Scholarship ($250 to over $40,000 per year) is based on financial need after other forms of aid have been applied. The Karr Achievement Scholarship ($2,500 annually) is a merit-based scholarship.

Special Opportunities

There is an Honors in Theatre program for students who demonstrate academic achievement and complete a senior year project. Additionally, theatre students may study abroad. Typically, theatre students take advantage of the study abroad opportunity with the British American Drama Academy in London.

Notable Alumni

Warren Beatty, Ann-Margret, Richard Benjamin, Greg Berlanti, Craig Bierko, Clancy Brown, Charles Busch, Stephen Colbert, Stephanie Shemin D'Abruzzo, Gregg Edelman, Frank Galati, Ana Gasteyer, Kathryn Hahn, Heather Headley, Marg Helgenberger, Brian d'Arcy James, Laura Innes, Charlton Heston, Rex Ingram, Jennifer Jones, Adam Kantor, Robert Kline, Sherry Lansing, Cloris Leachman, Seth Meyers, Tony Musante, George Newbern, James Olson, Jerry Orbach, Mary Beth Peil, Paula Prentiss, Lily Rabe, Charlotte Rae, Tony Randall, Robert Reed, Jeri Ryan, Dan Shor, Robin Lord Taylor, Michael Weston, and Fred Williamson

UNIVERSITY OF CHICAGO

Address: 915 E 60th St., Chicago, IL 60637
Website: *https://taps.uchicago.edu/undergraduate/major-minor*
Contact: *https://arts.uchicago.edu/about/contact*
Phone: (773) 702-2787
Email: collegeadmissions@uchicago.edu

COST OF ATTENDANCE:

Tuition & Fees: $60,552 | **Additional Expenses:** $20,979
Total: $81,531

Financial Aid: https://financialaid.uchicago.edu/

ADDITIONAL INFORMATION:

Additional Degree(s)

- BA Theater and Performance Studies

Artistic Review Requirement

There is no audition requirement. Applicants may submit an
optional creative portfolio that includes highlights from their
performances.

Scholarships Offered

UChicago offers merit scholarships ranging in value from $4,000-
$10,000 per year for four years. In addition, all first-generation
college students are awarded the UChicago Empower Scholarship.
The award is $20,000 over four years and no separate application is
required. Students enrolled in UChicago Arts may apply for grants
to fund various campus art activities as well.

Special Opportunities

University of Chicago houses the Chicago Performance Lab. This
interdisciplinary collaboration allows companies to come into the
university and host workshops and presentations for university
students. Furthermore, Theatre and Performance Studies (TAPS)
students complete a BA project that is presented during their senior
year.

Notable Alumni

Ed Asner, Anna Chlumsky, Misha Collins, Sessue Hayakawa, Marilu
Henner, Celeste Holm, Elaine May, Mike Nichols, Sheldon Patinkin,
Kimberly Peirce, Eddie Shin, Paul Sills, David Steinberg, and Fritz
Weaver

ILLINOIS

INDIANA

IOWA

KANSAS

MICHIGAN

MINNESOTA

MISSOURI

NEBRASKA

NORTH DAKOTA

OHIO

SOUTH DAKOTA

WISCONSIN

MIDWEST

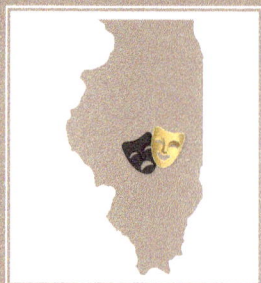

UNIVERSITY OF ILLINOIS URBANA-CHAMPAIGN (UIUC)

Address: 901 West Illinois Street, Urbana, IL 61801
Website: *https://theatre.illinois.edu/*
Contact: *https://admissions.illinois.edu/contact*
Phone: (217) 333-0302
Email: admissions@illinois.edu

COST OF ATTENDANCE:

In-State Tuition & Fees: $16,866 | **Additional Expenses:** $16,194
Total: $33,060

Out-of-State Tuition & Fees: $34,316 | **Additional Expenses:** $16,534
Total: $50,850

Financial Aid: https://admissions.illinois.edu/Invest/financial-aid

ADDITIONAL INFORMATION:

Available Degree(s)

- BFA Theatre, concentrations: Theatre Studies: Playwriting, Directing, & Dramaturgy; Acting; Arts & Entertainment Technology; Costume Design & Technology; Lighting Design & Technology; Scenic Design; Scenic Technology; Sound Design & Technology; Stage Management

Artistic Review Requirement

The BFA in Acting requires an audition. Applicants must prepare a headshot, resume, and 2 contrasting monologues, 1 of which is contemporary. Students may optionally prepare a song as well.

Scholarships Offered

Both in-state and out-of-state applicants are eligible for various scholarships. Applicants are selected for College of Fine & Applied Arts talent-based awards during their audition, interview, and/or portfolio review.

Special Opportunities

The performance spaces at Krannert Center for the Performing Arts serve as labs for all theatre students. Students have access to the Krannert costume shop, the CU Community Fablab, and the wig and makeup studio. There are also two lighting laboratories and three professionally-equipped audio suites on campus.

Notable Alumni

Ruth Attaway, Barbara Bain, Betsy Brandt, Timothy Carhart, Terrence Connor Carson, Arden Cho, Dominic Fumusa, Nancy Lee Grahn, Shanola Hampton, Margaret Judson, Ned Luke, Mary Elizabeth Mastrantonio, Ryan McPartlin, Ben Murphy, Lucas Neff, Nick Offerman, Jerry Orbach, Peter Palmer, Larry Parks, Andy Richter, Alan Ruck, Jonathan Sadowski, Allan Sherman, Sushanth, Lynne Thigpen, and Grant Williams

BALL STATE UNIVERSITY

Address: 2000 W University Ave, Muncie, IN 47306
Website: *https://www.bsu.edu/academics/collegesanddepartments/theatredance/what-we-offer*
Contact: *https://www.bsu.edu/admissions/undergraduate-admissions/contact-us*
Phone: (800) 482-4278
Email: askus@bsu.edu

COST OF ATTENDANCE:

In-State Tuition & Fees: $9,520 | **Additional Expenses:** $12,802
Total: $24,484

Out-of-State Tuition & Fees: $18,594 | **Additional Expenses:** $12,802
Total: $31,396

Financial Aid: https://www.bsu.edu/admissions/financial-aid-and-scholarships

ADDITIONAL INFORMATION:

Available Degree(s)

- BFA Theatre, options: Acting; Musical Theatre; Design and Technology

Artistic Review Requirement

Ball State requires a digital or in-person audition. Applicants to the Acting option must prepare 2 contemporary monologues. Students interested in the Musical Theatre option must prepare 2 contrasting songs, 2 contrasting monologues, and participate in a dance call.

Scholarships Offered

The Department of Theatre and Dance offers merit-based scholarships such as the University CFA Awards ($4,000 a year for in-state students and $2,000 a year for out-of-state students).

Special Opportunities

Ball State is an award-winning participant in the Kennedy Center American College Theatre Festival. Furthermore, musical theatre students are required to complete a senior capstone project, where they are part of a live group cabaret performance. Additionally, a BA or BS degree Is available In theatre, however the options underneath the degree relate to stage management, teaching, or design rather than performance.

Notable Alumni

Meghan "Collins" Conley, Jessica Ervin, Talley Beth Gale, Matt Glassner, Joe Lino, David Merten, Erin Neufer, Grace Rex, Adam B. Shapiro, Mary Taylor, and Meg Warner

ILLINOIS

INDIANA

IOWA

KANSAS

MICHIGAN

MINNESOTA

MISSOURI

NEBRASKA

NORTH DAKOTA

OHIO

SOUTH DAKOTA

WISCONSIN

MIDWEST

ILLINOIS

INDIANA

IOWA

KANSAS

MICHIGAN

MINNESOTA

MISSOURI

NEBRASKA

NORTH DAKOTA

OHIO

SOUTH DAKOTA

WISCONSIN

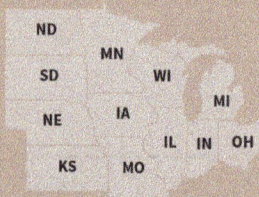

INDIANA UNIVERSITY BLOOMINGTON

Address: 107 S. Indiana Avenue, Bloomington, IN 47405
Website: *https://theatre.indiana.edu/*
Contact: *https://admissions.indiana.edu/contact/index.html*
Phone: (812) 855-4848
Email: admissions@indiana.edu

COST OF ATTENDANCE:

In-State Tuition & Fees: $11,332 | **Additional Expenses:** $15,966
Total: $27,298

Out-of-State Tuition & Fees: $38,352 | **Additional Expenses:** $15,966
Total: $54,318

Financial Aid: https://admissions.indiana.edu/cost-financial-aid/financial-aid.html

ADDITIONAL INFORMATION:

Available Degree(s)

- BA Theatre and Drama, concentration: Acting
- BFA Musical Theatre

Artistic Review Requirement

There is no artistic review requirement for the BA in Theatre and Drama. The BFA in Musical Theatre requires a prescreen and audition. At the audition, applicants must participate in a dance class, an acting class, and prepare 2 contrasting songs.

Scholarships Offered

Indiana University Bloomington offers a variety of scholarships for in-state, out-of-state, and international students. Students applying before the early action deadline will receive consideration for IU Academic Scholarships ($1,000–$11,000) and for the invitation-only Selective Scholarship.

Special Opportunities

At least eight on-campus productions are presented each year. Students have ample opportunity to gain on-stage experience.

Notable Alumni

Maddie Shea Baldwin, Jonathan Banks, Sarah Clarke, Laverne Cox, Matthew Daddario, David C. Giuntoli, Tan Kheng Hua, Patricia Kalember, Andraes Katsulas, Charles Kimbrough, Kevin Kline, J. Lee, Lee Majors, Arian Moayed, Nicole Parker, Julian Ramos, Ranveer Singh, Hana Slevin, Brian Stack, Jeri Taylor, Herb Vigran, Aaron Waltke, and Jaysen Wright

PURDUE UNIVERSITY

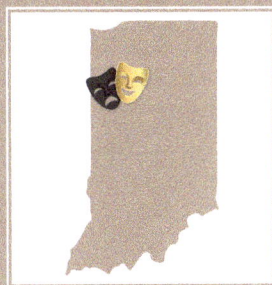

Address: Purdue University, West Lafayette, IN 47907
Website: *https://cla.purdue.edu/academic/rueffschool/theatre/*
academics/undergraduate/theatre.html
Contact: *https://www.admissions.purdue.edu/contact/index.php*
Phone: (765) 494-4600
Email: admissions@purdue.edu

COST OF ATTENDANCE:

In-State Tuition & Fees: $10,052 | **Additional Expenses:** $12,820
Total: $22,872

Out-of-State Tuition & Fees: $28,854 | **Additional Expenses:** $12,820
Total: $41,674

Financial Aid: https://www.purdue.edu/dfa/

ADDITIONAL INFORMATION:

Available Degree(s)

- BA Theatre

Artistic Review Requirement

There is no artistic review requirement.

Scholarships Offered

Purdue awards freshman scholarships based on academic merit
as well as financial need. The Trustees Scholarship awards $10,000
per year to in-state students and $16,000 per year to out-of-state
students. The Presidential Scholarship awards $4,000 per year to
in-state students and $10,000 per year to out-of-state students.
There are also scholarships available to Theatre majors that are
selected by The Scholarship Committee or faculty and staff of the
Department of Theatre.

Special Opportunities

Students may apply for the 5-year BS/MS degree in Computer
Graphics Technology. Additionally,

Purdue Study Abroad offers two programs of theatre study in
England through University of Coventry and University of Kent at
Canterbury.

Notable Alumni

Monte Blue, Kenneth Choi, Jim Gaffigan, Callie Khouri, Wayne
Lamb, Tom Moore, George Peppard, Bob Peterson, and Dulquer
Salmaan

ILLINOIS

INDIANA

IOWA

KANSAS

MICHIGAN

MINNESOTA

MISSOURI

NEBRASKA

NORTH DAKOTA

OHIO

SOUTH DAKOTA

WISCONSIN

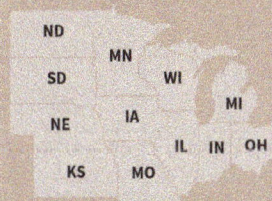

MIDWEST

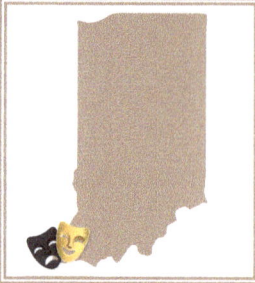

ILLINOIS

INDIANA

IOWA

KANSAS

MICHIGAN

MINNESOTA

MISSOURI

NEBRASKA

NORTH DAKOTA

OHIO

SOUTH DAKOTA

WISCONSIN

UNIVERSITY OF EVANSVILLE

Address: 1800 Lincoln Ave, Evansville, IN 47722
Website: *https://www.evansville.edu/majors/theatre/degrees.cfm*
Contact: *https://www.evansville.edu/contact/*
Phone: (833) 232-6223
Email: uerelations@evansville.edu

COST OF ATTENDANCE:

Tuition & Fees: $41,336 | **Additional Expenses:** $17,110
Total: $58,446

Financial Aid: https://www.evansville.edu/student-financial-services/

ADDITIONAL INFORMATION:

Available Degree(s)

- BFA Theatre Performance
- BS Theatre Performance

Artistic Review Requirement

University of Evansville requires an audition and an interview. Applicants must prepare a headshot, resume, and a memorized, 2-3 minute monologue from a contemporary play, 20-30 lines from a Shakespeare play, and a verse from a musical.

Scholarships Offered

Any remaining gap between a student's UE Scholarships, Indiana State Grant Funding, and Federal Grant Funding and full-time tuition and full-time fees will be covered through an Aces Opportunity Grant. Merit-based scholarships include Presidential Scholarship ($21,000 at minimum).

Special Opportunities

University of Evansville's Department of Theatre is highly selective. They see approximately 1700 auditions and accept only 40 students into the entire department. At Harlaxton College, UE's study abroad center in England, Theatre students may take Introduction to Theatre and Period Styles in Theatre: Costume History in the summer or British Studies: Literary Perspectives, Independent Study in British Theatre, and Shakespeare in a fall or spring semester.

Notable Alumni

David Emge, Crista Flanagan, Kelli Giddish, Ron Glass, Deirdre Lovejoy, Rami Malek, Jack McBrayer, Lennon Parham, Stephen Plunkett, Carrie Preston, and Rutina Wesley

UNIVERSITY OF NOTRE DAME

Address: University of Notre Dame, Notre Dame, IN 46556
Website: *https://ftt.nd.edu/*
Contact: *https://www.nd.edu/about/contact/*
Phone: (574) 631-5000
Email: admissions@nd.edu

COST OF ATTENDANCE:

Tuition & Fees: $57,699 | **Additional Expenses:** $19,184
Total: $76,883

Financial Aid: https://financialaid.nd.edu/

ADDITIONAL INFORMATION:

Available Degree(s)

- BA Film, Television, and Theatre, concentration: Theatre

Artistic Review Requirement

There is no audition requirement.

Scholarships Offered

Notre Dame offers institutional scholarships, club scholarships, and private scholarships. The university scholarships are both need-based and academic-based.

Special Opportunities

The Film, Television, and Theatre (FTT) major allow students to explore filmmaking while also gaining performance skills. Students may also do a thesis and write a research paper, create a film, direct a play, design a set, or do any other host of skills related to theatre. Furthermore, Notre Dame hosts an annual Notre Dame Student Film Festival that students may join in on. All students may audition for plays and musicals on campus as well.

Notable Alumni

Tony Bill, Jimmy Brogan, Mark Consuelos, Brain Kelly, William Mapother, Dan O'Brien, Richard Riehle, Tim Russell, Austin Swift, George Wendt, and Jason Zimbler

ILLINOIS

INDIANA

IOWA

KANSAS

MICHIGAN

MINNESOTA

MISSOURI

NEBRASKA

NORTH DAKOTA

OHIO

SOUTH DAKOTA

WISCONSIN

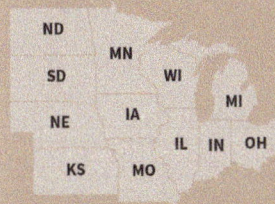

MIDWEST

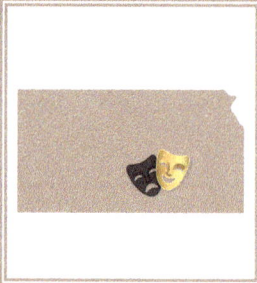

WICHITA STATE UNIVERSITY

Address: 1845 Fairmount St, Wichita, KS 67260
Website: *https://www.wichita.edu/academics/fine_arts/spa/3_THEATRE/index.php*
Contact: *https://www.wichita.edu/academics/academic_affairs/Contact.php*
Phone: (316) 978-3010
Email: uerelations@evansville.edu

COST OF ATTENDANCE:

In-State Tuition & Fees: $8,103 | **Additional Expenses:** $17,260
Total: $25,363

Out-of-State Tuition & Fees: $16,973 | **Additional Expenses:** $17,260
Total: $34,233

Financial Aid: https://www.wichita.edu/administration/financial_aid/

ADDITIONAL INFORMATION:

Available Degree(s)

- BA Theatre
- BFA Theatre Performance

Artistic Review Requirement

Auditions and interviews are required for the BA in Theatre if students would like to be considered for scholarships. Auditions and interviews are mandatory for the BFA in Theatre Performance. Audition requirements include 2 contrasting monologues, a resume, and a headshot.

Scholarships Offered

Wichita State University offers tuition discounts, financial aids, and scholarships. Both in-state students and out-of-state students are eligible for The Freshmen Merit Scholarship ($1,000 - $4,000 a year and $2,500 - $6,000 a year respectively). WSU's National Merit Scholarships (up to $50,000 over four years) are open to National Merit Finalists and National Hispanic Recognition Finalists. The Global Select Scholarships ($500 - $2,500 a year) are awarded to international students based on their performance at WSU.

Special Opportunities

The College of Fine Arts participates in WSU's cooperative education internship program, which aims to provide paid employment experiences that complement the curriculum. The Theatre Program offers a Certificate in Stage Management.

Notable Alumni

Karla Burns, James Billings, Karla Burns, Erin Dagon-Mitchell, Joyce DiDonato, Shirley Knight, Lance LeGault, Samuel Ramey, Kate Snodgrass, and Michael Sylvester

UNIVERSITY OF MICHIGAN

Address: 500 S. State St., Ann Arbor, MI 48109
Website: *https://smtd.umich.edu/departments/theatre-drama/*
Contact: *https://smtd.umich.edu/about/contact-us/*
Phone: (734) 764-0593
Email: smtd.admissions@umich.edu

COST OF ATTENDANCE:

In-State Tuition & Fees: $15,558 | **Additional Expenses:** $15,498
Total: $31,056

Out-of-State Tuition & Fees: $51,200 | **Additional Expenses:** $15,498
Total: $66,698

Financial Aid: https://finaid.umich.edu/

ADDITIONAL INFORMATION:

Available Degree(s)

- BTA Theatre
- BFA Interarts Performance
- BFA Theatre Performance: Acting
- BFA Musical Theatre

Artistic Review Requirement

The BTA in Theatre does not require an audition, however applicants must submit several writing pieces that follow the application prompts. The BFA in Theatre Performance: Acting and the BFA in Musical Theatre requires a prescreen and a live audition. THe BFA in Interarts Performance does not require a prescreen nor audition.

Scholarships Offered

The School of Music, Theatre, & Dance offers merit-based scholarships to theatre students. Additionally, University of Michigan offers several scholarships for incoming students. One of them is the Stamps Scholars Program, a prestigious merit-based program that offers the full cost of attendance. The HAIL Scholarship is an invitational award that covers four years of tuition and fees for low-income, high achieving Michigan students. Many scholarships are need-based, although some are merit-based as well.

Special Opportunities

The Department of Theatre and Drama hosts 4-5 main stage shows annually. Furthermore, Basement Arts, a student-run theatre organization presents 15-20 shows each year. These are all performance opportunities for students.

Notable Alumni

Maureen Anderman, Gavin Creel, Erin Dilly, Caleb Foote, Hunter Foster, David Allen Grier, Gregory Jbara, James Earl Jones, Andrew Keenan-Bolger, Celia Keenan-Bolger, Andrew Lippa, Michael L. Maguire, Marian Ethel Mercer, Benj Pasek, Justin Paul, Jeffrey Seller, James D. Stern, and Jacqueline Toboni

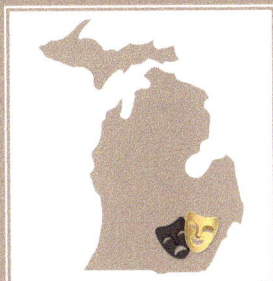

ILLINOIS

INDIANA

IOWA

KANSAS

MICHIGAN

MINNESOTA

MISSOURI

NEBRASKA

NORTH DAKOTA

OHIO

SOUTH DAKOTA

WISCONSIN

MIDWEST

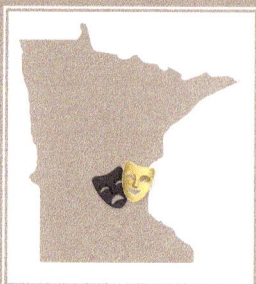

ILLINOIS

INDIANA

IOWA

KANSAS

MICHIGAN

MINNESOTA

MISSOURI

NEBRASKA

NORTH DAKOTA

OHIO

SOUTH DAKOTA

WISCONSIN

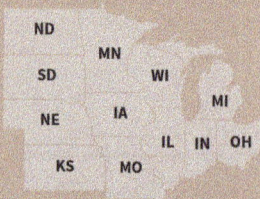

UNIVERSITY OF MINNESOTA

Address: 330 21st Ave S., Minneapolis, MN 55455
Website: *https://cla.umn.edu/theatre*
Contact: *http://umn.force.com/admissions/*
Phone: (612) 625-6699
Email: theatre@umn.edu

COST OF ATTENDANCE:

In-State Tuition & Fees: $15,236 | **Additional Expenses:** $16,082
Total: $31,318

Out-of-State Tuition & Fees: $33,534 | **Additional Expenses:** $17,582
Total: $51,116

Financial Aid: https://admissions.tc.umn.edu/costsaid/index.html

ADDITIONAL INFORMATION:

Available Degree(s)

- BA Theatre Arts, tracks: Generalist; History/Literature; Performance Creation; Design & Technology; Social Justice
- BFA Acting

Artistic Review Requirement

The BFA in Acting requires a prescreen via Acceptd and an callback audition. The prescreen requires 2 monologues and the callback is in the form of in-person workshops. Only 20 students are accepted into the program. There is no artistic review requirement for the BA in Theatre Arts.

Scholarships Offered

University of Minnesota offers numerous scholarship opportunities to all students, including in-state and out-of-state students. The University-Wide Academic Scholarships are highly competitive and have varying award amounts. In addition, all international students are automatically considered for the Global Excellence Scholarship ($10,000-$25,000 per year for up to four years).

Special Opportunities

All BFA Acting students spend their third year, fall semester abroad in London at the Globe Theater and CAPA Global Education Network. BA Theatre Arts students have the opportunity to study abroad the Theatre Arts Study Center in Dublin, Ireland.

Notable Alumni

Eddie Albert, Loni Anderson, James Arness, John Astin, Brad Beyer, Susan Blackwell, Jessica Blank, Michael Blodgett, Roman Bohnen, Guy Branum, Joel Brooks, Richard Carlson, Aya Cash, Arlene Dahl, Richard Dix, Kimberly Elise, Tovah Feldshuh, Stink Fisher, Henry Fonda, Santino Fontana, Frank Forest, Warren Frost, Jay Goede, Peter Michael Goetz, Peter Graves, Ari Herstand, James Hong, Ernie Hudson, Linda Kelsey, T.R. Knight, Jessica Lange, Jill Larson, Peter MacNicol, E.G. Marshall, Kevin McCarthy, Kate Mulgrew, Charles Nolte, Laurence Overmire, Ron Perlman, Arthur Peterson, Jr., David Soul, Robert Vaughn, Lenny Wolpe, and Tay Zonday

COLLEGE OF THE OZARKS

Address: 100 Opportunity Ave, Point Lookout, MO 65726
Website: *https://www.cofo.edu/Theatre*
Contact: *https://www.cofo.edu/contact*
Phone: (800) 222-0525
Email: https://www.cofo.edu/Contact/Email

COST OF ATTENDANCE:

Tuition & Fees: $19,660 | **Additional Expenses:** $11,104
Total: $30,764

Financial Aid: https://www.cofo.edu/Scholarships

ADDITIONAL INFORMATION:

Available Degree(s)

- BA Theatre
- BA/BS Music Theatre

Artistic Review Requirement

There is no artistic review requirement.

Scholarships Offered

Room and Board scholarships are available through the Summer Work Education Program. The General Scholarship Application is also available to all students and closes December 1st each year. Furthermore, College of the Ozarks offers alumni and external scholarships.

Special Opportunities

Students may audition for any of the four productions per year, including one spring musical. Furthermore, a degree in Speech and Theatre Education is also available within the department.

Notable Alumni

Lennie Aleshire, April Scott, and Tony Tost

ILLINOIS

INDIANA

IOWA

KANSAS

MICHIGAN

MINNESOTA

MISSOURI

NEBRASKA

NORTH DAKOTA

OHIO

SOUTH DAKOTA

WISCONSIN

MIDWEST

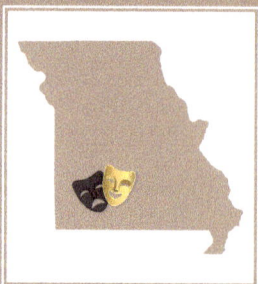

ILLINOIS

INDIANA

IOWA

KANSAS

MICHIGAN

MINNESOTA

MISSOURI

NEBRASKA

NORTH DAKOTA

OHIO

SOUTH DAKOTA

WISCONSIN

MISSOURI STATE UNIVERSITY

Address: 901 S National Ave, Springfield, MO 65897
Website: *https://theatreanddance.missouristate.edu/design-technology.htm*
Contact: *https://theatreanddance.missouristate.edu/Contact.aspx*
Phone: (417) 836-4400
Email: TheatreAndDance@MissouriState.edu

COST OF ATTENDANCE:

In-State Tuition & Fees: $8,294 | **Additional Expenses:** $14,874
Total: $23,168

Out-of-State Tuition & Fees: $16,498 | **Additional Expenses:** $14,874
Total: $31,372

Financial Aid: https://www.missouristate.edu/financialaid/

ADDITIONAL INFORMATION:

Available Degree(s)

- BS Theatre
- BA Theatre
- BFA Theatre and Dance, options: Acting
- BFA Musical Theatre

Artistic Review Requirement

The BFA Theatre & Dance: Acting and BFA Musical Theatre require an audition and interview. In the audition, applicants participate in a group warm-up, prepare 2 contrasting monologues, and interview with faculty. The BFA Musical Theatre requires a monologue, 2 contrasting songs, a dance combination, and an interview with faculty. The BA or BS in Theatre only requires an interview. Submit all materials via Acceptd.

Scholarships Offered

Missouri State University funds automatic scholarships based on students' GPA and standardized test score as well as competitive scholarships including the Presidential Scholarship (up to $60,000 over four years) and the Inclusive Excellence Scholarship (up to $21,000 over four years).

The theatre and dance department awards sixteen $2,000 activity scholarships as recommended by the faculty and six $2,000 scholarships associated with the department's student theatre troupe, In-School Players, are assigned via an audition process. Numerous other scholarships are awarded with various criteria.

Special Opportunities

The BFA Theatre & Dance, option: Acting offers a three-year transfer plan and a three-year plus one semester degree plan. Every other year, the department sponsors a group trip to Toronto to train and get certified with Fight Directors Canada's Stage Combat Certification Program. Theatre students may study away with the Theatre Academy London (TAL) in England.

Notable Alumni

Don S. Davis, John Goodman, Tess Harper, Kendra Kassebaum, Kyle Dean Massey, and Kathleen Turner

UNIVERSITY OF MISSOURI

Address: University of Missouri, Columbia, MO 65211
Website: *https://majors.missouri.edu/theatre-design-technical-ba/*
Contact: *https://admissions.missouri.edu/contact/*
Phone: (573) 882-7786
Email: askmizzou@missouri.edu

COST OF ATTENDANCE:

In-State Tuition & Fees: $13,128 | **Additional Expenses:** $10,964
Total: $24,092

Out-of-State Tuition & Fees: $31,734 | **Additional Expenses:** $10,964
Total: $42,698

Financial Aid: https://admissions.missouri.edu/financial-aid/

ADDITIONAL INFORMATION:

Available Degree(s)

- BA Theatre, emphases: Performance; Writing for Performance; Design/Technical

Artistic Review Requirement

There is no artistic review requirement.

Scholarships Offered

University of Missouri offers automatic scholarships to in-state students, out-of-state students, and international students. Applicants who apply test-optional and do not have official test scores are reviewed holistically for scholarships. Competitive awards include the Stamps Scholars Award (full scholarship). The Theatre Department established the Dan Springer Memorial Fund, which provides scholarships to Theatre students studying the technical arts involved in performance. There are also department-level scholarships awarded to current students.

Special Opportunities

MU's principal theatre, The Rhynsburger Theatre, houses a variety of light and sound equipment and control systems and a state-of-the-art professional computer graphics lab. Students also have access to a costume shop and a scene shop. Students may study abroad In Lancaster University and University of East Anglia in England.

Notable Alumni

Tom Berenger, Brent Briscoe, Kate Capshaw, Chris Cooper, Jon Hamm, Clista Jarrett, David Koechner, Gary Mickelson, Robert Loggia, Richard Matheson, Brad Pitt, George C. Scott, Tennessee Williams, Rhonda Weller-Stilson, and Ying Da

ILLINOIS

INDIANA

IOWA

KANSAS

MICHIGAN

MINNESOTA

MISSOURI

NEBRASKA

NORTH DAKOTA

OHIO

SOUTH DAKOTA

WISCONSIN

MIDWEST

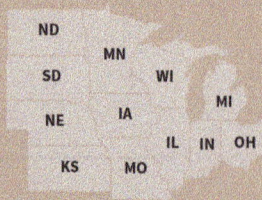

BALDWIN WALLACE UNIVERSITY

Address: 275 Eastland Rd, Berea, OH 44017
Website: *https://www.bw.edu/academics/undergraduate/theatre-design-technical/*
Contact: *https://www.bw.edu/admission/counselors/*
Phone: (440) 826-2222
Email: admission@bw.edu

COST OF ATTENDANCE:

Tuition & Fees: $35,366 | **Additional Expenses:** $13,024
Total: $48,390

Financial Aid: https://www.bw.edu/undergraduate-admission/first-year/tuition/

ADDITIONAL INFORMATION:

Available Degree(s)

- BFA Acting
- BA Theatre, concentrations: Acting & Directing; Dance & Movement; Stage Management; Design and Technical
- BM Music Theatre

Artistic Review Requirement

The BFA in Acting and BM in Music Theatre requires an audition and an interview. Students must prepare 2 contrasting monologues for the BFA in Acting. An optional prescreen for the BM in Music Theatre is available. Music Theatre applicants must submit a recorded monologue, wildcard component, and dance audition prior to their callback audition. The BA in Theatre does not require an artistic review.

Scholarships Offered

First-year applicants are automatically considered for merit scholarships ($12,000 to $21,000 a year) based on their cumulative weighted high school GPA. Baldwin Wallace University also offers numerous special awards.

Special Opportunities

Baldwin Wallace hosts an intensive theatre program with training in acting, voice, and movement. Individual mentoring and opportunities with the Great Lakes Theatre at Playhouse Square and partnerships with nationally-ranked theatre programs. Auditions are offered with Shakespeare festivals across the country. British theatre training in London offered. BW has a comedy troupe and both Mainstage and Black Box Theatre opportunities. BW offers opera, musicals, plays, dance concerts, and other opportunities.

Notable Alumni

Zach Adkins, Cleo DeOrio, Caitlin Houlahan, Kyle Jean-Baptiste, Corey Mach, Ali Manfredi, Lauren Marshall, Chris McCarrell, Trista Moldovan, Mawusi N Jill Paice, Kyle Post, Ciara Renee, Nicholas Moertl, and Kate Rockwell

KENT STATE UNIVERSITY

Address: 1325 Theatre Drive, Kent, OH 44242
Website: *https://www.kent.edu/theatredance*
Contact: *https://www.kent.edu/theatredance/contact-us*
Phone: (330) 672-2082
Email: theatre@kent.edu

COST OF ATTENDANCE:

In-State Tuition & Fees: $10,916 | **Additional Expenses:** $16,112
Total: $27,028

Out-of-State Tuition & Fees: $19,792 | **Additional Expenses:**
$16,112   **Total:** $35,904

Financial Aid: https://www.kent.edu/financialaid

ADDITIONAL INFORMATION:

Available Degree(s)

- BA Theatre Studies, concentrations: Theatre and Society; Performance; Theatre Management; Production
- BFA Musical Theatre

Artistic Review Requirement

There is no artistic review requirement for BA Theatre Studies applicants. However, BFA Musical Theatre applicants must audition. Students who opt for a live, virtual audition must also submit a prescreen. The audition consists of a monologue, 2 songs, and a dance call.

Scholarships Offered

Out-of-state students may be eligible for merit-based awards, including the President's Achievement Award ($4,000-$12,500), the Honors Distinction Award ($1,000-$3,000), the Founders Scholarship ($1,000-$2,000) among others. In-state students may be eligible for the same scholarships.

Special Opportunities

The BA program is good for students who would like to gain a traditional liberal arts education while simultaneously exploring theatre. The campus houses 3 theatres, rehearsal spaces, laboratories for costumes and scenery, and it oversees the outdoor venue Porthouse Theatre. In their senior year, students may participate in the New York City Musical Theatre Showcase.

Notable Alumni

Kaitlyn Black, Tee Boyich, Antoinette Comer, John de Lancie, Jeff Richmond, Alice Ripley, and Ray Wise

ILLINOIS

INDIANA

IOWA

KANSAS

MICHIGAN

MINNESOTA

MISSOURI

NEBRASKA

NORTH DAKOTA

OHIO

SOUTH DAKOTA

WISCONSIN

MIDWEST

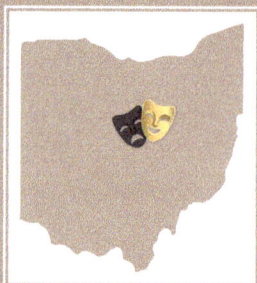

ILLINOIS

INDIANA

IOWA

KANSAS

MICHIGAN

MINNESOTA

MISSOURI

NEBRASKA

NORTH DAKOTA

OHIO

SOUTH DAKOTA

WISCONSIN

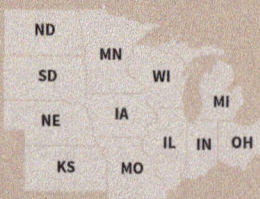

KENYON COLLEGE

Address: 103 College Rd, Gambier, OH 43022
Website: *https://www.kenyon.edu/academics/departments-programs/dance-drama-and-film/*
Contact: *https://www.kenyon.edu/admissions-aid/contact-admissions/*
Phone: (800) 848-2468
Email: admissions@kenyon.edu

COST OF ATTENDANCE:

Tuition & Fees: $60,800 | **Additional Expenses:** $13,130
Total: $73,930

Financial Aid: https://www.kenyon.edu/admissions-aid/financial-aid/

ADDITIONAL INFORMATION:

Available Degree(s)

- BA Drama

Artistic Review Requirement

There is no artistic review requirement.

Scholarships Offered

Kenyon College offers Honor, Science, and Trustee Opportunity Scholarships. These awards are worth $25,000 per year, renewable, and based on academic achievement. In addition, students in the top 10-15 percent of their graduating class may be eligible for the Distinguished Academic Scholarship Program ($15,000 per year for four years).

Special Opportunities

Kenyon College houses numerous facilities that students can enjoy, including a two-story film studio, a 30-seat screening room, the Bolton Theatre, and more. Kenyon presents multiple mainstage shows that students may find a role in.

Notable Alumni

Nick Bakay, Frank Dicopoulos, Chris Eigeman, Allison Janney, Paul Newman, Josh Radnor, Jonathan Winters, and Damian Young

OHIO STATE UNIVERSITY

Address: 1849 Cannon Drive, Columbus, OH 43210
Website: *https://theatre.osu.edu/*
Contact: *https://theatre.osu.edu/contact*
Phone: (614) 292-5821
Email: theatre-ugrad@osu.edu

COST OF ATTENDANCE:

In-State Tuition & Fees: $11,518 | **Additional Expenses:** $17,146
Total: $28,664

Out-of-State Tuition & Fees: $33,502 | **Additional Expenses:** $17,980
Total: $51,482

Financial Aid: https://sfa.osu.edu/

ADDITIONAL INFORMATION:

Available Degree(s)

* BA Theatre

Artistic Review Requirement

There is no audition requirement.

Scholarships Offered

University merit scholarships include the Eminence Fellows
Program and Scholarship (full cost of attendance for 8 semesters),
the Morrill Scholarship Program, the Maximus Scholarship ($3,000
per year), and several others.

Special Opportunities

Ohio State is located near the Wexner Center for the Arts and within
a dynamic theatre scene. Guest artists and professionals visit for
workshops and special classes for theatre students to enjoy.

Notable Alumni

Ross Butler, Ruby Elzy, Patricia Heaton, Eileen Heckart, Melina
Kanakaredes, Richard Lewis, Ron O'Neal, Ross Patterson, Jean
Peters, Gigi Rice, Kristen Ruhlin, and Dwight Yoakam

ILLINOIS

INDIANA

IOWA

KANSAS

MICHIGAN

MINNESOTA

MISSOURI

NEBRASKA

NORTH DAKOTA

OHIO

SOUTH DAKOTA

WISCONSIN

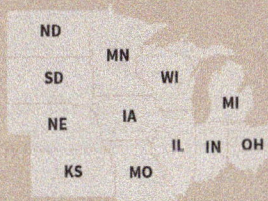

MIDWEST

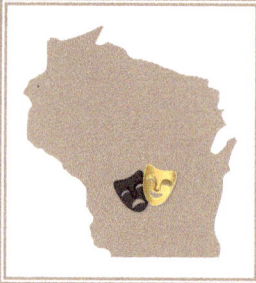

ILLINOIS

INDIANA

IOWA

KANSAS

MICHIGAN

MINNESOTA

MISSOURI

NEBRASKA

NORTH DAKOTA

OHIO

SOUTH DAKOTA

WISCONSIN

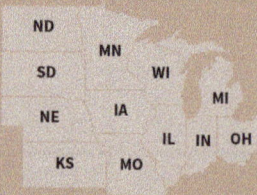

UNIVERSITY OF WISCONSIN

Address: 821 University Ave., 6173 Vilas Hall, Madison, WI 53706
Website: *https://theatre.wisc.edu/academics/*
Contact: *https://theatre.wisc.edu/contact/*
Phone: (608) 263-2329
Email: uwtheatre@theatre.wisc.edu

COST OF ATTENDANCE:

In-State Tuition & Fees: $10,766 | **Additional Expenses:** $16,764
Total: $27,530

Out-of-State Tuition & Fees: $38,654 | **Additional Expenses:** $17,234
Total: $55,888

MN Resident Tuition & Fees: $14,812 | **Additional Expenses:** $17,044
Total: $31,856

Financial Aid: https://financialaid.wisc.edu/

ADDITIONAL INFORMATION:

Available Degree(s)

- BS Theatre and Drama, option: Acting

Artistic Review Requirement

There is no artistic review requirement for incoming freshmen. However, once admitted, if the student is interested in the Acting concentration, they must audition during the semester.

Scholarships Offered

Theater-specific scholarships are available. Students are encouraged to browse through current offerings. The University of Wisconsin also offers various institutional awards. Students may apply through the Wisconsin Scholarship Hub (WiSH).

Special Opportunities

The UW-Madison Department of Theatre and Drama produces many productions that students may audition for.

Notable Alumni

Don Ameche, Joseph Anthony, Tamara Braun, Macdonald Carey, Robert Clarke, Carrie Coon, Joan Cusack, André DeShields, Honor Ford-Smith, Jason Gerhardt, Uta Hagen, Anders Holm, Jane Kaczmarek, Fredric March, Agnes Moorehead, Kevin Murphy, Tricia O'Kelley, Brad Rowe, Gena Rowlands, Jana Schneider, Seann William Scott, Joe Silver, Josh Stamberg, Daniel J. Travanti, Tom Wopat, and Charlotte Zucker

ALABAMA

ARKANSAS

DELAWARE

DISTRICT OF
COLUMBIA

FLORIDA

GEORGIA

KENTUCKY

LOUISIANA

MARYLAND

MISSISSIPPI

NORTH CAROLINA

OKLAHOMA

SOUTH CAROLINA

TENNESSEE

TEXAS

VIRGINIA

WEST VIRGINIA

CHAPTER 15

REGION THREE

SOUTH

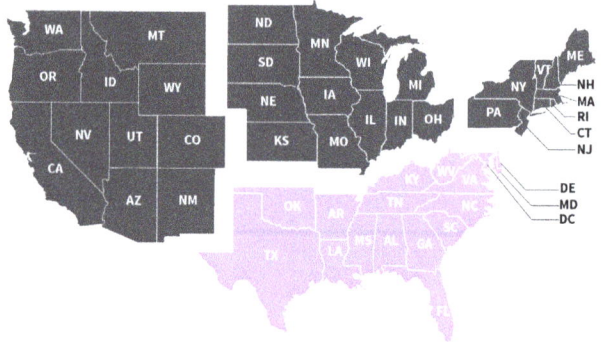

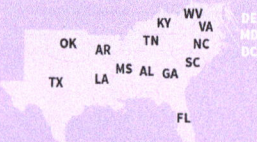

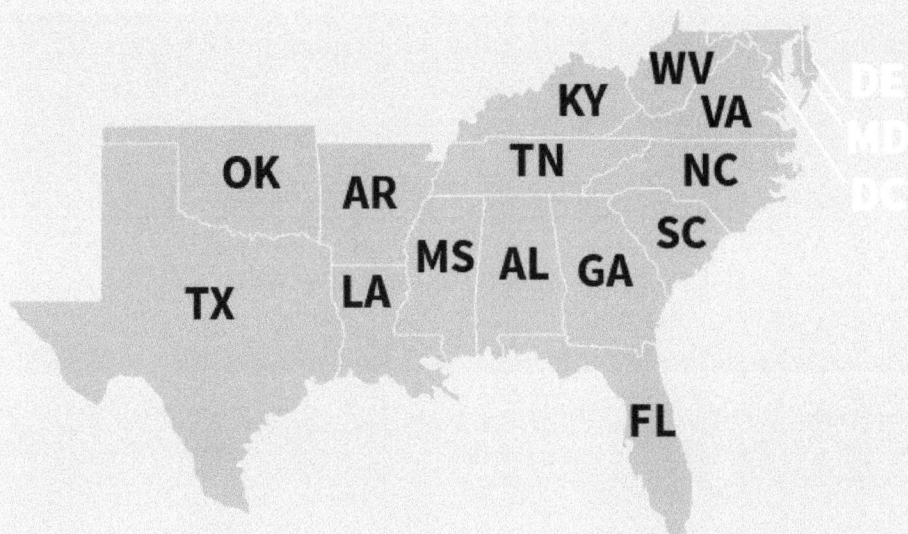

16 Programs | 16 States

1. AL - Auburn University
2. DC - The George Washington University
3. FL – Florida State University
4. GA - Emory University
5. LA - Tulane University
6. NC - Catawba College
7. NC - Duke University
8. NC - Elon University
9. NC - University of North Carolina at Chapel Hill
10. OK - Oklahoma City University
11. OK - University of Oklahoma
12. TN - Belmont University
13. TX - Baylor University
14. TX - Texas Christian University (TCU)
15. VA - Shenandoah University
16. VA - Virginia Commonwealth University

THEATRE PROGRAMS

School	Avg. GPA, SAT Evidence Based Reading and Writing (ERW), SAT Math (M), and ACT Composite (C) Early Decision (ED): Yes/No	Admission Statistics	Program(s) See website for additional options.	Artistic Review Required (Req.)
Auburn University	GPA: 3.97 SAT (ERW): 590-650 SAT (M): 580-680 ACT (C): 24-30 ED: No	Overall College Admit Rate: 71% Undergrad Enrollment: 24,931 Total Enrollment: 31,526	BA Theatre BFA Theatre Degrees Awarded in the Program(s): 19	None req.
The George Washington University (GWU)	GPA: N/A SAT (ERW): 640-720 SAT (M): 630-730 ACT (C): 29-33 ED: Yes	Overall College Admit Rate: 43% Undergrad Enrollment: 11,762 Total Enrollment: 27,017	BA Theatre Degrees Awarded in the Program(s): 4	None req.
Florida State University	GPA: 3.59 SAT (ERW): 620-670 SAT (M): 600-670 ACT (C): 27-31 ED: No	Overall College Admit Rate: 32% Undergrad Enrollment: 32,543 Total Enrollment: 43,569	BA Theatre BFA Acting BFA Music Theatre Degrees Awarded in the Program(s): 62	BA Theatre None req. BFA Acting and BFA Music Theatre Prescreen and audition req.
Emory University	GPA: 3.80 SAT (ERW): 680-740 SAT (M): 700-790 ACT (C): 31-34 ED: No	Overall College Admit Rate: 19% Undergrad Enrollment: 7,010 Total Enrollment: 14,002	BA Theater Studies Degrees Awarded in the Program(s): 10	None req.

THEATRE PROGRAMS

School	Avg. GPA, SAT Evidence Based Reading and Writing (ERW), SAT Math (M), and ACT Composite (C) Early Decision (ED): Yes/No	Admission Statistics	Program(s) See website for additional options.	Artistic Review Required (Req.)
Tulane University	GPA: 3.64 SAT (ERW): 680-740 SAT (M): 680-770 ACT (C): 30-33 ED: No	Overall College Admit Rate: 10% Undergrad Enrollment: 7,780 Total Enrollment: 13,127	BA Theatre Degrees Awarded in the Program(s): 9	Audition req. when student is already enrolled - only for the Performance concentration
Catawba College	GPA: 3.59 SAT (ERW): 470-570 SAT (M): 470-570 ACT (C): 17-22 ED: No	Overall College Admit Rate: 52% Undergrad Enrollment: 1,340 Total Enrollment: 1,371	BA Theatre Arts BFA Theatre Arts Degrees Awarded in the Program(s): 3	BA Theatre Arts None req. BFA Theatre Arts: Performance Audition req.
Duke University	GPA: N/A SAT (ERW): 720-770 SAT (M): 750-800 ACT (C): 34-35 ED: Yes	Overall College Admit Rate: 8% Undergrad Enrollment: 6,717 Total Enrollment: 16,172	BA Theater Studies Degrees Awarded in the Program(s): 1	None req.

SOUTH

THEATRE PROGRAMS

School	Avg. GPA, SAT Evidence Based Reading and Writing (ERW), SAT Math (M), and ACT Composite (C) Early Decision (ED): Yes/No	Admission Statistics	Program(s) See website for additional options.	Artistic Review Required (Req.)
Elon University	GPA: 4.04 SAT (ERW): 580-660 SAT (M): 560-660 ACT (C): 25-30 ED: Yes	Overall College Admit Rate: 72% Undergrad Enrollment: 6,291 Total Enrollment: 7,117	BA Drama & Theatre Studies BFA Acting BFA Music Theatre Degrees Awarded in the Program(s): 10	BA Drama & Theatre Studies None req. BFA Acting and BFA Music Theatre Prescreen and audition req.
University of North Carolina at Chapel Hill	GPA: 4.39 SAT (ERW): 640-730 SAT (M): 640-760 ACT (C): 28-33 ED: No	Overall College Admit Rate: 25% Undergrad Enrollment: 19,395 Total Enrollment: 30,092	BA Dramatic Art Degrees Awarded in the Program(s): 19	None req.
Oklahoma City University	GPA: N/A SAT (ERW): 550-650 SAT (M): 530-610 ACT (C): 22-29 ED: No	Overall College Admit Rate: 73% Undergrad Enrollment: 1,527 Total Enrollment: 2,617	BA Theatre BFA Acting Degrees Awarded in the Program(s): 4	Audition and interview req.
University of Oklahoma	GPA: 3.63 SAT (ERW): 560-650 SAT (M): 540-650 ACT (C): 23-29 ED: No	Overall College Admit Rate: 83% Undergrad Enrollment: 21,383 Total Enrollment: 27,772	BFA Theatre BFA Musical Theatre Degrees Awarded in the Program(s): 38	BFA Theatre: Acting Audition req. BFA Musical Theatre Prescreen and audition req.

THEATRE PROGRAMS

School	Avg. GPA, SAT Evidence Based Reading and Writing (ERW), SAT Math (M), and ACT Composite (C) **Early Decision (ED): Yes/No**	Admission Statistics	Program(s) **See website for additional options.**	Artistic Review Required (Req.)
Belmont University	GPA: 3.83 SAT (ERW): 580-660 SAT (M): 540-640 ACT (C): 23-30 ED: No	Overall College Admit Rate: 83% Undergrad Enrollment: 6,631 Total Enrollment: 8,204	BA Theatre and Drama BFA Theatre BFA Musical Theatre BM Musical Theatre BA Voice, emphasis: Musical Theatre Degrees Awarded in the Program(s): 3	BA Theatre and Drama None req. BFA Theatre, BFA Musical Theatre, BM Musical Theatre, and BA Voice Audition req.
Baylor University	GPA: N/A SAT (ERW): 600-680 SAT (M): 590-680 ACT (C): 26-31 ED: Yes	Overall College Admit Rate: 68% Undergrad Enrollment: 14,399 Total Enrollment: 19,297	BA Theatre Arts BFA Theatre Performance Degrees Awarded in the Program(s): 23	Prescreen, audition, interview, and portfolio req.

SOUTH

THEATRE PROGRAMS

School	Avg. GPA, SAT Evidence Based Reading and Writing (ERW), SAT Math (M), and ACT Composite (C) Early Decision (ED): Yes/No	Admission Statistics	Program(s) See website for additional options.	Artistic Review Required (Req.)
Texas Christian University (TCU)	GPA: N/A SAT (ERW): 560-660 SAT (M): 550-660 ACT (C): 25-31 ED: No	Overall College Admit Rate: 48% Undergrad Enrollment: 9,704 Total Enrollment: 11,379	BA Theatre BFA Theatre Degrees Awarded in the Program(s): 11	BA Theatre None req. BFA Theatre Prescreen and audition for Acting and Musical Theatre. Portfolio also req. for the Theatre Studies emphasis
Shenandoah University	GPA: 3.55 SAT (ERW): 510-630 SAT (M): 500-600 ACT (C): 19-26 ED: No	Overall College Admit Rate: 74% Undergrad Enrollment: 2,267 Total Enrollment: 4,174	BFA Acting BFA Musical Theatre Degrees Awarded in the Program(s): N/A	BFA Acting Audition req. BFA Musical Theatre Prescreen and audition req.
Virginia Commonwealth University (VCU)	GPA: 3.72 SAT (ERW): 540-640 SAT (M): 520-610 ACT (C): 21-28 ED: No	Overall College Admit Rate: 91% Undergrad Enrollment: 21,943 Total Enrollment: 29,070	BA Theatre BFA Theatre Degrees Awarded in the Program(s): 36	BA Theatre Interview req. BFA Theatre Prescreen and audition req.

AUBURN UNIVERSITY

Address: Auburn University, Auburn, AL 36849
Website: *https://cla.auburn.edu/theatre/*
Contact: *http://www.auburn.edu/enrollment/contact_us.php*
Phone: (334) 844-4084
Email: ulricpv@auburn.edu

COST OF ATTENDANCE:

In-State Tuition & Fees: $11,796 | **Additional Expenses:** $21,648
Total: $33,444

Out-of-State Tuition & Fees: $31,956 | **Additional Expenses:** $21,648
Total: $53,604

Financial Aid: http://www.auburn.edu/administration/business-finance/finaid/

ADDITIONAL INFORMATION:

Available Degree(s)

- BA Theatre
- BFA Theatre, options: Performance; Music Theatre; Management; Design/Technology

Artistic Review Requirement

There is no artistic review requirement for incoming freshmen. Interested BFA students enter as BA students and only gain acceptance to the BFA program after a successful portfolio review towards the end of their second year.

Scholarships Offered

Applicants are eligible for merit-based and achievement scholarships. Non-resident scholarships are up to $16,500 and resident scholarships go up to $10,500. Auburn University also awards general scholarships and department scholarships.

Special Opportunities

The Telfair Peet Theatre houses multi-story costume and scenery shops and a black box theatre with a state-of-the-art digital lighting system.

Notable Alumni

Ashley Crow, Thom Gossom, Jr., Justice Leak, Michael O'Neill, Kimberly Page, and Octavia Spencer

ALABAMA

ARKANSAS

DELAWARE

DISTRICT OF COLUMBIA

FLORIDA

GEORGIA

KENTUCKY

LOUISIANA

MARYLAND

MISSISSIPPI

NORTH CAROLINA

OKLAHOMA

SOUTH CAROLINA

TENNESSEE

TEXAS

VIRGINIA

WEST VIRGINIA

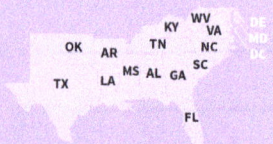

THE GEORGE WASHINGTON UNIVERSITY

Address: 814 20th Street NW, 3rd Floor, Washington, DC 20052
Website: *https://corcoran.gwu.edu/theatre-undergraduate*
Contact: *https://corcoran.gwu.edu/contact*
Phone: (202) 994-1700
Email: corcoranschool@gwu.edu

COST OF ATTENDANCE:

Tuition & Fees: $59,780 | **Additional Expenses:** $19,540
Total: $79,320

Financial Aid: https://financialaid.gwu.edu/

ADDITIONAL INFORMATION:

Available Degree(s)

- BA Theatre

Artistic Review Requirement

There is no artistic review requirement for admission to the program. However, applicants must audition for consideration for the Corcoran Scholars program.

Scholarships Offered

Students who are admitted as Corcoran Scholars receive a renewable award. Furthermore, all GWU students may be eligible for Presidential Academic Scholarships, the Cisneros Scholars program, or the International Baccalaureate (IB) Scholarship. No additional application is necessary to be considered for the Presidential Academic Scholarship.

Special Opportunities

Students are encouraged to audition for any of the performance opportunities held on campus. Corcoran School of the Arts & Design hosts a mainstage production, a cabaret, and a spring dance concert. Furthermore, students may audition and apply to be a Corcoran Scholar. This group of students receive a renewable scholarship and priority housing placement in the Arts + Design Living Learning Community.

Notable Alumni

Casey Affleck, Emily Axford, Alec Baldwin, Courtney Cox, Manish Dayal, Donna Dixon, Kevin Peter Hall, Rooney Mara, Ross Martin, Dina Merrill, T.J. Miller, Lee Phillip, Kerry Washington, and Scott Wolf

ALABAMA

ARKANSAS

DELAWARE

DISTRICT OF COLUMBIA

FLORIDA

GEORGIA

KENTUCKY

LOUISIANA

MARYLAND

MISSISSIPPI

NORTH CAROLINA

OKLAHOMA

SOUTH CAROLINA

TENNESSEE

TEXAS

VIRGINIA

WEST VIRGINIA

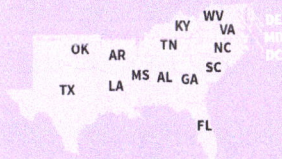

SOUTH

FLORIDA STATE UNIVERSITY

Address: 540 W. Call Street, 239 Fine Arts Building, Tallahassee, FL 32306
Website: *https://theatre.fsu.edu/*
Contact: *https://admissions.fsu.edu/contact/*
Phone: (850) 644-6200
Email: admissions@fsu.edu

COST OF ATTENDANCE:

In-State Tuition & Fees: $6,516 | **Additional Expenses:** $16,512
Total: $23,028

Out-of-State Tuition & Fees: $21,683 | **Additional Expenses:** $16,512
Total: $38,195

Financial Aid: https://financialaid.fsu.edu/

ADDITIONAL INFORMATION:

Available Degree(s)
- BA Theatre
- BFA Acting
- BFA Music Theatre

Artistic Review Requirement
The BA in Theatre does not require an artistic review, however a separate application is required for entry to the major. Prospective students must submit a prescreen and complete a callback audition. The BFA Acting prescreen supplement consists of a one-page essay, a headshot, theatrical resume, three letters of recommendation, and a monologue. The BFA in Music Theatre requires a prescreen and a callback audition.

Scholarships Offered
The School of Theatre awards scholarships to selected incoming and continuing students. BFA students can qualify based on academic ability and potential.

Special Opportunities
FSU's London Theatre Program is a comprehensive one-year program designed and led by the School of Theatre faculty; a summer program is also available. The Academy offers a wide range of playwriting, acting, design, and stage management classes. classes with leading theatre artists. This comprehensive program focused on professional theatre and the entertainment industry. Coursework includes stage combat, makeup, dialects, and audition techniques. Seniors present a Showcase in NYC or L.A. for agents and casting directors.

Notable Alumni
Frankie Alvarez, Senait Ashenafi, King Bach, Vanessa Baden, Dan Bakkedahl, Trenesha Biggers, Ricou Browning, Cody Burger, Matt Cohen, Gregor Collins, Mekia Cox, Valerie Cruz, Dimitri Diatchenko, Faye Dunaway, Tiffany Fallon, Luis Fonsi, Suzanne Friedline, Joanna Garcia, Paul Gleason, Montego Glover, Andre Gordon, Jennifer Hammon, Joey Haro, Cheryl Hines, Andre Holland, Polly Holliday, Traylor Howard, Nancy Kulp, Billy Lane, Jon Locke, DeLane Matthews, Michelle McCool, Gerald McCullouch, Vic Morrow, Henry Polic II, John Preston, Burt Reynolds, Chay Santini, Amy Seimetz, Sonny Shroyer, Richard Simmons, Pat Skipper, J Smith-Cameron, Tonea Stewart, Erik Stolhanske, Gabriel Traversari, Robert Urich, Casper Van Dien, and Joseph Will

ALABAMA

ARKANSAS

DELAWARE

DISTRICT OF COLUMBIA

FLORIDA

GEORGIA

KENTUCKY

LOUISIANA

MARYLAND

MISSISSIPPI

NORTH CAROLINA

OKLAHOMA

SOUTH CAROLINA

TENNESSEE

TEXAS

VIRGINIA

WEST VIRGINIA

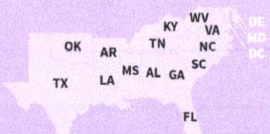

EMORY UNIVERSITY

Address: 201 Dowman Dr, Atlanta, GA 30322
Website: *http://theater.emory.edu/home/index.html*
Contact: *http://theater.emory.edu/home/about/contact.html*
Phone: (404) 727-6123
Email: admission@emory.edu

COST OF ATTENDANCE:

Tuition & Fees: $55,998 | **Additional Expenses:** $19,426
Total: $75,424

Financial Aid: https://studentaid.emory.edu/index.html

ADDITIONAL INFORMATION:

Available Degree(s)

- BA Theater Studies

Artistic Review Requirement

There is no audition requirement. However, some applicants may be asked to include an optional arts supplement. The supplement consists of a resume and 2 contrasting monologues.

Scholarships Offered

Emory offers scholarships/awards to undergraduates of any major. The Woodruff Dean's Achievement Scholarship is a $10,000 merit scholarship that is awarded to Emory freshmen. The Emory University Grant is a need-based award. The Emory Opportunity Award is a renewable merit award offered to accepted applicants.

Special Opportunities

Theater students are encouraged to study abroad at the various programs specific to theater majors. These include a semester at the Accademia dell'Arte in Italy, a semester at the London Academy of Music and Dramatic Art (LAMDA), or Emory's British Studies Program at Oxford University.

Notable Alumni

Orny Adams, Erica Ash, Fala Chen, Justin Lazard, Natalia Livingston, Adam Richman, Jim Sarbh, Stephen Schneider, and Eugene Williams

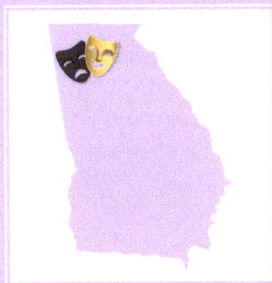

ALABAMA

ARKANSAS

DELAWARE

DISTRICT OF COLUMBIA

FLORIDA

GEORGIA

KENTUCKY

LOUISIANA

MARYLAND

MISSISSIPPI

NORTH CAROLINA

OKLAHOMA

SOUTH CAROLINA

TENNESSEE

TEXAS

VIRGINIA

WEST VIRGINIA

SOUTH

ALABAMA

ARKANSAS

DELAWARE

DISTRICT OF
COLUMBIA

FLORIDA

GEORGIA

KENTUCKY

LOUISIANA

MARYLAND

MISSISSIPPI

NORTH CAROLINA

OKLAHOMA

SOUTH CAROLINA

TENNESSEE

TEXAS

VIRGINIA

WEST VIRGINIA

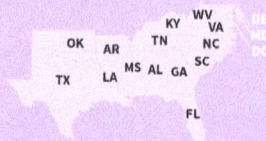

TULANE UNIVERSITY

Address: 6823 St Charles Ave, New Orleans, LA 70118
Website: *https://liberalarts.tulane.edu/departments/theatre-dance/*
programs/undergraduate/theatre
Contact: *https://liberalarts.tulane.edu/departments/theatre-dance/*
contact-us
Phone: (504) 865-5389
Email: undergrad.admission@tulane.edu

COST OF ATTENDANCE:

Tuition & Fees: $60,814 | **Additional Expenses:** $18,828
Total: $80,232

Financial Aid: https://admission.tulane.edu/tuition-aid

ADDITIONAL INFORMATION:

Available Degree(s)

- BA Theatre, concentrations: Performance (Acting and
  Directing); Design/Technology; Theatre Generalist

Artistic Review Requirement

Applicants must audition if they choose the Performance
concentration. Auditions take place after the student is already
enrolled in the program.

Scholarships Offered

Tulane University offers two full-tuition merit scholarships: the
Deans' Honor Scholarship and the Paul Tulane Award. They also
offer one total-cost merit scholarship: the Stamps Scholarship.

Special Opportunities

Theatre majors take coursework in the Suzuki Method, clowning
and improvisation, dialects, and more.

Notable Alumni

Bryan Batt, Evan Farmer, Paul Michael Glaser, Rick Hurst, Anthony
Laciura, Christian LeBlanc, Enrique Murciano, Ed Nelson, Al Shea,
and Harold Sylvester

CATAWBA COLLEGE

Address: 2300 W Innes St, Salisbury, NC 28144
Website: *https://catawba.edu/academics/programs/undergraduate/theatre-arts/*
Contact: *https://catawba.edu/contact-catawba/*
Phone: (704) 637-4402
Email: admission@catawba.edu

COST OF ATTENDANCE:

Tuition & Fees: $32,380 | **Additional Expenses:** $15,964
Total: $48,344

Financial Aid: https://catawba.edu/about/offices/finaid/

ADDITIONAL INFORMATION:

Available Degree(s)

- BA Theatre Arts
- BFA Theatre Arts, tracks: Performance

Artistic Review Requirement

Applicants for the BA Theatre Arts program are not required to undergo an artistic review. However, auditions are required for Theatre Arts Scholarship consideration. BFA: Theatre Arts, track: Performance applicants must submit a headshot, resume, essay, 2 contrasting monologues, and a short answer response. Submit all materials via Acceptd.

Scholarships Offered

Merit-based scholarships offered at Catawba College include two full-tuition scholarships: the Socratic Scholarship and the Spirit of Catawba Scholarship. The Theatre Arts program awards an invitation-only full-tuition scholarship—the Burnet Hobgood Theatre Arts Scholarship.

Special Opportunities

Through a unique partnership with Lee Street theatre in Salisbury, Theatre Arts majors at Catawba College may take advantage of a semester-long production internship. Theatre Arts majors have studied abroad in U.K., Italy, Costa Rica, Greece, Germany, Japan, and Estonia.

Notable Alumni

Katie Carpenter and Jasika Nicole

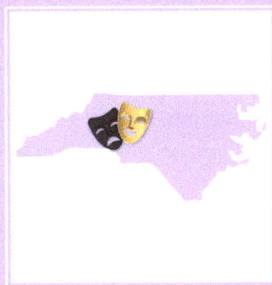

ALABAMA
ARKANSAS
DELAWARE
DISTRICT OF COLUMBIA
FLORIDA
GEORGIA
KENTUCKY
LOUISIANA
MARYLAND
MISSISSIPPI
NORTH CAROLINA
OKLAHOMA
SOUTH CAROLINA
TENNESSEE
TEXAS
VIRGINIA
WEST VIRGINIA

SOUTH

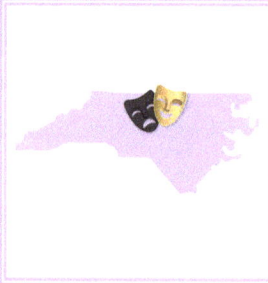

ALABAMA

ARKANSAS

DELAWARE

DISTRICT OF COLUMBIA

FLORIDA

GEORGIA

KENTUCKY

LOUISIANA

MARYLAND

MISSISSIPPI

NORTH CAROLINA

OKLAHOMA

SOUTH CAROLINA

TENNESSEE

TEXAS

VIRGINIA

WEST VIRGINIA

DUKE UNIVERSITY

Address: Duke University, Durham, NC 27708
Website: *https://theaterstudies.duke.edu/*
Contact: *https://admissions.duke.edu/contact/*
Phone: (919) 684-3214
Email: undergrad-admissions@duke.edu

COST OF ATTENDANCE:

Tuition & Fees: $60,408 | Additional Expenses: $20,894
Total: $81,302

Financial Aid: https://financialaid.duke.edu/

ADDITIONAL INFORMATION:

Available Degree(s)

- BA Theater Studies

Artistic Review Requirement

There is no audition requirement. However, students may submit an optional arts supplement via Slideroom. The arts supplement requires a personal statement, resume, and 2 contrasting monologues (or 1 monologue and 1 song).

Scholarships Offered

Duke University mainly offers need-based grants and scholarships to students. Students are welcome to apply to outside scholarships.

Special Opportunities

Duke encourages theater students to study away at programs such as the Duke in London – Drama program, the Duke in New York Arts & Media program, or the Duke in New York Summer Internships in the City program. For more information, visit: https://theaterstudies.duke.edu/academics/global-education

Notable Alumni

Andy Baldwin, Jayne Brooke, Ryan Carnes, Bailey Chase, Jack Coleman, Paul W. Downs, Sean Flynn, Annabeth Gish, Kevin Gray, Jared Harris, Ken Jeong, Keith Lucas, Ellary Porterfield, David H. Steinberg, Rita Volk, and Randall Wallace

ELON UNIVERSITY

Address: 100 Campus Drive, Elon, NC 27244
Website: *https://www.elon.edu/u/academics/arts-and-sciences/performing-arts/*
Contact: *https://www.elon.edu/u/about/contact-elon/*
Phone: (336) 278-2000
Email: admissions@elon.edu

COST OF ATTENDANCE:

Tuition & Fees: $38,725 | **Additional Expenses:** $16,922
Total: $55,647

Financial Aid: https://www.elon.edu/u/admissions/undergraduate/financial-aid/

ADDITIONAL INFORMATION:

Available Degree(s)

- BA Drama & Theatre Studies
- BFA Acting
- BFA Music Theatre

Artistic Review Requirement

An audition is required for the following programs: Acting and Theatrical Design & Technology. All items must be submitted via Acceptd.

The BFA Acting and BFA Music Theatre require a prescreen and callback audition. The BFA Acting prescreen includes a resume, headshot, recorded personal statement, and two contrasting monologues. The audition may take place in person or live, virtually. An interview takes place during the audition. The BFA Music Theatre includes monologues, songs, and a dance requirement. The BA in Drama & Theatre Studies does not require an artistic review.

Scholarships Offered

Elon University offers numerous merit-based scholarships, talent-based scholarships including Performing Arts Scholarships, as well as Fellows and Scholars programs (scholarships ranging from $7,500 to $13,500 per year).

Special Opportunities

The Center for the Arts is a 75,000-square-foot facility for performance and teaching. It includes the following facilities: McCrary Theatre, Yeager Recital Hall, Black Box Theatre, three dance studios, practice rooms and studios, costume shops, Pilates Studio, and more.

Notable Alumni

John Bucchino, Rich Blomquist, Dave Clemmons, Reno Collier, Lisa Goldstein, Grant Gustin, Katie Hillard, Kelli O'Hara, Geof Pilkington, Martin Ritt, Ben Seay, Brent Sexton, Mike Trainor, Taylor Trensch, Kenneth Utt, Barrett Wilbert Weed, and Chris Wood

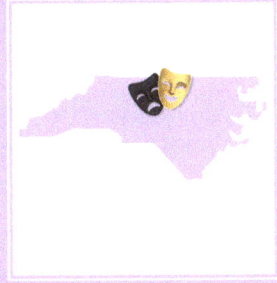

ALABAMA

ARKANSAS

DELAWARE

DISTRICT OF COLUMBIA

FLORIDA

GEORGIA

KENTUCKY

LOUISIANA

MARYLAND

MISSISSIPPI

NORTH CAROLINA

OKLAHOMA

SOUTH CAROLINA

TENNESSEE

TEXAS

VIRGINIA

WEST VIRGINIA

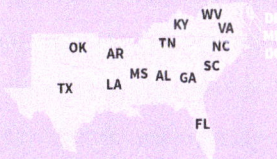

SOUTH

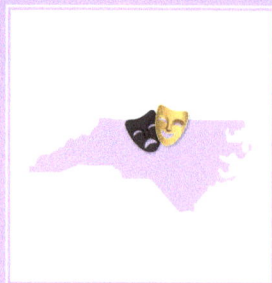

UNIVERSITY OF NORTH CAROLINA AT CHAPEL HILL

Address: Center for Dramatic Art, Chapel Hill, NC 27599
Website: *http://drama.unc.edu/*
Contact: *https://www.unc.edu/about/contact-us/*
Phone: (919) 962-2211
Email: Contact via contact form or phone.

COST OF ATTENDANCE:

In-State Tuition & Fees: $9,018 | **Additional Expenses:** $15,248
Total: $24,266

Out-of-State Tuition & Fees: $36,000 | Additional Expenses: $16,026
Total: $52,026

Financial Aid: https://studentaid.unc.edu/

ADDITIONAL INFORMATION:

Available Degree(s)

- BA Dramatic Art

Artistic Review Requirement

There is no artistic review requirement.

Scholarships Offered

UNC at Chapel Hill offers many need-based and merit-based scholarship opportunities for students. Most are for students who are residents of North Carolina. Students may consider applying for external opportunities as well. Some require students to apply by the early action deadline.

Special Opportunities

Drama students are encouraged to study abroad at Trinity College Dublin, the London Academy of Music and Dramatic Art (LAMDA), and the Gaiety School of Acting in Dublin. Students may also be eligible for the Elizabeth Malone Roughton Study Abroad Scholarship.

Notable Alumni

Whit Bissell, Lewis Black, Wyatt Cenac, Kelen Coleman, Dan Cortese, Billy Crudup, Michael Cumpsty, Melissa Claire Egan, John Forsythe, Louise Fletcher, Rick Fox, Ed Grady, Andy Griffith, George Grizzard, Anne Haney, Mamrie Hart, Liza Huber, Ken Jeong, Ben Jones, Darwin Joston, Kay Kyser, Sharon Lawrence, Michael Louden, Crystal McLaurin-Coney, Jane McNeill, Nolan North, Jack Palance, Jim Rash, Adam Reed, Jeff Richards, Randolph Scott, Nick Searcy, Lionel Stander, and Christine White

ALABAMA

ARKANSAS

DELAWARE

DISTRICT OF COLUMBIA

FLORIDA

GEORGIA

KENTUCKY

LOUISIANA

MARYLAND

MISSISSIPPI

NORTH CAROLINA

OKLAHOMA

SOUTH CAROLINA

TENNESSEE

TEXAS

VIRGINIA

WEST VIRGINIA

OKLAHOMA CITY UNIVERSITY

Address: 2501 N. Blackwelder, Oklahoma City, OK 73106
Website: *https://www.okcu.edu/theatre/home/*
Contact: *https://www.okcu.edu/main/contact/*
Phone: (405) 208-5000
Email: N/A

COST OF ATTENDANCE:

Tuition & Fees: $33,404 | **Additional Expenses:** $16,276
Total: $49,680

Financial Aid: https://www.okcu.edu/financialaid/home/

ADDITIONAL INFORMATION:

Available Degree(s):

- BA Theatre
- BFA Acting

Artistic Review Requirement

The BA Theatre program requires an audition, interview, theatre resume, headshot, and 2 letters of recommendation. The BFA Acting requires 2 contrasting monologues, an improvisation session, resume, headshot, and interview. All materials must be submitted via Acceptd.

Scholarships Offered

Students in the School of Theatre are eligible for academic scholarships based on high school GPA and standardized test scores (up to $7,800 a year).

Special Opportunities

The Schools of Dance, Music, and Theatre produce 55 productions each year. There are numerous opportunities for students to audition and earn roles.

Notable Alumni

Belinda Allyn, Colin Anderson, Heather Botts, Jane Bunting, Kristin Chenoweth, Jacob Gutierrez, Wes Hart, Jeremy Hays, Eryn LeCroy, Stacey Logan, Elliott Mattox, Tiffany Mann, Will Mann, Matt McMahan, Manna Nichols, Kelli O'Hara, Minami Okamura, Destan Owens, Ernie Pruneda, Ron Raines, Molly Rushing, Jennifer Sanchez, Abby C. Smith, and Darius Wright

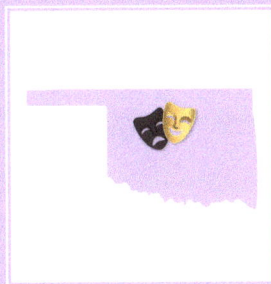

ALABAMA

ARKANSAS

DELAWARE

DISTRICT OF COLUMBIA

FLORIDA

GEORGIA

KENTUCKY

LOUISIANA

MARYLAND

MISSISSIPPI

NORTH CAROLINA

OKLAHOMA

SOUTH CAROLINA

TENNESSEE

TEXAS

VIRGINIA

WEST VIRGINIA

SOUTH

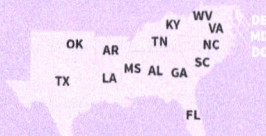

UNIVERSITY OF OKLAHOMA

Address: 660 Parrington Oval, Norman, OK 73019
Website: *https://www.ou.edu/finearts/degrees*
Contact: *http://www.ou.edu/web/about_ou/contact*
Phone: (405) 325-2151
Email: admissions@ou.edu

COST OF ATTENDANCE:

In-State Tuition & Fees: $13,065 | **Additional Expenses:** $11,700
Total: $24,765

Out-of-State Tuition & Fees: $28,869 | **Additional Expenses:** $18,757
Total: $40,569

Financial Aid: http://www.ou.edu/admissions/affordability/financial-aid

ADDITIONAL INFORMATION:

Available Degree(s)

- BFA Theatre, emphasis: Acting
- BFA Musical Theatre

Artistic Review Requirement

Applicants interested in applying for the BFA in Theatre: Acting Emphasis must submit a headshot, theatre resume, statement, letters of recommendation, and an optional submission of 2 contrasting monologues. The BFA Musical Theatre requires a prescreen and audition. Submit materials via Acceptd.

Scholarships Offered

University of Oklahoma offers numerous test score and high school GPA-based scholarships (up to $16,000 over four years for in-state students and $60,000 over four years for out-of-state students and and international students) as well as National Merit Scholarships, Oklahoma State Regents' Academic Scholars Program scholarship and test-optional scholarships.

Special Opportunities

The University of Oklahoma houses numerous facilities for students, including Oklahoma's only European-style performance hall, costume and scene shops, state-of-the-art lighting and sound equipment, and more. Additionally, the University of Oklahoma's Weitzenhoffer School of Musical Theatre hosts the only full musical theatre program in the nation.

Notable Alumni

Skyler Adams, Lou Antonio, Lindsey Bliven, Stephen Dickson, Larry Drake, C.K. Edwards, Ronnie Claire Edwards, Annie Funke, James Garner, Alice Ghostley, Ed Harris, Van Heflin, Adrianna Hicks, Rance Howard, Christian Kane, Roberta Knie, Kelly Mantle, Olivia Munn, Meg Randall, Hollis Scarborough, Iqbal Theba, Matt Villines, and Dennis Weaver, and Kristen Beth Williams

ALABAMA

ARKANSAS

DELAWARE

DISTRICT OF COLUMBIA

FLORIDA

GEORGIA

KENTUCKY

LOUISIANA

MARYLAND

MISSISSIPPI

NORTH CAROLINA

OKLAHOMA

SOUTH CAROLINA

TENNESSEE

TEXAS

VIRGINIA

WEST VIRGINIA

BELMONT UNIVERSITY

Address: 1900 Belmont Blvd, Nashville, TN 37212
Website: *https://www.belmont.edu/cmpa/theatre-dance/undergrad/index.html*
Contact: *https://www.belmont.edu/admissions/index.html*
Phone: (615) 460-6000
Email: N/A

COST OF ATTENDANCE:

Tuition & Fees: $38,430 | **Additional Expenses:** $19,875
Total: $58,305

Financial Aid: https://www.belmont.edu/sfs/aid/undergrad.html

ADDITIONAL INFORMATION:

Available Degree(s)

- BA Theatre & Drama, emphasis: Performance
- BFA Theatre
- BFA Musical Theatre
- BM Musical Theatre
- BA Voice, emphasis: Musical Theatre

Artistic Review Requirement

The BA Theatre & Drama does not require an artistic review. Belmont University does not require a pre-screen. Auditions are required for the BFA Theatre, the BFA and BM in Musical Theatre. The BFA Theatre requires 2 contrasting monologues. The BFA and BM in Musical Theatre require 1 aria song, 2 musical theatre songs, 1 monologue, a group dance class, headshot, and resume. The BA Voice: Musical Theatre requires 2 classical pieces, 1 musical theatre song, a repertory list, and resume.

Scholarships Offered

All applicants are automatically considered for merit scholarships when they submit their Belmont University application. Students who apply as test-optional will be considered for merit scholarships based on their high school GPA and overall strength of their application. General Freshman Academic Merit Scholarships ($3,000 to $10,000 annually) are awarded on a rolling basis following the offer of admission. Belmont also offers named awards, which recognize approximately the top two percent of all freshman applicants.

Special Opportunities

Several of Belmont University's productions have won the American Prize in Musical Theatre Performance. Students in Belmont's Musical Theatre program are known for the "Belmont Belt" - their open and healthy vocal sound.

Notable Alumni

McKinley Belcher III, Sean Hetherington, DJ Qualls, and Tony Vincent

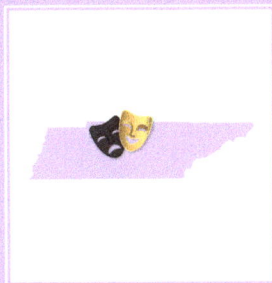

ALABAMA
ARKANSAS
DELAWARE
DISTRICT OF COLUMBIA
FLORIDA
GEORGIA
KENTUCKY
LOUISIANA
MARYLAND
MISSISSIPPI
NORTH CAROLINA
OKLAHOMA
SOUTH CAROLINA
TENNESSEE
TEXAS
VIRGINIA
WEST VIRGINIA

SOUTH

BAYLOR UNIVERSITY

Address: 1311 S 5th St, Waco, TX 76706
Website: *https://www.baylor.edu/theatre/index.php?id=947375*
Contact: *https://www.baylor.edu/admissions/index.php?id=871966*
Phone: (254) 710-3436
Email: admissions@baylor.edu

COST OF ATTENDANCE:

Tuition & Fees: $50,232 | **Additional Expenses:** $12,682
Total: $62,914

Financial Aid: https://www.baylor.edu/admissions/index.php?id=871964

ADDITIONAL INFORMATION:

Available Degree(s)

- BA Theatre Arts, concentration: Musical Theatre
- BFA Theatre Performance, concentration: Musical Theatre

Artistic Review Requirement

All programs in the Department of Theatre Arts require a prescreen, interview, audition, and portfolio. The audition consists of 2 contrasting monologues and an optional song.

Scholarships Offered

All applicants to Baylor University, including students who apply as test optional and first-time international students, are automatically considered for academic scholarships. Other scholarships include a scholarship valued at approximately $60,000 per year at the Getterman Scholars Program and a full-tuition scholarship at the Invitation to Excellence program.

Special Opportunities

The Theatre Department gathers weekly to observe student-produced work and other presentations, which prospective students are encouraged to attend. Every two years, students may participate in a European study abroad program, which has included lengthy stays in England or France. This program has also brought students to Italy, Greece, Belgium, and Ireland. Additionally, the Theatre Department co-sponsors the Fine Arts Living Learning Center, a community of student artists just next door to Baylor's premiere Fine Arts facilities.

Notable Alumni

Nancy Barrett, Crystal Bernard, Carole Cook, Elizabeth A. Davis, Randy Flagler, Jackson Hurst, Kara Killmer, Angela Kinsey, Brooklyn McKnight, Bailey McKnight, Austin Miller, Derek Phillips, David Sullivan, Allison Tolman, Noble Willingham, Jennifer Vasquez, and Stephanie Young

ALABAMA

ARKANSAS

DELAWARE

DISTRICT OF COLUMBIA

FLORIDA

GEORGIA

KENTUCKY

LOUISIANA

MARYLAND

MISSISSIPPI

NORTH CAROLINA

OKLAHOMA

SOUTH CAROLINA

TENNESSEE

TEXAS

VIRGINIA

WEST VIRGINIA

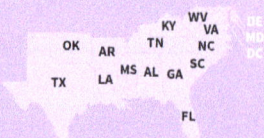

TEXAS CHRISTIAN UNIVERSITY (TCU)

Address: 2800 South University Dr., Fort Worth, TX 76109
Website: *https://finearts.tcu.edu/theatre/academics/areas-of-study/*
Contact: *https://admissions.tcu.edu/connect.php*
Phone: (817) 257-7000
Email: frogmail@tcu.edu

COST OF ATTENDANCE:

Tuition & Fees: $51,660 | **Additional Expenses:** $20,168
Total: $71,828

Financial Aid: https://financialaid.tcu.edu/

ADDITIONAL INFORMATION:

Available Degree(s)

- BA Theatre
- BFA Theatre, emphases: Theatre Studies; Acting; Musical Theatre

Artistic Review Requirement

All emphases of the BFA Theatre degree require a prescreen and audition. The BFA Theatre: Theatre Studies requires a portfolio as well. Submit via Acceptd. The BA Theatre does not require an artistic review.

Scholarships Offered

The Nordan Fine Arts Awards are competitive scholarships for students in the College of Fine Arts. The Nordan Young Artist Award is $10,000+ for incoming freshmen, based on application audition. Students may then renew this scholarship for their remaining years.

Special Opportunities

The student to faculty ratio for BFA performance classes is 12:1. All theatre students train together in fundamental performance coursework. BFA Musical Theatre students also get specific training on musical theatre performance, musical theatre dance, theory, history, and private voice lessons. Students are encouraged to audition for local theatres while they are enrolled at TCU.

Notable Alumni

Norman Alden, Betty Buckley, Tudi Rouche, Travis Schuldt, Shantel VanSanten, Van Williams, and Travis Willingham

ALABAMA

ARKANSAS

DELAWARE

DISTRICT OF COLUMBIA

FLORIDA

GEORGIA

KENTUCKY

LOUISIANA

MARYLAND

MISSISSIPPI

NORTH CAROLINA

OKLAHOMA

SOUTH CAROLINA

TENNESSEE

TEXAS

VIRGINIA

WEST VIRGINIA

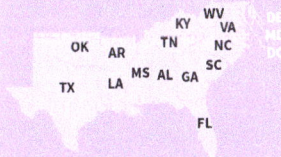

SOUTH

ALABAMA

ARKANSAS

DELAWARE

DISTRICT OF COLUMBIA

FLORIDA

GEORGIA

KENTUCKY

LOUISIANA

MARYLAND

MISSISSIPPI

NORTH CAROLINA

OKLAHOMA

SOUTH CAROLINA

TENNESSEE

TEXAS

VIRGINIA

WEST VIRGINIA

SHENANDOAH UNIVERSITY

Address: 1460 University Dr, Winchester, VA 22601
Website: *https://www.su.edu/conservatory/areas-of-study/acting/*
Contact: *https://www.su.edu/admissions/contact-us/*
Phone: (540) 665-4581
Email: Admit@su.edu

COST OF ATTENDANCE:

Tuition & Fees: $33,140 | **Additional Expenses:** $16,442
Total: $49,582

Financial Aid: https://www.su.edu/financial-aid/

ADDITIONAL INFORMATION:

Available Degree(s)

- BFA Acting
- BFA Musical Theatre

Artistic Review Requirement

The BFA in Acting requires an audition that consists of 2 monologues, a headshot, and a resume. The BFA in Musical Theatre requires a prescreen and audition.

Scholarships Offered

Theatre students may be eligible for the Shenandoah University Conservatory Scholarship, valued at $2,000-$19,500 per year. This renewable scholarship is based on the student's application and the audition. Students may also be eligible for other merit-based awards, ranging in value from $3,000-$20,000 per year.

Special Opportunities

Students in Shenandoah University's acting program utilize the Meisner technique and learn other methods throughout their studies. They also learn contact improvisation, stage combat, and performance styles.

Notable Alumni

Carter Beauford, Kate Flannery, Scott Monahan, Harold Perrineau, Josh Schauder, Carl Tanner, Mac Wiseman, and Richard Zarou

VIRGINIA COMMONWEALTH UNIVERSITY

Address: Virginia Commonwealth University, Richmond, VA 23284
Website: *https://arts.vcu.edu/academics/departments/theatre/*
Contact: *https://www.vcu.edu/contacts/*
Phone: (804) 828-0100
Email: ugrad@vcu.edu

COST OF ATTENDANCE:

In-State Tuition & Fees: $17,140 | **Additional Expenses:** $17,549
Total: $34,689

Out-of-State Tuition & Fees: $38,478 | **Additional Expenses:** $17,549
Total: $56,027

Financial Aid: https://finaid.vcu.edu/

ADDITIONAL INFORMATION:

Available Degree(s)

- BA Theatre
- BFA Theatre, concentrations: Performance; Musical Theatre

Artistic Review Requirement

The BA Theatre requires a resume, statement of intent, and an interview. The BFA Theatre: Performance requires a prescreen and audition. The prescreen consists of two contrasting monologues (or 1 monologue, 1 song). The BFA Theatre: Musical Theatre requires a prescreen and audition. The prescreen consists of 1 monologue, 2 songs, 1 dance solo, and 1 wild card video. Submit all materials via SlideRoom.

Scholarships Offered

First-year students are automatically considered for VCUarts talent scholarships ($5,000-$12,000 annually) based on academic merit and artistic talent. University scholarship awards vary based on the scholarship, but range from $8,000 per year to $16,000 plus room and board per year.

Special Opportunities

VCUarts Qatar is the sister campus located in Doha, Qatar. Design students may apply to spend a semester at this campus. Additionally, students may study abroad through faculty-led programs in Korea and Italy as well as VCU-affiliated programs.

Notable Alumni

Macon Blair, Stephen Furst, Jason Butler Harner, Bilal Khan, Zachary Knighton, and Boris Kodjoe

ALABAMA
ARKANSAS
DELAWARE
DISTRICT OF COLUMBIA
FLORIDA
GEORGIA
KENTUCKY
LOUISIANA
MARYLAND
MISSISSIPPI
NORTH CAROLINA
OKLAHOMA
SOUTH CAROLINA
TENNESSEE
TEXAS
VIRGINIA
WEST VIRGINIA

SOUTH

CHAPTER 16

REGION FOUR

WEST

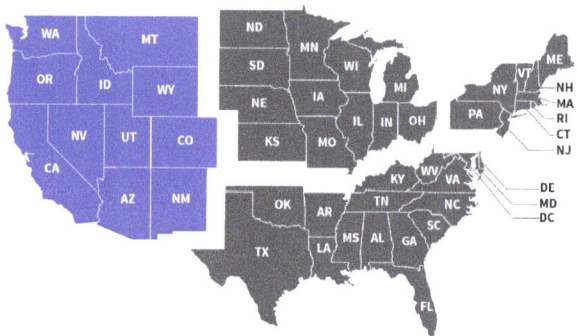

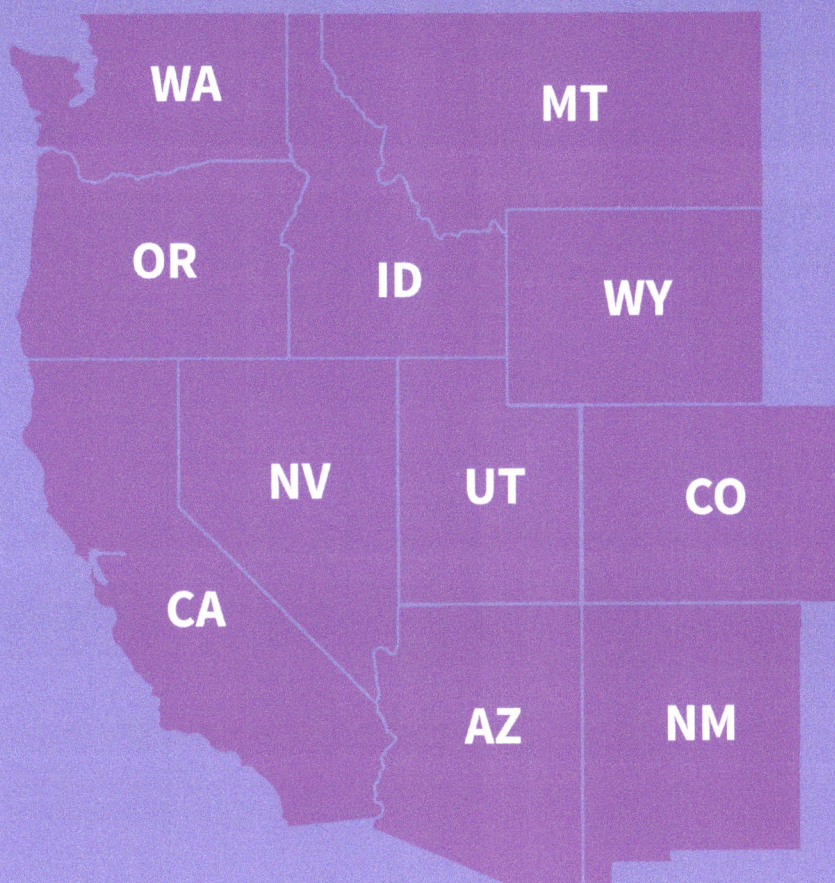

12 Programs | 13 States

1. AZ – University of Arizona
2. CA – American Musical and Dramatic Academy (AMDA)
3. CA - California Institute of the Arts
4. CA - Chapman University
5. CA - Loyola Marymount University (LMU)
6. CA - Pepperdine University
7. CA – University of California, Los Angeles (UCLA)
8. CA - University of California, San Diego (UCSD)
9. CA - University of Southern California (USC)
10. NV - University of Nevada, Las Vegas (UNLV)
11. WA - Cornish College of the Arts
12. WA - Gonzaga University

School	Avg. GPA, SAT Evidence Based Reading and Writing (ERW), SAT Math (M), and ACT Composite (C) Early Decision (ED): Yes/No	Admission Statistics	Program(s) See website for additional options.	Artistic Review Required (Req.)
University of Arizona	GPA: 3.43 SAT (ERW): 550-660 SAT (M): 540-690 ACT (C): 21-29 ED: No	Overall College Admit Rate: 85% Undergrad Enrollment: 36,503 Total Enrollment: 46,932	BA Theatre Arts BFA Musical Theatre BFA Theatre Production: Professional Actor Training Degrees Awarded in the Program(s): 56	BA Theatre Arts None req. BFA Musical Theatre and BFA Theatre Production: Professional Actor Training Prescreen and audition req.
American Musical & Dramatic Academy (AMDA)	GPA: N/A SAT (ERW): N/A* SAT (M): N/A* ACT (C): N/A* *Test-optional ED: No	Overall College Admit Rate: 44% Undergrad Enrollment: 1,395 Total Enrollment: 1,399	BFA Acting BFA Dance Theatre BFA Music Theatre BFA Performing Arts BA Theatre Arts Degrees Awarded in the Program(s): 213	Audition req.
California Institute of the Arts (CalArts)	GPA: N/A SAT (ERW): N/A* SAT (M): N/A* ACT (C): N/A* *Test-optional ED: Yes	Overall College Admit Rate: 32% Undergrad Enrollment: 783 Total Enrollment: 1,189	BFA Acting Degrees Awarded in the Program(s): 29	Audition req.

School	Avg. GPA, SAT Evidence Based Reading and Writing (ERW), SAT Math (M), and ACT Composite (C) Early Decision (ED): Yes/No	Admission Statistics	Program(s) See website for additional options.	Artistic Review Required (Req.)
Chapman University	GPA: N/A SAT (ERW): 590-670 SAT (M): 580-680 ACT (C): 25-30 ED: Yes	Overall College Admit Rate: 58% Undergrad Enrollment: 7,404 Total Enrollment: 9,761	BFA Theatre Performance BFA Screen Acting BA Theatre Degrees Awarded in the Program(s): 25	BFA Theatre Performance and BFA Screen Acting Audition req. BA Theatre Portfolio req.
Loyola Marymount University (LMU)	GPA: 3.92 SAT (ERW): 620-700 SAT (M): 630-720 ACT (C): 28-32 ED: Yes	Overall College Admit Rate: 46% Undergrad Enrollment: 7,127 Total Enrollment: 10,184	BA Theatre Arts Degrees Awarded in the Program(s): 59	Audition req.
Pepperdine University	GPA: 3.69 SAT (ERW): 600-690 SAT (M): 600-720 ACT (C): 26-31 ED: No	Overall College Admit Rate: 42% Undergrad Enrollment: 3,459 Total Enrollment: 9,554	BA Theatre Arts BA Theatre and Screen Arts Degrees Awarded in the Program(s): 16	BA Theatre Arts: Musical Theatre Prescreen and audition req. BA Theatre and Screen Arts: Acting Audition req.

WEST

THEATRE PROGRAMS

School	Avg. GPA, SAT Evidence Based Reading and Writing (ERW), SAT Math (M), and ACT Composite (C) Early Decision (ED): Yes/No	Admission Statistics	Program(s) See website for additional options.	Artistic Review Required (Req.)
University of California, Los Angeles (UCLA)	GPA: 3.90 SAT (ERW): 650-740 SAT (M): 640-780 ACT (C): 29-34 ED: No	Overall College Admit Rate: 14% Undergrad Enrollment: 31,636 Total Enrollment: 46,000	BA Theater Degrees Awarded in the Program(s): 62	None req. for admittance, unless explicitly asked to interview and audition
University of California, San Diego (UCSD)	GPA: 4.09 SAT (ERW): 620-710 SAT (M): 640-770 ACT (C): 26-33 ED: No	Overall College Admit Rate: 38% Undergrad Enrollment: 31,842 Total Enrollment: 39,576	BA Theatre Degrees Awarded in the Program(s): 40	Audition optional
University of Southern California (USC)	GPA: 3.83 SAT (ERW): 660-740 SAT (M): 680-790 ACT (C): 30-34 ED: No	Overall College Admit Rate: 16% Undergrad Enrollment: 19,606 Total Enrollment: 46,107	BFA Acting for Stage, Screen and New Media BFA Musical Theatre BA Theatre Degrees Awarded in the Program(s): 50	BFA Acting for Stage, Screen, and New Media and BFA Musical Theatre Prescreen and audition req. BA Theatre Portfolio req.
University of Nevada, Las Vegas (UNLV)	GPA: 3.43 SAT (ERW): 520-620 SAT (M): 510-630 ACT (C): 19-25 ED: No	Overall College Admit Rate: 81% Undergrad Enrollment: 25,862 Total Enrollment: 31,140	BA Theatre Degrees Awarded in the Program(s): 40	BA Theatre: Theatre Studies None req. BA Theatre: Stage and Screen Acting Audition req.

School	Avg. GPA, SAT Evidence Based Reading and Writing (ERW), SAT Math (M), and ACT Composite (C) Early Decision (ED): Yes/No	Admission Statistics	Program(s) See website for additional options.	Artistic Review Required (Req.)
Cornish College of the Arts	GPA: N/A SAT (ERW): N/A* SAT (M): N/A* ACT (C): N/A* *Test-optional ED: No	Overall College Admit Rate: 79% Undergrad Enrollment: 482 Total Enrollment: 482	BFA Acting & Original Works BFA Musical Theater Degrees Awarded in the Program(s): 39	BFA Acting & Original Works Audition and interview req. BFA Musical Theatre Audition req.
Gonzaga University	GPA: 3.69 SAT (ERW): 580-670 SAT (M): 580-680 ACT (C): 25-30 ED: No	Overall College Admit Rate: 73% Undergrad Enrollment: 4,852 Total Enrollment: 7,295	BA Theatre Arts Degrees Awarded in the Program(s): 2	None req.

WEST

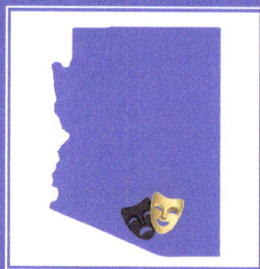

ALASKA

ARIZONA

CALIFORNIA

COLORADO

HAWAII

IDAHO

MONTANA

NEVADA

NEW MEXICO

OREGON

UTAH

WASHINGTON

WYOMING

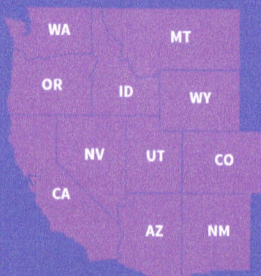

UNIVERSITY OF ARIZONA

Address: The University of Arizona, Tucson, AZ 85721
Website: *https://tftv.arizona.edu/prospective-students/theatre-studies/*
Contact: *https://www.arizona.edu/contact-us*
Phone: (520) 621-2211
Email: admissions@arizona.edu

COST OF ATTENDANCE:

In-State Tuition & Fees: $12,700 | **Additional Expenses:** $18,050
Total: $30,750

Out-of-State Tuition & Fees: $37,200 | **Additional Expenses:** $18,050
Total: $55,250

Financial Aid: https://financialaid.arizona.edu/

ADDITIONAL INFORMATION:

Available Degree(s)

- BA Theatre Arts
- BFA Musical Theatre
- BFA Theatre Production: Professional Actor Training

Artistic Review Requirement

There is no artistic review requirement for the BA in Theatre. For the BFA Theatre Production: Professional Actor Training (i.e., Acting) and BFA Musical Theatre, a prescreen and an audition is required. The BFA Acting requires 2 contrasting monologues and a wildcard video. The BFA Musical Theatre requires 2 contrasting songs, 1 monologue, a dance video, and a wildcard video.

Scholarships Offered

University of Arizona offers several merit-based and need-based awards. Arizona residents are eligible for the Resident Wildcat Awards, based on GPA and test scores. Awards range from $3,000-$15,000. The Non-Resident Arizona Awards range from $2,000-$35,000. The School of Theatre, Film & Television offers Theatre Student Awards such as the Baker Theatrical Lighting Scholarship and the G. Ann Blackmarr Endowment.

Special Opportunities

BFA Acting students have the opportunity to intern with Arizona Theatre Company and perform in featured roles as ensemble members or as understudies. This internship opportunity allows students to receive academic credit as well.

Notable Alumni

Samaire Armstrong, Michael Biehn, Lynn Borden, Jerry Bruckheimer, Fred Christenson, Rick Hoffman, Nicole Randall Johnson, Kourtney Kardashian, Greg Kinnear, Don Knotts, Tamika Lawrence, Marie MacKnight, Dipti Mehta, Labina Mitevska, Peter Murrieta, Craig T. Nelson, Caroline Rhea, Nicole Richie, Ron Shelton, Stephen Spinella, Barret Swatek, Jack Wagner, Kate Walsh, Kristen Wiig, and Christine Woods

AMERICAN MUSICAL & DRAMATIC ACADEMY (AMDA)

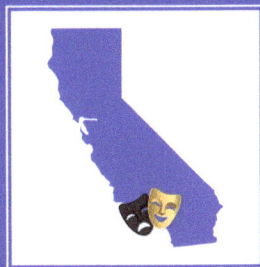

Address: 6305 Yucca Street, Los Angeles, CA 90028
Website: *https://www.amda.edu/programs#find-program*
Contact: *https://www.amda.edu/contact-us*
Phone: (800) 367-7908
Email: admissionsteam@amda.edu

COST OF ATTENDANCE:

Tuition & Fees: $44,260 | **Additional Expenses:** $19,560
Total: $63,820

Financial Aid: https://www.amda.edu/scholarships-financial-aid

ADDITIONAL INFORMATION:

Available Degree(s)

- BFA Acting
- BFA Dance Theatre
- BFA Music Theatre
- BFA Performing Arts, concentrations: Acting; Music Theatre; Dance Theatre; Acting & Creative Content Development; Music Theatre & Creative Content Development;
- BA Theatre Arts, concentrations: General; Performance

Artistic Review Requirement

An audition and phone interview are required for all programs. The audition consists of 2 contrasting monologues.

Scholarships Offered

Institutional scholarships are need and/or merit-based. These awards are based on the audition and other factors seen during the application process. In addition, the AMDA offers institutional need-based grants to students who have a demonstrated financial need. Furthermore, the AMDA accepts scholarship nominations for students. For more information, visit: https://www.amda.edu/scholarships-financial-aid#scholarships

Special Opportunities

AMDA offers an accelerated undergraduate degree track that takes 2.5 years, as opposed to the traditional 4 years. They also have a New York campus, where students may earn a certificate.

Notable Alumni

Nina Arianda, Nicole Byer, Tyne Daly, Bailey De Young, Jason Derulo, Asia Kate Dillon, Erik Estrada, Mike Faist, Jesse Tyler Ferguson, Brita Filter, Ray Fisher, Adam Grace, Christopher Jackson, Neil Kaplan, Dita Karang, Hailey Kilgore, Caissie Levy, Rizwan Manji, Carolyne Mas, Gretchen Mol, Janelle Monáe, Anthony Ramos, Paul Sorvino, Lee Tergesen, Becca Tobin, Michelle Visage, Marissa Jaret Winokur, Michael-Leon Wooley, Natalie Zea, and Jessica White

ALASKA

ARIZONA

CALIFORNIA

COLORADO

HAWAII

IDAHO

MONTANA

NEVADA

NEW MEXICO

OREGON

UTAH

WASHINGTON

WYOMING

WEST

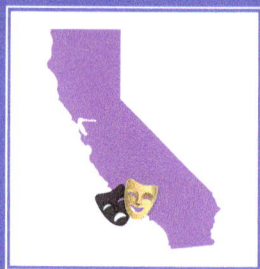

ALASKA

ARIZONA

CALIFORNIA

COLORADO

HAWAII

IDAHO

MONTANA

NEVADA

NEW MEXICO

OREGON

UTAH

WASHINGTON

WYOMING

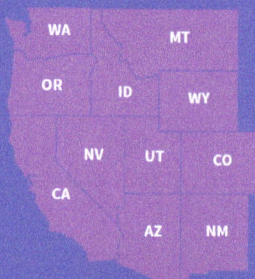

CALIFORNIA INSTITUTE OF THE ARTS

Address: 24700 McBean Pkwy., Valencia, CA 91355
Website: *https://theater.calarts.edu/*
Contact: *https://calarts.edu/about/contact*
Phone: (661) 255-1050
Email: admissions@calarts.edu

COST OF ATTENDANCE:

Tuition & Fees: $53,466 | **Additional Expenses:** $20,792
Total: $74,258

Financial Aid: https://calarts.edu/tuition-and-financial-aid/financial-aid/overview

ADDITIONAL INFORMATION:

Available Degree(s)

- BFA Acting

Artistic Review Requirement

The BFA in Acting requires an audition. The audition consists of an artist statement, headshot, resume, 2 contrasting monologues, and optional supplements such as scripts, voice work, etc.

Scholarships Offered

CalArts offers institutional scholarships that are awarded to students based on need and merit. All awards cover tuition only. In addition, they offer endowed and annually funded scholarships.

Special Opportunities

In the BFA Acting program, first-year students study and perform texts from American canon. In the second year, students focus on classical world texts. The third year has students engaging in contemporary dramatic classics.

Notable Alumni

Amanda Aday, Lamar Aguilar, Kathy Baker, Cameron Bancroft, Dorie Barton, Jesse Borrego, Barbara Bosson, Alison Brie, Merritt Butrick, Stephanie Barton-Farcas, Don Cheadle, Eliza Coupe, Jennifer Elise Cox, Michael Cudlitz, Ed Harris, David Hasselhof, Bill Irwin, Simbi Khali-Williams, Michael Lassell, Scott McDonald, Kim Milford, Dana Morosini, Laraine Newman, Condola Rashad, Paul Reubens, Michael Richards, Michael D. Roberts, Katey Sagal, Cecily Strong, Julie Taymor, Mageina Tovah, and Deborah Joy Winans

CHAPMAN UNIVERSITY

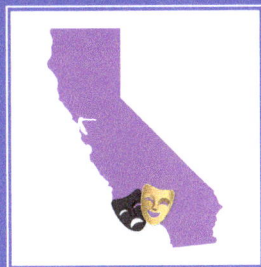

Address: 1 University Drive, Orange, CA 92866
Website: *https://www.chapman.edu/copa/theatre/index.aspx*
Contact: *https://www.chapman.edu/about/connect/index.aspx*
Phone: (714) 997-6815
Email: admit@chapman.edu

COST OF ATTENDANCE:

Tuition & Fees: $60,672 | **Additional Expenses:** $21,874
Total: $82,546

Financial Aid: https://www.chapman.edu/students/tuition-and-aid/
financial-aid/undergraduate/index.aspx

ADDITIONAL INFORMATION:

Available Degree(s)

- BA Theatre, tracks: Performance and Directing; Dramaturgy;
  Playwriting; Theatre Technology
- BFA in Screen Acting
- BFA Theatre Performance

Artistic Review Requirement

The BFA Screen Acting and the BFA Theatre Performance require
an audition. The audition consists of 2 monologues, a resume,
headshot, and goal statement. The BA Theatre requires a resume,
statement, headshot, portfolio, and an optional monologue video.

Scholarships Offered

First-year scholarships range in amounts up to $36,000 per year.
Select admitted students will also be offered institutional awards.
These include awards for first-generation and underrepresented
students, as well as awards from departments and schools/colleges.
The Department of Theatre has a limited number of Talent Awards
for incoming first-year and transfer students. Students must be
theatre majors. Consideration is made at the audition/interview and
notified afterward.

Special Opportunities

Chapman University offers a unique collaboration with the Dodge
College of Film and Media Arts. Theatre majors can take part in one
of the film program's eight film productions each year. Students may
work professionally but must attend all classes. CAST is a student
group that organizes student-run productions, workshops, and guest
artists. They produce events such as the 24-Hour Play Festival, From
the Ground Up, Guerilla Shakespeare, and Beyond Stage (musical
productions). USITT also organizes events and activities in technical
theatre. Students can participate in Chapman On Broadway or the
Player's Society. Film students at Dodge College hold open auditions
for films.

Notable Alumni

Samantha Brown, Colin Hanks, Leslie Jones,
Kellan Lutz, Linh Nga, Justin Simien, Roger
Craig Smith, Joan Staley, Jodie Sweetin, Robin
Thoren, and Esther Liang Veronin

ALASKA

ARIZONA

CALIFORNIA

COLORADO

HAWAII

IDAHO

MONTANA

NEVADA

NEW MEXICO

OREGON

UTAH

WASHINGTON

WYOMING

WEST

ALASKA

ARIZONA

CALIFORNIA

COLORADO

HAWAII

IDAHO

MONTANA

NEVADA

NEW MEXICO

OREGON

UTAH

WASHINGTON

WYOMING

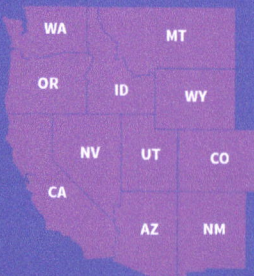

LOYOLA MARYMOUNT UNIVERSITY (LMU)

Address: 1 LMU Dr., Los Angeles, CA 90045
Website: *https://cfa.lmu.edu/programs/theatrearts/*
Contact: *https://cfa.lmu.edu/programs/theatrearts/contactus/*
Phone: (310) 338-2700
Email: admission@lmu.edu

COST OF ATTENDANCE:

Tuition & Fees: $52,553 | **Additional Expenses:** $19,633
Total: $72,186

Financial Aid: https://financialaid.lmu.edu/

ADDITIONAL INFORMATION:

Available Degree(s)

- BA Theatre Arts, emphasis: Performance

Artistic Review Requirement

The BA Theatre requires a video introduction, 2 monologues, and 2 contrasting songs. There are no live auditions.

Scholarships Offered

The Arrupe Scholarship ranges in value from $12,500 to full tuition. This scholarship is available to domestic and international students. It is renewable for four years. The Trustee Scholarship is an extremely competitive scholarship program that requires an on-campus interview. The award is full tuition, room, and board for four years. Ten Trustee Scholarship awards are gifted annually. The Presidential Scholarship is also a merit-based opportunity that gifts $25,000 annually for four years. It also includes a "paid summer research opportunity through [the] Summer Undergraduate Research Program (SURP)…". For more information, visit: https://financialaid.lmu.edu/prospectivestudents/scholarships/

Special Opportunities

Theatre majors are encouraged to study abroad at the Moscow Art Theater (MXAT). This program is a four-month conservatory-style program where students train with European theatre experts and LMU faculty. For more information, visit: https://cfa.lmu.edu/programs/theatrearts/academics/studyabroad/

Notable Alumni

John Bailey, Maria Blasucci, Jennifer Candy, Linda Cardellini, Mindy Cohn, Bob Denver, Clark Duke, Scott Eastwood, Chase Ellison, Mark Haapala, Jack Haley, Jr., Colin Hanks, Emily Harper, Dwayne Hickman, Kaliko Kauahi, Gloria Calderón Kellet, Mila Kunis, Emma Lockhart, Kate Micucci, Kate Mitchell, Taylour Paige, Busy Phillips, Tony Plana, Jessica Rey, Steve Rossi, Chris Sullivan, Desean Terry, Daniel J. Travanti, Michael Wayne, Patrick Wayne, and James Wong

PEPPERDINE UNIVERSITY

Address: 24255 Pacific Coast Hwy, Malibu, CA 90263
Website: *https://seaver.pepperdine.edu/fine-arts/undergraduate/theatre/*
Contact: *https://www.pepperdine.edu/contact/*
Phone: (310) 506-4000
Email: admission-seaver@pepperdine.edu

COST OF ATTENDANCE:

Tuition & Fees: $59,450 | **Additional Expenses:** $20,770
Total: $80,220

Financial Aid: https://seaver.pepperdine.edu/admission/financial-aid/undergraduate/

ADDITIONAL INFORMATION:

Available degree(s)

- BA Theatre Arts, emphases: Musical Theatre
- BA Theatre and Screen Arts, emphasis: Acting

Artistic Review Requirement

The BA Theatre & Screen Arts: Acting require an audition that consists of 2 contrasting monologues and optional songs. Upload via Slideroom. The BA Theatre Arts: Musical Theatre does not require a prescreen, however an audition is required.

Scholarships Offered

Merit and need-based scholarships are available for Theatre students. Approximately 75% of theatre majors receive scholarships in varying amounts. Students must complete a FAFSA form. The Theatre program awards a Special Achievement Scholarship as well as the Ubben Endowed Scholarship for Production Design Majors ($25,000 per year).

Special Opportunities

In addition to rigorous training and workshops with professional actors, Pepperdine's 8-week Theatre Program offers summer training through the Edinburgh Summer Program in Scotland. Pepperdine's Theatre department has participated in the International Edinburgh Fringe Festival since 1985. This popular, bi-annual, international program is exclusively for theatre majors. The Edinburgh program draws on the strengths of both Scottish and American theatre traditions, with a commitment to international collaboration through co-creation by artists from both Pepperdine and Scotland. Students employ the Linklater Voice technique.

Notable Alumni

Marshall Colt, Cami Edwards, Douglas Emerson, Kim Fields, Darby Hinton, Kelly Hu, Ashley Jones, Kate Mansi, Tahj Mowry, Tamera Mowry, Tia Mowry, Brandy Norwood, Eric Christian Olsen, Meredith Salenger, Francesca Marie Smith, and Clayton Snyder

ALASKA

ARIZONA

CALIFORNIA

COLORADO

HAWAII

IDAHO

MONTANA

NEVADA

NEW MEXICO

OREGON

UTAH

WASHINGTON

WYOMING

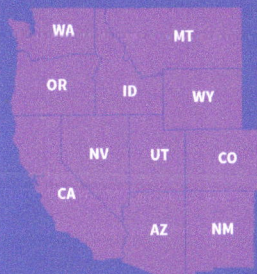

WEST

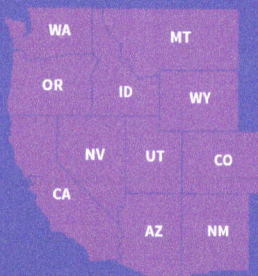

UNIVERSITY OF CALIFORNIA, LOS ANGELES

Address: 405 Hilgard Avenue, Los Angeles, CA 90095
Website: *http://www.tft.ucla.edu/programs/theater-department/*
Contact: *http://www.tft.ucla.edu/contact/*
Phone: (310) 206-8441
Email: info@tft.ucla.edu

COST OF ATTENDANCE:

In-State Tuition & Fees: $13,239 | **Additional Expenses:** $22,096
Total: $35,335

Out-of-State Tuition & Fees: $42,993 | **Additional Expenses:** $22,096
Total: $65,089

Financial Aid: https://www.financialaid.ucla.edu/

ADDITIONAL INFORMATION:

Available Degree(s)
- BA Theater, areas of emphasis: Acting; Musical Theater

Artistic Review Requirement
Not all applicants are required to submit an audition or interview for admittance to the program. If an interview/audition is requested, applicants must prepare 2 monologues.

Scholarships Offered
Aside from institutional scholarships, the UCLA School of Theater, Film and Television offers numerous scholarship opportunities. The Army Archerd Fellowship in Theater, Film, and Television is a need-based and merit-based award that is available to all TFT majors. The Hollywood Foreign Press Association Endowed Scholarship offers need-based aid to TFT students.

Special Opportunities
Theatre students have access to numerous facilities, including theaters, sound stages, TV studios, prop and costume shops, and more. Furthermore, students may earn Dean's Honors in the School of Theater, Film and Television.

Notable Alumni
Corey Allen, Rachel Ames, Victoria Ann Lewis, Sean Astin, Sunkrish Bala, Beth Behrs, Catherine Bell, Corbin Bernsen, Sarah Uriarte Berry, Mayim Bialik, Jack Black, Shane Black, Lo Bosworth, Beau Bridges, Dorothy Bridges, Lloyd Bridges, Carol Burnett, Ana Brenda Contreras, Michael Burns, Nicolas Cage, Sofia Carson, Nancy Cartwright, Tanya Chisholm, James Coburn, Josh Cooke, Wyatt Emory Cooper, James Dean, Joyce DeWitt, Deepti Divakar, David Dorfman, Merrin Dungey, Robert Englund, Josh Evans, Will Forte, James Franco, Eddie Frierson, Brad Garrett, Kathy Garver, Caitlin Gerard, Christopher Gorham, Horace Hahn, Chris Hardwick, Mariska Hargitay, Mark Harmon, Michael Hitchcock, Laurie Holden, Earl Holliman, Allan Hunt, Brittany Ishibashi, Anne-Marie Johnson, Judy Kaye, Staci Keanan, Joanna Kerns, Taran Killam, Derek Klena, Walter Koenig, Mila Kunis, Carlos Lacámara, Christine Lakin, Robert Lehrer, Heather Locklear, Josie Loren, Masiela Lusha, Meredith MacRae, Jayne Mansfield, Doug McClure, Elizabeth McGovern, Danica McKellar, Scott Mechlowicz, Nigel Miguel, Victor Millan, Leonard Nimoy, Danielle Panabaker, Kay Panabaker, Bryce Papenbrook, Randall Park, Nasim Pedrad, Kal Penn, Autumn Reeser, Rob Reiner, Tim Robbins, Harry Shearer, Dax Shepard, Armin Shimerman, Jeremy Sisto, Tom Skerritt, John Smith, Ben Stiller, Cynthia Szigeti, George Takei, Chris Tashima, Tamlyn Tomita, Kelly Marie Tran, Gabrielle Union, Milo Ventimiglia, Michael Warren, Jaleel White, Eric Winter, Leonard Wu, and Daphne Zuniga

ALASKA

ARIZONA

CALIFORNIA

COLORADO

HAWAII

IDAHO

MONTANA

NEVADA

NEW MEXICO

OREGON

UTAH

WASHINGTON

WYOMING

UNIVERSITY OF CALIFORNIA, SAN DIEGO

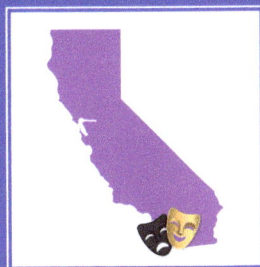

Address: 9500 Gilman Drive, La Jolla, CA 92093
Website: *https://theatre.ucsd.edu/academics/undergraduate/theatre.html*
Contact: *https://theatre.ucsd.edu/about/contact-us.html*
Phone: (858) 534-2230
Email: tdadvising@ucsd.edu

COST OF ATTENDANCE:

In-State Tuition & Fees: $14,733 | **Additional Expenses:** $19,377
Total: $34,110

Out-of-State Tuition & Fees: $44,487 | **Additional Expenses:** $19,377
Total: $63,864

Financial Aid: https://fas.ucsd.edu/

ADDITIONAL INFORMATION:

Available Degree(s)

- BA Theatre

Artistic Review Requirement

Applicants may submit an audition if they choose to. It is not required. The audition consists of a video response, resume, one letter of recommendation, and a monologue.

Scholarships Offered

UCSD offers first-year merit scholarships such as the Regents Scholarship or the Ellen and Roger Revelle Scholarship. There are also first-year scholarships based on merit and need combined. There are numerous other merit-based awards available.

Special Opportunities

UCSD stages 3 productions per quarter in the Theatre District, which is shared with La Jolla Playhouse. Students are encouraged to apply to these productions and for the numerous graduate shows and other shows hosted by guest artists.

Notable Alumni

Yareli Arizmendi, James Avery, David Barrera, Marsha Stephanie Blake, Hart Bochner, Robert Buckley, Danny Burstein, Zoë Chao, Ricardo Chavira, Charlet Chung, Benicio del Toro, Emily Donahoe, Maria Dizzia, Johnny Ray Gill, Matt Hoverman, Zora Howard, Chane't Johnson, Ty Granderson Jones, Sagan Lewis, Jefferson Mays, Silas Weir Mitchell, Toby Onwumere, Joy Osmanski, Jeanne Paulsen, Maria Striar, Milana Vayntrub, Kellie Waymire, John Wesley, and Jimmy O. Yang

ALASKA

ARIZONA

CALIFORNIA

COLORADO

HAWAII

IDAHO

MONTANA

NEVADA

NEW MEXICO

OREGON

UTAH

WASHINGTON

WYOMING

WEST

ALASKA

ARIZONA

CALIFORNIA

COLORADO

HAWAII

IDAHO

MONTANA

NEVADA

NEW MEXICO

OREGON

UTAH

WASHINGTON

WYOMING

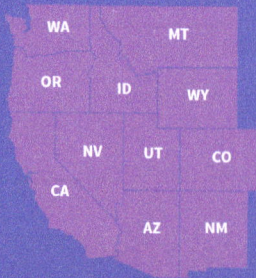

UNIVERSITY OF SOUTHERN CALIFORNIA (USC)

Address: 1029 Childs Way, Los Angeles, CA 90089
Website: *https://dramaticarts.usc.edu/*
Contact: *https://dramaticarts.usc.edu/contact/*
Phone: (213) 821-2744
Email: sdainfo@usc.edu

COST OF ATTENDANCE:

Tuition & Fees: $57,256 | **Additional Expenses:** $19,264
Total: $76,520

Financial Aid: https://financialaid.usc.edu/undergraduates/students.html

ADDITIONAL INFORMATION:

Available Degree(s)

- BFA Acting for Stage, Screen and New Media
- BFA Musical Theatre
- BA Theatre, emphases: Acting; Comedy; Design

Artistic Review Requirement

The BA Theatre requires a portfolio that consists of a headshot, resume, 3 images, letter of recommendation, essay responses, and a self-intro video. The BFA in Acting for Stage, Screen, and New Media requires a prescreen and audition. The BFA Musical Theatre requires a prescreen and audition.

Scholarships Offered

The School of Dramatic Arts provides awards to students who have completed at least one year as a dramatic arts major at USC. These awards are merit-based. USC offers several scholarships for all students. The Mork Family Scholarship offers a full tuition award plus a $5,000 stipend. The Trustee Scholarship offers full tuition. In addition, the Presidential Scholarship includes a half tuition award.

Special Opportunities

Students in the USC School of Dramatic Arts have numerous global opportunities, including global fellowships, a conservatory experience at the British American Drama Academy in London, the Global Scholars Program, and other overseas experiences.

Notable Alumni

Patrick J. Adams, Shiri Appleby, McKinley Belcher III, Troian Bellisario, Beck Bennett, Todd Black, Nichole Bloom, Charl Brown, LeVar Burton, Tate Donovan, Timothy Dowling, Anthony Edwards, Ryan Eggold, Greer Grammer, Daryl Hannah, Briga Heelan, Grant Heslov, Devin Kelley, Swoosie Kurtz, Eric Ladin, James Lesure, Jaren Lewison, Chris Lowell, Alexander Ludwig, Joseph Mazzello, Bentley Mitchum, Fess Parker, Kelly Preston, Michael Pataki, Kyra Sedgwick, Tom Selleck, Cybill Shepherd, Chima Simone, Karan Soni, Robert Stack, Marlo Thomas, Robert Vaughn, John Wayne, Forest Whitaker, Mary Kate Wiles, Deborah Ann Woll, Anton Yelchin, and Lee Thompson Young

UNIVERSITY OF NEVADA, LAS VEGAS

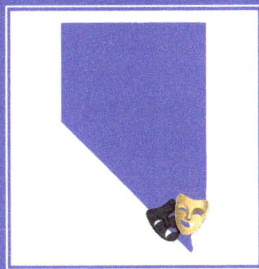

Address: 4505 S Maryland Pkwy, Las Vegas, NV 89154
Website: *https://www.unlv.edu/degree/ba-theatre*
Contact: *https://www.unlv.edu/admissions/contact*
Phone: (702) 774-8658
Email: admissions@unlv.edu

COST OF ATTENDANCE:

In-State Tuition & Fees: $8,893 | **Additional Expenses:** $17,678
Total: $26,571

Out-of-State Tuition & Fees: $24,984 | **Additional Expenses:**
$18,887   **Total:** $43,871

Financial Aid: https://www.unlv.edu/finaid

ADDITIONAL INFORMATION:

Available Degree(s)

- BA Theatre, concentrations: Theatre Studies; Stage and
  Screen Acting

Artistic Review Requirement

The BA Theatre, concentration: Stage and Screen Acting requires an
audition. The BA Theatre, concentration: Theatre Studies program
does not require an artistic review.

Scholarships Offered

Applicants are automatically considered for scholarships when they
submit their UNLV application and FAFSA. Students who submit their
applications prior to November 15th receive priority consideration.
The Department of Theatre awards approximately $20-$25,000 in
undergraduate scholarships and grant-in-aid funds each academic
year. Traditionally, students receive $1,000 to $2,500 annually.

Special Opportunities

The BA Theatre, concentration: Stage and Screen Acting is relatively
new and offers conservatory-style training. Coursework includes
Play Structure and Analysis, Scene Study: Stage Acting, Speech for
the Actor, and more.

Notable Alumni

Michael Bunin, Gina Carano, Lindsay Hartley, Giovanna Sardelli, Eric
Whitacre, and Anthony E. Zuiker

ALASKA

ARIZONA

CALIFORNIA

COLORADO

HAWAII

IDAHO

MONTANA

NEVADA

NEW MEXICO

OREGON

UTAH

WASHINGTON

WYOMING

WEST

ALASKA

ARIZONA

CALIFORNIA

COLORADO

HAWAII

IDAHO

MONTANA

NEVADA

NEW MEXICO

OREGON

UTAH

WASHINGTON

WYOMING

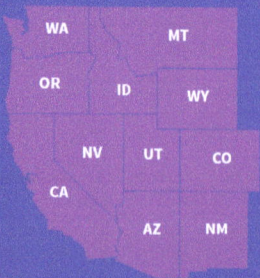

CORNISH COLLEGE OF THE ARTS

Address: 1000 Lenora St, Seattle, WA 98121
Website: *https://www.cornish.edu/cornish-programs/performance-production/*
Contact: *https://www.cornish.edu/contact/*
Phone: (206) 726-2787
Email: hello@cornish.edu

COST OF ATTENDANCE:

Tuition & Fees: $40,464 | **Additional Expenses:** $16,080
Total: $56,544

Financial Aid: https://www.cornish.edu/tuition-financial-aid/

ADDITIONAL INFORMATION:

Available Degree(s)

- BFA Acting & Original Works
- BFA Musical Theater

Artistic Review Requirement

Both BFA programs require an audition. Applicants may audition in person, live virtually, or via recorded audition.

Scholarships Offered

Cornish merit scholarships are based on students' application and audition/portfolio review. No separate application is required for scholarship consideration. The BFA Acting & Original Works audition requires 2 contemporary monologues and an interview. The BFA Musical Theater requires 1 monologue, 2 contrasting songs, and a dance call.

Special Opportunities

Incoming freshmen participate in the First-Year Experience in Theater. Students take coursework in voice, text analysis, acting, singing, musicianship, physical technique, improvisation, and collaboration.

Notable Alumni

Brendan Fraser, David Gasman, C.S. Lee, Jinkx Monsoon, and Lady Rizo

GONZAGA UNIVERSITY

Address: 502 E Boone Ave, Spokane, WA 99258
Website: *https://www.gonzaga.edu/college-of-arts-sciences/ departments/theatre-dance/theatre*
Contact: *https://www.gonzaga.edu/contact-us*
Phone: (509) 328-4220
Email: admissions@gonzaga.edu

COST OF ATTENDANCE:

Tuition & Fees: $48,470 | **Additional Expenses:** $18,191
Total: $66,661

Financial Aid: https://www.gonzaga.edu/admission/tuition-scholarships-aid

ADDITIONAL INFORMATION:

Available Degree(s)

- BA Theatre Arts, concentrations: Performance

Artistic Review Requirement

There is no artistic review requirement. Interviews are optional.

Scholarships Offered

All applicants to Gonzaga University are automatically considered for test-optional merit scholarships. The Act Six Scholarship awards full-tuition or full-need scholarships to emerging urban and community leaders from Tacoma, Seattle, or Spokane areas.

Special Opportunities

The Theatre & Dance Department offers a minor in Interdisciplinary Arts. Additionally, the Theatre Program participates in the Kennedy Center American College Theatre Festival and is a wonderful opportunity for students seeking internships with theatre companies.

Notable Alumni

Bing Crosby and Dan Cummins

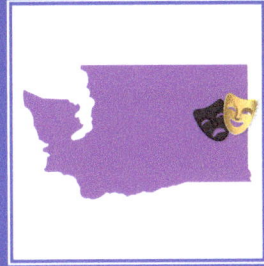

ALASKA

ARIZONA

CALIFORNIA

COLORADO

HAWAII

IDAHO

MONTANA

NEVADA

NEW MEXICO

OREGON

UTAH

WASHINGTON

WYOMING

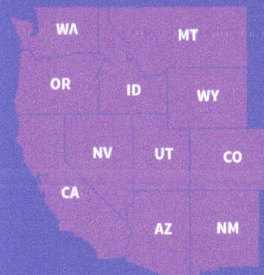

WEST

CHAPTER 17

THEATRE & DRAMATIC ARTS SCHOOLS ALPHABETIZED BY CITY/STATE

School	City	State
Auburn University	Auburn	Alabama
University of Arizona	Tucson	Arizona
University of California, San Diego (UCSD)	La Jolla	California
American Musical & Dramatic Academy (AMDA)	Los Angeles	California
Loyola Marymount University (LMU)	Los Angeles	California
University of California, Los Angeles (UCLA)	Los Angeles	California
University of Southern California (USC)	Los Angeles	California
Pepperdine University	Malibu	California
Chapman University	Orange	California
California Institute of the Arts (CalArts)	Valencia	California
Wesleyan University	Middletown	Connecticut
Yale University	New Haven	Connecticut
University of Connecticut (UConn)	Storrs	Connecticut
The George Washington University (GWU)	Washington	DC
Florida State University	Tallahassee	Florida
Emory University	Atlanta	Georgia
University of Illinois Urbana-Champaign (UIUC)	Champaign	Illinois
Columbia College Chicago	Chicago	Illinois
DePaul University	Chicago	Illinois
University of Chicago	Chicago	Illinois
Northwestern University	Evanston	Illinois
Indiana University Bloomington	Bloomington	Indiana
University of Evansville	Evansville	Indiana
Ball State University	Muncie	Indiana
University of Notre Dame	Notre Dame	Indiana
Purdue University	West Lafayette	Indiana
Wichita State University	Wichita	Kansas
Tulane University	New Orleans	Louisiana
University of Massachusetts, Amherst	Amherst	Massachusetts
Boston University	Boston	Massachusetts
Emerson College	Boston	Massachusetts
University of Michigan	Ann Arbor	Michigan
University of Minnesota	Minneapolis	Minnesota
University of Missouri	Columbia	Missouri
College of the Ozarks	Point Lookout	Missouri
Missouri State University	Springfield	Missouri
University of Nevada, Las Vegas (UNLV)	Las Vegas	Nevada

School	City	State
Montclair State University	Montclair	New Jersey
Rutgers, The State University of New Jersey	New Brunswick	New Jersey
State University of New York at Binghamton	Binghamton	New York
Fordham University	Bronx	New York
University at Buffalo	Buffalo	New York
Ithaca College	Ithaca	New York
Barnard College	New York	New York
The Juilliard School	New York	New York
Marymount Manhattan College	New York	New York
New York University (NYU)	New York	New York
Pace University	New York	New York
Long Island University (LIU)	Orangeburg	New York
Vassar College	Poughkeepsie	New York
Skidmore College	Saratoga Springs	New York
Syracuse University	Syracuse	New York
University of North Carolina at Chapel Hill	Chapel Hill	North Carolina
Duke University	Durham	North Carolina
Elon University	Elon	North Carolina
Catawba College	Salisbury	North Carolina
Baldwin Wallace University	Berea	Ohio
Ohio State University	Columbus	Ohio
Kenyon College	Gambier	Ohio
Kent State University	Kent	Ohio
University of Oklahoma	Norman	Oklahoma
Oklahoma City University	Oklahoma City	Oklahoma
University of the Arts (UArts)	Philadelphia	Pennsylvania
Carnegie Mellon University	Pittsburgh	Pennsylvania
Pennsylvania State University	University Park	Pennsylvania
Belmont University	Nashville	Tennessee
Texas Christian University (TCU)	Fort Worth	Texas
Baylor University	Waco	Texas
Middlebury College	Middlebury	Vermont
Virginia Commonwealth University (VCU)	Richmond	Virginia
Shenandoah University	Winchester	Virginia
Cornish College of the Arts	Seattle	Washington
Gonzaga University	Spokane	Washington
University of Wisconsin	Madison	Wisconsin

CHAPTER 18

TOP 30 THEATRE & DRAMATIC ARTS SCHOOLS

Ranking	School
1	The Juilliard School
2	New York University
3	Carnegie Mellon University
4	University of North Carolina School of the Arts
5	Syracuse University
6	Ithaca College
7	Northwestern University
8	Cal Arts
9	UCLA
10	USC
11	Emerson College
12	SUNY Purchase
13	Elon College
14	Rutgers University
15	Boston University
16	Pace University
17	DePaul University
18	University of the Arts
19	University of Texas at Austin
20	Chapman University
21	University of Miami
22	Hamilton College
23	Southern Methodist University
24	University of Notre Dame
25	University of Minnesota
26	University of Michigan
27	Pennsylvania State University
28	Florida State University
29	Texas State University
30	University of Central Florida

CHAPTER 19

THEATRE & DRAMATIC ARTS SCHOOLS BY AVERAGE TEST SCORE

THEATRE & DRAMATIC ARTS SCHOOLS BY AVERAGE SAT SCORE

School	Avg. SAT
College of the Ozarks	470-540 (ERW)
	480-560 (M)
Catawba College	470-570 (ERW)
	470-570 (M)
Marymount Manhattan College	500-580 (ERW)
	460-620 (M)
Montclair State University	500-600 (ERW)
	510-610 (M)
	*Test optional
Kent State University	510-610 (ERW)
	510-600 (M)
Missouri State University	510-610 (ERW)
	510-610 (M)
Shenandoah University	510-630 (ERW)
	500-600 (M)
Wichita State University	510-630 (ERW)
	520-630 (M)
University of Nevada, Las Vegas (UNLV)	520-620 (ERW)
	510-630 (M)
Baldwin Wallace University	520-640 (ERW)
	520-620 (M)
DePaul University	530-640 (ERW)
	530-640 (M)
Pace University	540-630 (ERW)
	520-610 (M)
Virginia Commonwealth University (VCU)	540-640 (ERW)
	520-610 (M)
Long Island University (LIU)	540-640 (ERW)
	540-650 (M)
Oklahoma City University	550-650 (ERW)
	530-610 (M)
University of Arizona	550-660 (ERW)
	540-690 (M)
University at Buffalo	560-640 (ERW)
	580-670 (M)

School	Avg. SAT
University of Oklahoma	560-650 (ERW)
	540-650 (M)
Texas Christian University (TCU)	560-660 (ERW)
	550-660 (M)
University of Missouri	560-660 (ERW)
	550-660 (M)
Belmont University	580-660 (ERW)
	540-640 (M)
Elon University	580-660 (ERW)
	560-660 (M)
Gonzaga University	580-670 (ERW)
	580-680 (M)
Pennsylvania State University	580-670 (ERW)
	580-700 (M)
University of Connecticut (UConn)	580-680 (ERW)
	590-710 (M)
Rutgers, The State University of New Jersey	580-680 (ERW)
	600-730 (M)
Indiana University Bloomington	580-700 (ERW)
	560-680 (M)
Auburn University	590-650 (ERW)
	580-680 (M)
Chapman University	590-670 (ERW)
	580-680 (M)
Purdue University	590-690 (ERW)
	600-740 (M)
Ohio State University	590-690 (ERW)
	620-740 (M)
University of Illinois Urbana-Champaign (UIUC)	590-700 (ERW)
	620-770 (M)
Ithaca College	600-680 (ERW)
	580-670 (M)
Baylor University	600-680 (ERW)
	590-680 (M)
Pepperdine University	600-690 (ERW)
	600-720 (M)

School	Avg. SAT
University of Minnesota	600-700 (ERW)
	640-760 (M)
Emerson College	610-690 (ERW)
	580-690 (M)
University of Wisconsin	610-690 (ERW)
	650-770 (M)
Florida State University	620-670 (ERW)
	600-670 (M)
Fordham University	620-700 (ERW)
	620-740 (M)
Loyola Marymount University (LMU)	620-700 (ERW)
	630-720 (M)
University of Massachusetts, Amherst	620-710 (ERW)
	630-750 (M)
University of California, San Diego (UCSD)	620-710 (ERW)
	640-770 (M)
Skidmore College	630-720 (ERW)
	640-720 (M)
State University of New York at Binghamton	640-710 (ERW)
	650-740 (M)
The George Washington University (GWU)	640-720 (ERW)
	630-730 (M)
Boston University	640-720 (ERW)
	670-780 (M)
University of North Carolina at Chapel Hill	640-730 (ERW)
	640-760 (M)
University of California, Los Angeles (UCLA)	650-740 (ERW)
	640-780 (M)
Kenyon College	660-730 (ERW)
	620-730 (M)
University of Michigan	660-740 (ERW)
	680-780 (M)
University of Southern California (USC)	660-740 (ERW)
	680-790 (M)
New York University (NYU)	670-740 (ERW)
	700-800 (M)

School	Avg. SAT
Wesleyan University	670-750 (ERW)
	670-770 (M)
Middlebury College	670-750 (ERW)
	670-770 (M)
Tulane University	680-740 (ERW)
	680-770 (M)
Emory University	680-740 (ERW)
	700-790 (M)
Barnard College	680-747.5 (ERW)
	670-770 (M)
Vassar College	680-750 (ERW)
	680-770 (M)
University of Notre Dame	690-760 (ERW)
	710-790 (M)
Northwestern University	700-760 (ERW)
	730-790 (M)
Carnegie Mellon University	700-760 (ERW)
	760-800 (M)
Duke University	720-770 (ERW)
	750-800 (M)
Yale University	720-780 (ERW)
	740-800 (M)
University of Chicago	730-770 (ERW)
	770-800 (M)
Syracuse University	N/A
American Musical & Dramatic Academy (AMDA)	N/A *Test optional
California Institute of the Arts (CalArts)	N/A *Test optional
Columbia College Chicago	N/A *Test optional
Cornish College of the Arts	N/A *Test optional
The Juilliard School	N/A *Test optional
Ball State University	N/A *Test optional
University of the Arts (UArts)	N/A *Test optional
University of Evansville	N/A *Test optional

THEATRE & DRAMATIC ARTS SCHOOLS BY AVERAGE ACT SCORE

School	Avg. ACT
Catawba College	17-22 (ACT C)
College of the Ozarks	18-23 (ACT C)
University of Nevada, Las Vegas (UNLV)	19-25 (ACT C)
Shenandoah University	19-26 (ACT C)
Kent State University	20-26 (ACT C)
Wichita State University	20-27 (ACT C)
Marymount Manhattan College	20-28 (ACT C)
	*Test optional
Baldwin Wallace University	21-27 (ACT C)
Missouri State University	21-27 (ACT C)
Montclair State University	21-28
	*Test optional
Virginia Commonwealth University (VCU)	21-28 (ACT C)
University of Arizona	21-29 (ACT C)
Pace University	22-28 (ACT C)
	*Test optional
Long Island University (LIU)	22-29 (ACT C)
Oklahoma City University	22-29 (ACT C)
University at Buffalo	23-29 (ACT C)
University of Missouri	23-29 (ACT C)
University of Oklahoma	23-29 (ACT C)
Belmont University	23-30 (ACT C)
Auburn University	24-30 (ACT C)
Chapman University	25-30 (ACT C)
Elon University	25-30 (ACT C)
Gonzaga University	25-30 (ACT C)
Pennsylvania State University	25-30 (ACT C)
Texas Christian University (TCU)	25-31 (ACT C)
University of Minnesota	25-31 (ACT C)
Rutgers, The State University of New Jersey	25-32 (ACT C)
Purdue University	25-33 (ACT C)
Baylor University	26-31 (ACT C)
Pepperdine University	26-31 (ACT C)
Indiana University Bloomington	26-32 (ACT C)
Ohio State University	26-32 (ACT C)
University of California, San Diego (UCSD)	26-33 (ACT C)

School	Avg. ACT
Florida State University	27-31 (ACT C)
Emerson College	27-31 (ACT C)
	*Test optional
Ithaca College	27-31 (ACT C)
	*Test optional
University of Connecticut (UConn)	27-32 (ACT C)
University of Wisconsin	27-32 (ACT C)
University of Illinois Urbana-Champaign (UIUC)	27-33 (ACT C)
Fordham University	28-32 (ACT C)
Loyola Marymount University (LMU)	28-32 (ACT C)
University of Massachusetts, Amherst	28-33 (ACT C)
University of North Carolina at Chapel Hill	28-33 (ACT C)
State University of New York at Binghamton	29-32 (ACT C)
Skidmore College	29-33 (ACT C)
The George Washington University (GWU)	29-33 (ACT C)
University of California, Los Angeles (UCLA)	29-34 (ACT C)
Kenyon College	30-33 (ACT C)
Tulane University	30-33 (ACT C)
University of Southern California (USC)	30-34 (ACT C)
Boston University	30-34 (ACT C)
Barnard College	31-34 (ACT C)
Emory University	31-34 (ACT C)
Middlebury College	31-34 (ACT C)
New York University (NYU)	31-34 (ACT C)
University of Michigan	31-34 (ACT C)
Wesleyan University	31-34 (ACT C)
	*Test optional
Vassar College	32-34 (ACT C)
University of Notre Dame	32-35 (ACT C)
Carnegie Mellon University	33-35 (ACT C)
Yale University	33-35 (ACT C)
Northwestern University	33-35 (ACT)
Duke University	34-35 (ACT C)
University of Chicago	34-35 (ACT C)
DePaul University	N/A
Syracuse University	N/A

School	Avg. ACT
American Musical & Dramatic Academy (AMDA)	N/A *Test optional
California Institute of the Arts (CalArts)	N/A *Test optional
Columbia College Chicago	N/A *Test optional
Cornish College of the Arts	N/A *Test optional
The Juilliard School	N/A *Test optional
Ball State University	N/A *Test optional
University of the Arts (UArts)	N/A *Test optional
University of Evansville	N/A *Test optional

THEATRE & DRAMATIC ARTS SCHOOLS BY AVERAGE GPA

School	Avg. GPA
College of the Ozarks	3.37
University of Arizona	3.43
University of Nevada, Las Vegas (UNLV)	3.43
Emerson College	3.5
Wichita State University	3.51
Ball State University	3.52
Shenandoah University	3.55
Catawba College	3.59
Florida State University	3.59
Kent State University	3.61
University of Oklahoma	3.63
Baldwin Wallace University	3.64
Fordham University	3.64
Tulane University	3.64
Purdue University	3.67
Syracuse University	3.67
Gonzaga University	3.69
Pepperdine University	3.69
University at Buffalo	3.7
New York University (NYU)	3.71
Virginia Commonwealth University (VCU)	3.72
Missouri State University	3.73
Indiana University Bloomington	3.74
Boston University	3.76
DePaul University	3.8
Emory University	3.8
Belmont University	3.83
University of Southern California (USC)	3.83
Carnegie Mellon University	3.85
University of Michigan	3.87
University of Wisconsin	3.87
University of California, Los Angeles (UCLA)	3.9
Loyola Marymount University (LMU)	3.92
Auburn University	3.97
University of Massachusetts, Amherst	3.99
Elon University	4.04

School	Avg. GPA
University of California, San Diego (UCSD)	4.09
University of North Carolina at Chapel Hill	4.39
American Musical & Dramatic Academy (AMDA)	N/A
Barnard College	N/A
Baylor University	N/A
California Institute of the Arts (CalArts)	N/A
Chapman University	N/A
Columbia College Chicago	N/A
Cornish College of the Arts	N/A
Duke University	N/A
Ithaca College	N/A
Kenyon College	N/A
Long Island University (LIU)	N/A
Marymount Manhattan College	N/A
Middlebury College	N/A
Montclair State University	N/A
Northwestern University	N/A
Ohio State University	N/A
Oklahoma City University	N/A
Pace University	N/A
Pennsylvania State University	N/A
Rutgers, The State University of New Jersey	N/A
Skidmore College	N/A
State University of New York at Binghamton	N/A
Texas Christian University (TCU)	N/A
The George Washington University (GWU)	N/A
The Juilliard School	N/A
University of Chicago	N/A
University of Connecticut (UConn)	N/A
University of Evansville	N/A
University of Illinois Urbana-Champaign (UIUC)	N/A
University of Minnesota	N/A
University of Missouri	N/A
University of Notre Dame	N/A
University of the Arts (UArts)	N/A
Vassar College	N/A
Wesleyan University	N/A
Yale University	N/A

JOURNEY TO ART, DANCE, MUSIC, THEATRE, FILM, AND FASHION SERIES

JOURNEY TO
Fashion Design
COLLEGE ADMISSIONS & PROFILES
RACHEL A. WINSTON, PH.D.

JOURNEY TO
Fashion Merchandising
COLLEGE ADMISSIONS & PROFILES
RACHEL A. WINSTON, PH.D.

JOURNEY TO
Costume Design & Technical Theatre
COLLEGE ADMISSIONS & PROFILES
RACHEL A. WINSTON, PH.D.

JOURNEY TO
Theatre and the Dramatic Arts
COLLEGE ADMISSIONS & PROFILES
RACHEL A. WINSTON, PH.D.

JOURNEY TO
Musical
Theatre
COLLEGE ADMISSIONS & PROFILES

RACHEL A. WINSTON, PH.D.

Live your dreams today remembering that discipline is the
bridge between dreams and achievement!

"We believe in the American Dream that all people rich or poor can
go as far in life as their talents and persistence will take them."
– Lizard Publishing Vision

At Lizard, we help you make your dreams come true.

CONTACT INFORMATION

Phone: 949-833-7706
E-mail: collegeguide@yahoo.com
Website: collegelizard.com and Lizard-publishing.com

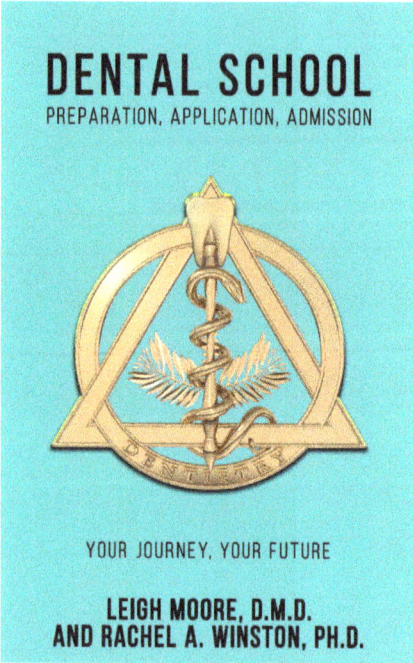

DENTAL SCHOOL
PREPARATION, APPLICATION, ADMISSION

YOUR JOURNEY, YOUR FUTURE

LEIGH MOORE, D.M.D.
AND RACHEL A. WINSTON, PH.D.

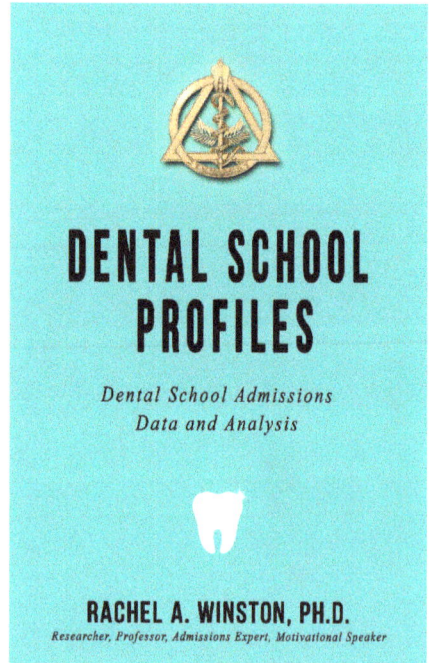

DENTAL SCHOOL PROFILES

Dental School Admissions Data and Analysis

RACHEL A. WINSTON, PH.D.
Researcher, Professor, Admissions Expert, Motivational Speaker

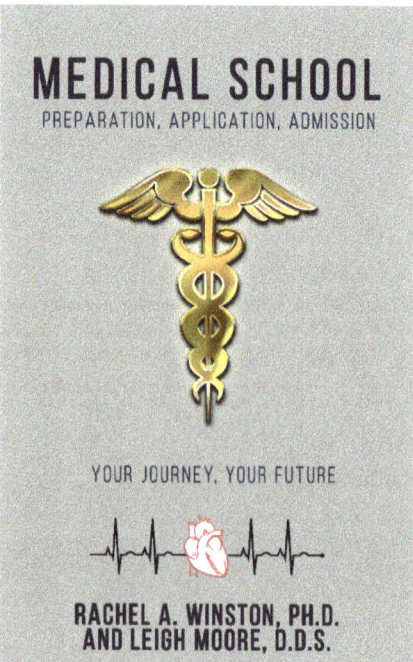

MEDICAL SCHOOL
PREPARATION, APPLICATION, ADMISSION

YOUR JOURNEY, YOUR FUTURE

RACHEL A. WINSTON, PH.D.
AND LEIGH MOORE, D.D.S.

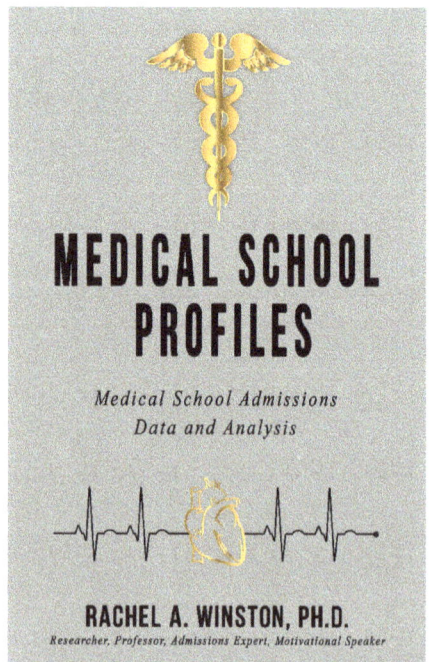

MEDICAL SCHOOL PROFILES

Medical School Admissions Data and Analysis

RACHEL A. WINSTON, PH.D.
Researcher, Professor, Admissions Expert, Motivational Speaker

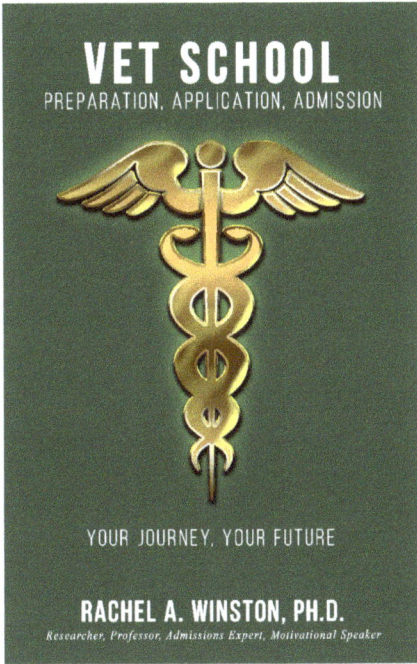

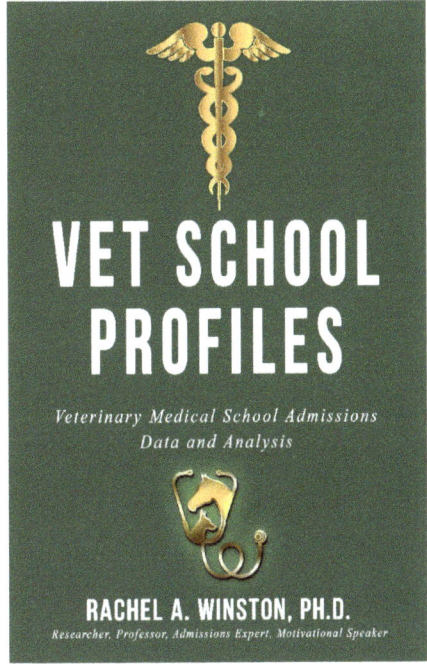

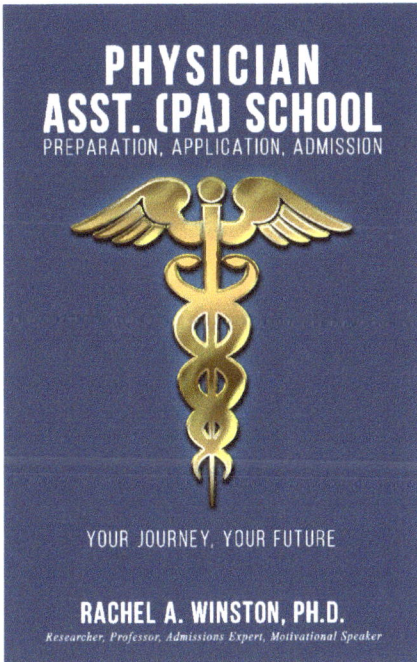

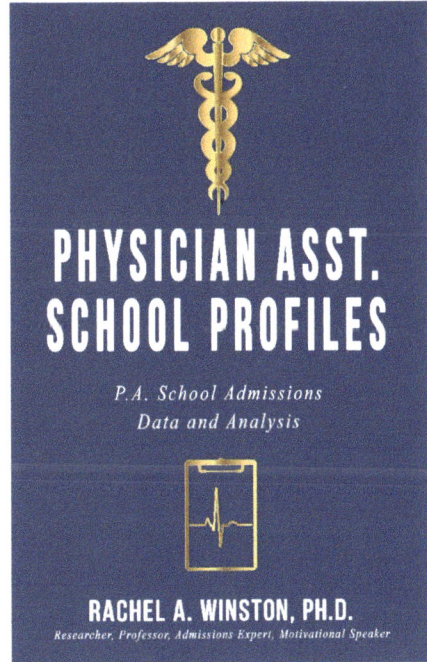

PHARM.D. SCHOOL
PREPARATION, APPLICATION, ADMISSION

YOUR JOURNEY, YOUR FUTURE

RACHEL A. WINSTON, PH.D.
Researcher, Professor, Admissions Expert, Motivational Speaker

PHARM.D. SCHOOL PROFILES

Pharmacy School Admissions Data and Analysis

RACHEL A. WINSTON, PH.D.
Researcher, Professor, Admissions Expert, Motivational Speaker

OSTEOPATHIC MEDICAL SCHOOL
PREPARATION, APPLICATION, ADMISSION

YOUR JOURNEY, YOUR FUTURE

RACHEL A. WINSTON, PH.D.
Researcher, Professor, Admissions Expert, Motivational Speaker

OSTEO SCHOOL PROFILES

Osteopathic Medical School Admissions Data and Analysis

RACHEL A. WINSTON, PH.D.
Researcher, Professor, Admissions Expert, Motivational Speaker

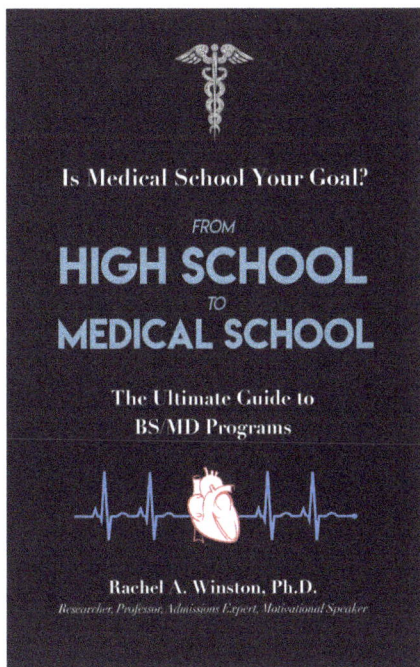

This comprehensive healthcare series is designed in full color to aid the growing number of applicants seeking clear, comprehensive materials. As a college admissions expert and former UCLA College Counseling Certificate Program faculty member, Dr. Winston is dedicated to helping students obtain the information they need.

FOR MORE INFORMATION

bsmdguide.com

medschoolexpert.com

Purchase books at Lizard-publishing.com

Is Medical School Your Goal?

FROM

HIGH SCHOOL
TO
MEDICAL SCHOOL

The Ultimate Guide to
BS/MD Programs

Rachel A. Winston, Ph.D.
Researcher, Professor, Admissions Expert, Motivational Speaker

SERVICES OFFERED BY LIZARD EDUCATION:

- College Counseling
- Admissions News/Resources
- Essay Support and Editing
- Interview Preparation
- Road Trips to Visit Colleges
- Career Planning/Majors/ Resumes
- BS/MD, BS/DO, BS/JD, BS/DDS
- Medical School
- Graduate School (Masters & Doctorate)
- Film Studio and Editing
- Portfolio Assistance/SlideRoom
- Athletics Recruiting/Highlight Films
- International Admissions/Visa/ TOEFL
- Financial Aid and Scholarships
- UCs, Ivy Leagues, and Colleges Nationwide
- Book Publishing
- Engineering, Robotics, STEM
- Art Portfolios

Email: collegeguide@yahoo.com

Website: collegelizard.com

LIZARD

INDEX

Symbols

B

C

D

E

N

O

P

R

U

W

Z